Implementing Microsoft Dynamics 365 Customer Engagement

Configure, customize, and extend Dynamics 365 CE in order to create effective CRM solutions

Mahender Pal

BIRMINGHAM - MUMBAI

Implementing Microsoft Dynamics 365 Customer Engagement

Commissioning Editor: Kunal Chaudhari
Acquisition Editor: Ashitosh Gupta
Content Development Editor: Divya Vijayan
Senior Editor: Mohammed Yusuf Imaratwale
Technical Editor: Jane Dsouza
Copy Editor: Safis Editing
Language Support Editor: Safis Editing
Project Coordinator: Kinjal Bari
Proofreader: Safis Editing
Indexer: Pratik Shirodkar
Production Designer: Jyoti Chauhan

First published: March 2020

Production reference: 1060320

Published by Packt Publishing Ltd.
Livery Place
35 Livery Street
Birmingham
B3 2PB, UK.

ISBN 978-1-83855-687-7

www.packt.com

To my family, all Dynamics 365 CE Community members, and to the memory of my father, Joginder Singh, for his sacrifices and hard work.
To my wife, Sonia, for being my loving partner throughout our joint life journey.
To my kids, Diksha and Arnav, for their love and support.

– Mahender Pal

`Packt.com`

Subscribe to our online digital library for full access to over 7,000 books and videos, as well as industry leading tools to help you plan your personal development and advance your career. For more information, please visit our website.

Why subscribe?

- Spend less time learning and more time coding with practical eBooks and Videos from over 4,000 industry professionals

- Improve your learning with Skill Plans built especially for you

- Get a free eBook or video every month

- Fully searchable for easy access to vital information

- Copy and paste, print, and bookmark content

Did you know that Packt offers eBook versions of every book published, with PDF and ePub files available? You can upgrade to the eBook version at `www.packt.com` and as a print book customer, you are entitled to a discount on the eBook copy. Get in touch with us at `customercare@packtpub.com` for more details.

At `www.packt.com`, you can also read a collection of free technical articles, sign up for a range of free newsletters, and receive exclusive discounts and offers on Packt books and eBooks.

Contributors

About the author

Mahender Pal is a Microsoft Dynamics 365 CE solution architect, trainer, and author. He started working with Dynamics CRM 3.0 and has used Microsoft Dynamics products professionally for more than 12 years. He loves to contribute to the community and has been awarded the Most Valuable Professional award 7 times. Mahender is the author of *Microsoft Dynamics CRM 2011 Application Design* and *Microsoft Dynamics 2015 Application Design*, for Packt Publishing, both of which cover developing xRM solutions using Dynamics CRM.

About the reviewers

Joergen Schladot is Microsoft Dynamics 365 CE and Power Platform solution architect and Dynamics CRM senior consultant with 6 years of experience. Joergen leads the Dynamics 365 CE and Power Platform team at Sycor GmbH, a Microsoft **Independent Software Vendor** (**ISV**) partner based in Germany, where he helped to develop a Microsoft Dynamics App Source solution for the life sciences industry.

He has been working in the CRM business since 2011 and helps customers to implement their business processes with the help of Dynamics 365 CE, Office 365, and since the beginning of 2019, also on basis of the Microsoft Power Platform. Besides being a Microsoft Certified Professional, he is a Professional Scrum Master and is an IREB Certified Professional for Requirement Engineering.

Rita Pereira is a Dynamics consultant with more than one year of experience in sales, customer service and field service across different industries. Her experience includes customization, administration (Dynamics and Office365), client support, and expertise with some Microsoft ISVs. Before that, she worked as a data analyst for multiple companies in the UK.

Packt is searching for authors like you

If you're interested in becoming an author for Packt, please visit `authors.packtpub.com` and apply today. We have worked with thousands of developers and tech professionals, just like you, to help them share their insight with the global tech community. You can make a general application, apply for a specific hot topic that we are recruiting an author for, or submit your own idea.

Table of Contents

Preface

Implementing Microsoft Dynamics 365 Customer Engagement is about implementing Dynamics 365 Customer Engagement for your customers. Microsoft Dynamics 365 Customer Engagement is one of the leading **customer relationship management (CRM)** solutions, helping companies to effectively communicate with their customers and allowing them to transform their business strategies. It provides different apps that can be used for different purposes.

Who this book is for

This book is for users, administrators, and consultants who wish to implement Dynamics 365 Customer Engagement for their businesses. This book will guide you through new features that Dynamics 365 Customer Engagement has to offer and help you implement them in your organization and for clients.

What this book covers

Chapter 1, *Introduction to Dynamics 365 CE*, provides basic details about Dynamics 365 Customer Engagement.

Chapter 2, *Implementation Methodology*, explains different project implementation methodologies.

Chapter 3, *Requirement Gathering and Analysis*, covers different techniques for requirements gathering and analysis.

Chapter 4, *Preparing Functional and Technical Design Documents*, explains how to prepare functional and technical design documents for your project.

Chapter 5, *Configuring Your Dynamics 365 CE Organization*, covers configuring different Dynamics 365 CE settings.

Chapter 6, *Customizing Dynamics 365 CE*, introduces ways to customize the Dynamics 365 CE application.

Chapter 7, *Extending Dynamics 365 CE*, covers writing code for the Dynamics 365 CE application.

Chapter 8, *Integrating Dynamics 365 CE with Other Applications*, covers integrating Dynamics 365 CE with other applications, such as Power Automate and Power Apps.

Chapter 9, *Business Intelligence and Reporting*, introduces the business intelligence capabilities of Dynamics 365 and covers how to create reports.

Chapter 10, *Testing and User Training Planning*, explains how to plan and perform testing for your project.

Chapter 11, *Migration and Upgrade*, introduces migration techniques and different upgrade paths.

Chapter 12, *Deployment and Go-Live Support*, explains how to deploy your project to production and how to provide go-live support.

To get the most out of this book

This book assumes you are familiar with earlier versions of Dynamics CRM and have programming knowledge. You should have access to a Dynamics 365 CE environment or you can set up a Dynamics 365 CE trial instance to work with different chapters. This book has the following software and hardware requirements:

Software/Hardware covered in the book	OS requirements
Visual Studio 2012 or later	Windows 7 SP1 or later
Windows Identity Foundation	Windows 7 SP1 or later
Microsoft Dynamics 365 Report Authoring Extension	Windows 7 SP1 or later
SQL Server Data Tools for Visual Studio 2012 or later	Windows 7 SP1 or later

If you are using the digital version of this book, we advise you to type the code yourself or access the code via the GitHub repository (link available in the next section). Doing so will help you avoid any potential errors related to the copying/pasting of code.

Download the example code files

You can download the example code files for this book from your account at www.packt.com. If you purchased this book elsewhere, you can visit www.packtpub.com/support and register to have the files emailed directly to you.

You can download the code files by following these steps:

1. Log in or register at www.packt.com.
2. Select the **Support** tab.
3. Click on **Code Downloads**.
4. Enter the name of the book in the **Search** box and follow the onscreen instructions.

Once the file is downloaded, please make sure that you unzip or extract the folder using the latest version of:

- WinRAR/7-Zip for Windows
- Zipeg/iZip/UnRarX for Mac
- 7-Zip/PeaZip for Linux

The code bundle for the book is also hosted on GitHub at https://github.com/ PacktPublishing/Implementing-Microsoft-Dynamics-365-Customer-Engagement. In case there's an update to the code, it will be updated on the existing GitHub repository.

We also have other code bundles from our rich catalog of books and videos available at https://github.com/PacktPublishing/. Check them out!

Conventions used

There are a number of text conventions used throughout this book.

CodeInText: Indicates code words in text, database table names, folder names, filenames, file extensions, pathnames, dummy URLs, user input, and Twitter handles. Here is an example: "Please refer to the Appendix1 folder on the GitHub repository for this book."

A block of code is set as follows:

```
req.open("GET", globalContext.getClientUrl() + "/api/data/v9.1/contacts(" +
contactid + ")?$select=emailaddress1", true);
```

When we wish to draw your attention to a particular part of a code block, the relevant lines or items are set in bold:

```
if (this.readyState === 4) {
  req.onreadystatechange = null;
  if (this.status === 200) {
//code to process result
}}
```

Bold: Indicates a new term, an important word, or words that you see on screen. For example, words in menus or dialog boxes appear in the text like this. Here is an example: "Start Visual Studio, go to **New Project**, and select **Console App**."

 Warnings or important notes appear like this.

 Tips and tricks appear like this.

Get in touch

Feedback from our readers is always welcome.

General feedback: If you have questions about any aspect of this book, mention the book title in the subject of your message and email us at customercare@packtpub.com.

Errata: Although we have taken every care to ensure the accuracy of our content, mistakes do happen. If you have found a mistake in this book, we would be grateful if you would report this to us. Please visit www.packtpub.com/support/errata, selecting your book, clicking on the Errata Submission Form link, and entering the details.

Piracy: If you come across any illegal copies of our works in any form on the internet, we would be grateful if you would provide us with the location address or website name. Please contact us at copyright@packt.com with a link to the material.

If you are interested in becoming an author: If there is a topic that you have expertise in, and you are interested in either writing or contributing to a book, please visit authors.packtpub.com.

Reviews

Please leave a review. Once you have read and used this book, why not leave a review on the site that you purchased it from? Potential readers can then see and use your unbiased opinion to make purchase decisions, we at Packt can understand what you think about our products, and our authors can see your feedback on their book. Thank you!

For more information about Packt, please visit packt.com.

Introduction to Dynamics 365 CE

This chapter will help you get started with Dynamics 365 **Customer Engagement** (**CE**), as well as help you understand its business applications and their uses. You will learn about the history of the Microsoft Dynamics family, as well as about the products that were part of the Microsoft Dynamics family before Microsoft Dynamics 365. You will also learn about the various Dynamics 365 CE editions, which will help you understand which edition is most suited for your organization.

Then, you will learn about the different apps that are available as part of Dynamics 365 and their uses. Later, we will discuss the different deployment options that will be useful for Dynamics 365 CE implementation planning. We will also discuss the different ways we can access Dynamics 365 CE based on our user requirements. Finally, you will be able to set up a quick trial for Dynamics 365 CE online.

The main topics that we are going to discuss in this chapter are as follows:

- Introduction to Dynamics 365
- Introduction to Dynamics 365 apps
- Introduction to Dynamics 365 CE
- Understanding deployment options
- Dynamics 365 CE clients
- Understanding subscription options
- Setting up a Dynamics 365 online trial

Technical requirements

This chapter doesn't have any technical requirements; we are merely helping you get started with Dynamics 365 CE. We will be covering the introduction of earlier versions of Dynamics **Customer Relationship Management (CRM)** to give you an added advantage in this area.

Introduction to Dynamics 365

If you are new to the Microsoft Dynamics product family and haven't worked with Dynamics before, you can consider it a collection of business applications. Now, you might be wondering, what a business application is? This is a piece of software that is specially built for automating business activities. In this case, business activities mean the processes used in the various departments of a business. These processes are dependent on the type of business you are doing.

For example, if you are running a service-based company, your process automation will be related to the services that you provide to your customer. An automobile service company can use business applications to manage their daily service requests, handle roadside assistance inquiries, deal with maintenance requests, and workorder generations. Similarly, if you are running a company that deals in sales and purchases, then your process automation will be more specific to sales, such as handling customer inquiries, managing leads, and providing quotations to customers.

Now that you have enough knowledge of a business application, let's go back to our main topic, that is, Dynamics 365. In 2003, the Microsoft Dynamics family included two types of business applications: **Enterprise Resource Planning (ERP)** and CRM. Within these two applications, **Great Plains (GP)**, **Axapta (Ax)**, **Navision (NAV)**, and **Solomon (SL)** came under the ERP category, while Dynamics CRM was the only product in the CRM category. These applications can be seen in the following diagram:

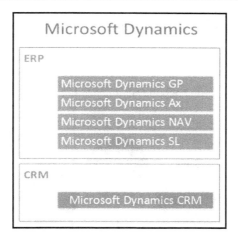

Microsoft released Dynamics 365 on November 1, 2016 for its online customers. Dynamics 365 includes different tailor-made business applications for your business needs. It also provides a strong platform called **Power Apps**, so you can customize these business applications based on specific business needs, and has out-of-the-box features for building new applications.

 Out-of-the-box features are the features that are available in any software so that it can be used without modification.

Dynamics 365 intelligent business applications can be used to digitally transform your business. Here, digital transformation does not just mean utilizing advanced technological machines for your business but using Dynamics 365 apps to enhance different business processes so that your business operations can be optimized to their maximum level. These processes could be as simple as interacting with your clients in a more organized manner, providing them with a 360-degree view of their data using **Business Intelligence** (**BI**) so that they have a better understanding of their sales, or using its **artificial intelligence** (**AI**) and **Internet of Things** (**IoT**) capabilities to get more data insights so that a more personalized experience can be provided to its customers.

 You can find out more about how to use Dynamics 365 AI capabilities by referring to https://dynamics.microsoft.com/en-in/ai/overview/.

Now that we have a good understanding of Dynamics 365, let's start discussing different Dynamics 365 apps.

Introduction to Dynamics 365 apps

Instead of individual applications in the earlier version of Microsoft Dynamics, Dynamics 365 broke down the functionality of its applications into smaller apps and brought them under a single roof. The following diagram explains the different apps under Dynamics 365:

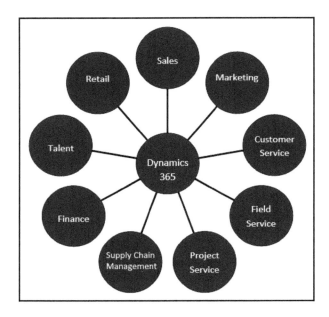

The aforementioned apps include different functionalities and can be used for different purposes. We'll take a closer look at these different apps in the following subsections.

Sales

The Sales app can be used to implement an end-to-end sales process. This app provides generic guided sales processes that help users close their sales quickly and manage their customers, leads, opportunities, orders, invoices, and other sales records. Leads can be captured using different sources, such as cold calling, campaign responses, websites, or incoming emails. The sales process that's started by the leads ends with generating an invoice after fulfilling the customer's order.

This app is equipped with different components that help salespeople define their goals, monitor lead progress, and move leads from one stage to another stage based on the lead score. The Sales app has inbuilt reporting capabilities that allow the salespeople to get the most up-to-date information and provide a 360-degree view of their customer's data. It supports salespeople in building strong relationships with organizations and delivers great service experience. The following is a screenshot of the **Leads** entity form for the Sales Hub app:

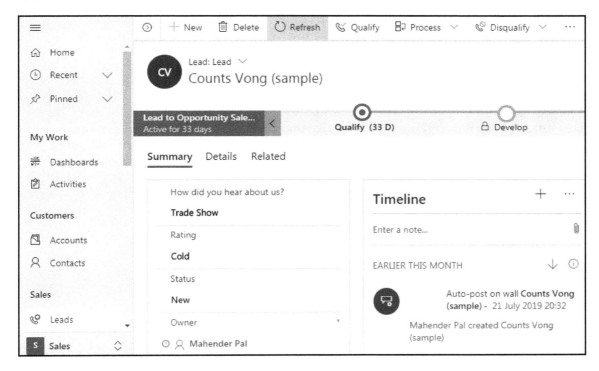

Apart from the traditional Sales app, which is similar to the sales module in earlier versions of Dynamics 365, it has a new Sales Hub app that is built on the **Unified Interface Framework** (UIF).

 You can find out more about the Dynamics 365 Sales app at https://docs.microsoft.com/en-us/dynamics365/customer-engagement/sales-enterprise/overview.

Marketing

The Dynamics 365 Marketing app brings long-awaited features for Microsoft Dynamics family users, such as an email editor, event management, and multi-channel campaign support. Previously, most Dynamics customers had to utilize third-party tools or the **Microsoft Dynamics Marketing** (**MDM**) application.

MDM was a separate cloud application, but with the release of Dynamics 365, Microsoft also announced that the MDM tool wouldn't be available for new customers from November 2016. Later, from May 2018, they finally discontinued this product and announced a new marketing tool for Dynamics 365.

The Dynamics 365 Marketing app is not available with Dynamics 365 plans, but it is available for purchase separately under a different plan, which is based on the number of contacts recorded in Dynamics 365 CE. This app also works seamlessly with other Dynamics 365 apps as it shares the same **Common Data Model** (**CDM**) for storing customer data as the other Dynamics 365 apps. This app is built on the Unified User Interface and can be used on different devices, such as mobiles, tablets, and desktops. It includes features such as multi-channel campaigning, event management, webinars, and a drag-and-drop email editor for sending personalized emails and lead scoring.

 You can find out more about the Dynamics 365 Marketing app at `https:/ /docs.microsoft.com/en-us/dynamics365/customer-engagement/ marketing/overview`.

Customer Service

The Customer Service app is similar to the service module that's present in Dynamics CRM. This app provides features that will help you provide better customer service experience to your clients. This app has built-in features for creating and managing cases, case routing, product management, service scheduling, knowledgebase management, and case entitlement management, has a service calendar, and also has business intelligence features for a 360-degree view of customer cases.

The following is a screenshot of a case form in the Unified Interface client. Here, you can see how sections such as **Summary**, **Details**, and **Case Relationships** and command buttons are rendered:

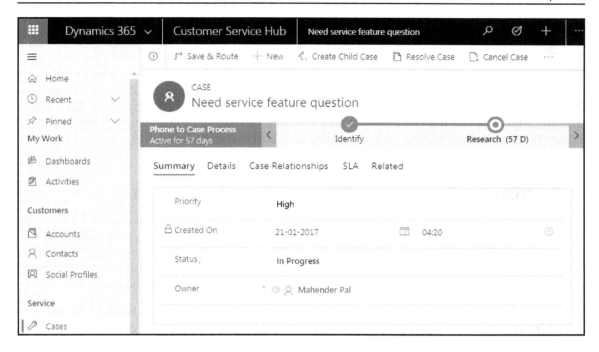

If you open a **case form** (you can open an existing case record by navigating to **Service |
Cases**) in the web client, you will be able to see how the different command buttons such as
New, **Cancel Case**, and **Save & Route** are presented there and how they are presented in
Unified Interface.

Apart from the Customer Service app, Dynamics 365 also has a Customer Service Hub that
was built using the UIF.

Field Service

The Field Service app is another way of providing better customer service. This app is all
about providing services to customers at their current location. These services include work
order management, interactive resource scheduling, customer assets management,
inventory management, and handling orders. The Field Service app reuses the same core
entities from the Sales, Marketing, and Service apps. This app has inbuilt reports that can be
used to measure key performance indicators and customer interaction.

The Field Service app is also built using the UIF and provides a responsive design
experience to customers and service technicians across various devices, such as desktops,
mobiles, and tablets.

Project Service

The Project Service app is built for project-based companies and provides a full suite for project management, allowing you to successfully start and finish a project. The Project Service app allows you to plan a project, get project approvals, track project costs, make entries in the project timesheet, and project resource planning and management. This app also has inbuilt reporting capabilities so that you can track the performance of the project, which helps in delivering the project on time and at the appropriate cost.

Finance and Supply Chain Management

The Finance and Supply Chain Management apps in Dynamics 365 are from the ERP category. These apps are replacements for earlier ERP products in the Dynamics family, such as AX, GP, and NAV. Both the Finance and Supply Chain Management apps include features for managing the financial and operational activities of an organization, such as accounts payable and receivable, inventory management, and assets management.

If required, these financial and supply chain management processes can be customized based on any specific needs. These apps also include business intelligence features that help in getting operational insights on financial and supply chain management from customers.

Talent

If you work in a company that deals with human resource management, then this Dynamics 365 app can definitely help you manage all your HR operations. Talent has inbuilt features for managing how a new resource is hired, managing jobs, leave management, salary management, and skills management.

This app also helps recruiters utilize their LinkedIn data by integrating Dynamics 365 for Talent with LinkedIn.

 You can find out more about the Dynamics 365 Talent app at `https://docs.microsoft.com/en-us/dynamics365/unified-operations/talent/`.

Retail

The Dynamics 365 app for Retail helps retailers fulfill the continuously changing demands of their customers. It can also be used by e-commerce business organizations. It provides end-to-end retail solutions and works seamlessly across multiple channels, along with finance and operation apps. Retail includes features such as multi-channel support, merchandising, business intelligence, customization options for retail processes, loyalty management, and inventory management.

This app also helps retailers utilize their social media capabilities by helping them gain new customers and provide them with personalized experiences.

 You can find out more about Dynamics 365 Retail at `https://docs.microsoft.com/en-us/dynamics365/unified-operations/retail/`.

Now, we know about all the apps for Dynamics 365 and how old modules from Dynamics CRM are available. Every app in Dynamics 365 has significance, where the Sales app is important for a customer to implement their end-to-end sales process, while the Marketing app is required if you wish to promote your product and services to increase your sales. If your customer is a service-providing company or project consulting organization, they can use the Project Service Automation app to effectively manage their projects.

Now that you've learned about all the apps, we can discuss Dynamics 365 CE in more detail.

Introduction to Dynamics 365 CE

After Dynamics CRM 2016 update 8.1 (in earlier versions, it was known as Dynamics CRM), we got the service update 8.2 release and Microsoft rebranded Dynamics CRM to Dynamics 365 CE. Just like other versions, Dynamics 365 did not come with a major release but with a service update for their online customers that was applied to on-premise customers as well. Dynamics 365 CE is a combination of sales, marketing, customer service, field service, project service apps, and other services. It is a new generation intelligence CRM application. All first-party apps, such as Sales, Marketing, Customer Service, Field Service, and Product Service Automation, are highly customizable and extendable, and all these apps provide out-of-the-box integration support for different Microsoft projects, such as SharePoint, OneNote, Microsoft Flow, Power BI, Azure, and Microsoft Teams. Using its out-of-the-box service support, it can be integrated with any other application if we write custom code or use customer connectors.

Dynamics 365's inbuilt business intelligence capability gives you real data insights and helps you make data-driven decisions. Dynamics 365 also utilizes Power BI and AI capabilities to provide real-time data insights that help you make logical business decisions.

Dynamics 365 CE is now part of the Power Platform. Basically, the **Power Platform** is a web and mobile application development platform that utilizes the capability of Azure Cloud Services. All the Dynamics 365 CE first-party apps are developed using the same platform. Dynamics 365 CE not only provides end-to-end solutions to boost your sales, manage your marketing activities effectively, and provide a personalized customer service experience to your customers, but we can use its Power Platform capabilities to develop customized apps that cater to your specific business needs. These apps can be used across various devices (such as mobiles, tablets, and desktops), which increases their user adaptability.

The Power Platform includes the following three main applications:

- **Power Apps**: Provides us with a visual designer so that we can design our apps using rich Power Apps controls. We can also use this to connect to different business applications. We can build two types of apps in Power Apps. We will discuss this in more detail in Chapter 8, *Integrating Dynamics 365 CE with Other Applications*.
- **Power Automate**: Helps us develop a workflow so that we can automate our activities. We can also connect to different applications using hundreds of connectors in just a few clicks. We will be working with Power Automate in Chapter 8, *Integrating Dynamics 365 CE with Other Applications*.
- **Power BI**: Is the next-generation business intelligence app that provides users with an interactive experience so that they can get and share data insights across your organization. We will be working with Power BI in Chapter 9, *Business Intelligence and Reporting*.

While discussing the Power Platform, some other important terminologies I want to mention are CDM and **Common Data Service (CDS)**. CDM is where we can store our data in different common business entities. These business entities include common business entities such as account, contact, and lead opportunity, but, if required, we can create new custom entities and extend existing entities. Further, data that's stored in these entities can be shared with different applications. CDS allows us to store data in business entities based on the CDM. We can use CDS to build an application in Power Apps. When creating an application in Power Apps, CDS helps us set database, security, and business logic for our application.

Dynamics 365 CE features

Dynamics 365 v 9.0 brought many exciting changes to Dynamics 365 CE customers that improved its productivity and user adaptability. We'll discuss some of these new features in the following subsections.

UI enhancement

I've been working with CRM since version 3.0 and I have seen drastic changes to the CRM UI with every new major release. Similarly, this service update also brought new UI changes to Dynamics CE users. If you have already worked with the earlier version, you might be aware of the frustrating amount of unnecessary spaces on the entity forms. The new UI has removed the unnecessary spaces and improved the fonts.

In the following screenshot, you can see that the border is added around sections and that the gap between the columns is also minimized:

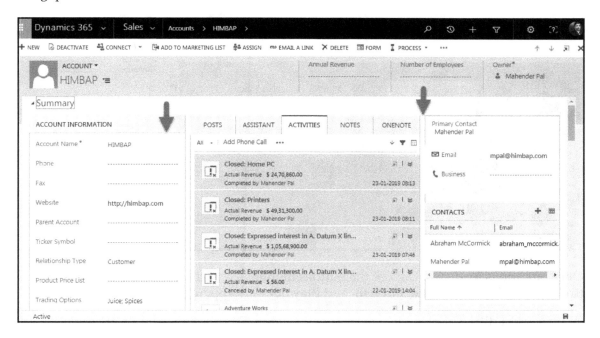

Another drastic change is the new Unified Interface design for Dynamics 365 apps, which gives the same user experience across various devices. Microsoft has already announced that from September 2019, the legacy web client will be deprecated. All customers need to move to Unified Interface before October 1, 2020.

Custom apps

We know that Dynamics 365 CE is now a part of the Power Apps platform. Power Apps is a collection of different services and connectors so that you can build custom mobile and web apps for your business. The Power Apps platform provides you with an inbuilt designer that contains a set of controls that you can simply drag and drop. This means that by using Power Apps, you can build non-code apps, but, if required, we can write code so that we can interact with other applications and external databases. It has many inbuilt connectors and, if required, we can also build custom connectors.

When I say Dynamics 365 CE is part of the Power Apps platform, it means all the aforementioned features can be used in Dynamics 365 CE for building no-code apps. We can build custom apps using Power Apps; such apps are known as model-driven apps. Power Apps also provides a custom app editor, as shown in the following screenshot:

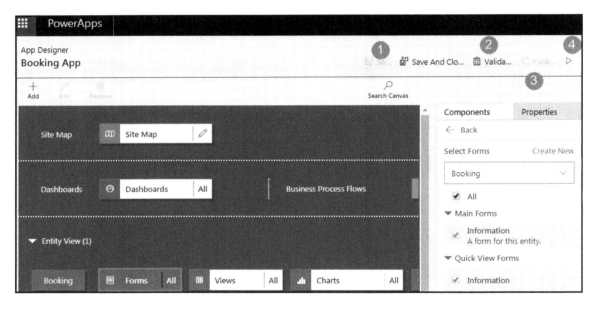

Once our app is ready, we can use the buttons highlighted in the preceding screenshot (from **1-4**) to **Save**, **Validate**, **Publish**, and **Play** our new app, respectively.

We can select different components such as **Site Map**, **Dashboards**, and **Entity** details from the windows on the right-hand side. Once selected, we can configure their properties accordingly. When our app is ready, we can save and validate it to check for errors. We can use the **Publish** button to make the app available to users and the **Play** button to see what it will look like. We can also control the custom app's security using Dynamics 365 CE security roles and control what the user can access.

Inbuilt Sitemap Designer

Sitemap is an XML file that is responsible for controlling the navigation of Dynamics 365 CE. If you have worked with Dynamics CRM before, do you remember how many times you have used the custom Sitemap editors to improve your navigation based on user requirements? Or did you have to manually edit the navigation features in Visual Studio? Of course, you can still use these now, but Dynamics 365 CE also has an out-of-the-box Sitemap editor.

The following screenshot shows the different commands we can use to **Add**, **Delete**, **Cut**, or **Copy** Sitemap components:

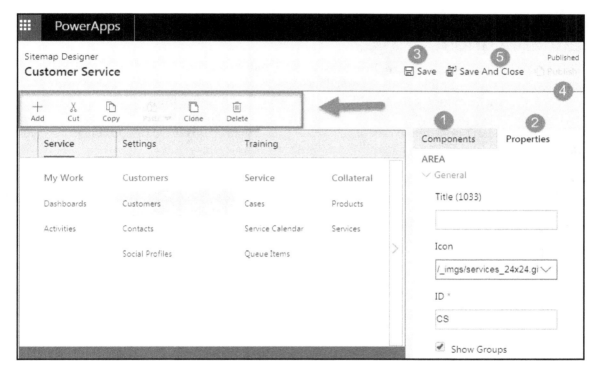

As you can see, if we want to add a new component to Sitemap, then we can pick it from the **Components** section (**1**) or we can configure their properties from the right-hand side **Properties** window (**2**). Once our Sitemap changes are completed, we can **Publish** our changes and use the **Save And Close** button to close the Sitemap editor. We can use the Sitemap editor to control navigation based on the user's security role.

Under the **Properties** tab, if you scroll down, you will be able to see the **Privileges** option under the **Advanced** section. We can use the privilege property of the subarea to check whether the current user has a specific privilege on some entity, if required. Privilege is the basic security unit in Dynamics 365 CE and defines the actions a user can perform.

You can find more details about privileges at `https://docs.microsoft.com/en-us/dynamics365/customer-engagement/admin/security-roles-privileges`.

You can also use custom the Sitemap editor from XrmToolBox: `https://www.xrmtoolbox.com/plugins/MsCrmTools.SiteMapEditor/`.

Editable grids

This was a long-awaited feature. Previously, users had to use third-party frameworks or develop their own editable grids using client-side code. We got an inline editable grid capability in the previous version of Dynamics 365 CE, but it was limited to line item entities such as opportunity products, quote orders, order details, and invoice details. However, it wasn't possible to customize these grids. With the release of editable grids, we can now apply editable grid capabilities to both grids and sub-grids.

The following screenshot shows the editable grid enabled for the **Active Accounts** view. Here, you can see how it is rendered based on the grouping:

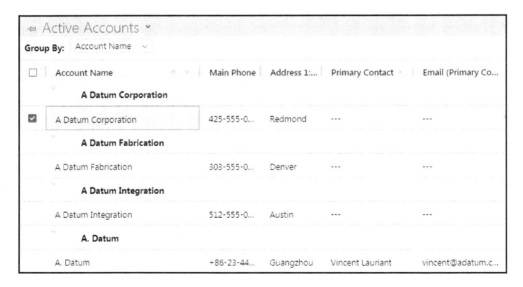

Editable grids also support JavaScript and allow us to have an event associated with each grid. We can apply groups based on the column of the grid. Most of the columns can be used in the editable grid and these grids are available for all the clients.

Business process flow enhancement

A business process flow is a visual representation of various stages a record can have. It can be used with the system or a custom entity. Dynamics 365 CE provides an inbuilt business process flow for generic business scenarios, such as, the lead to the opportunity sales process, phone to case process, and case to work order process. Dynamics 365 CE brought many new features to the business process flow. One of them is the new business process flow editor, as shown in the following screenshot:

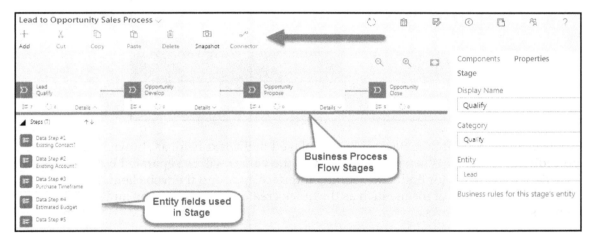

While designing processes, we can simply drag stages, conditions, data steps, workflows, or action steps to the canvas from the right-hand side property windows and configure their properties using the **Properties** tab. Then, we can use the action step to run the workflow on demand. This can be very useful in some scenarios, such as when notifying a user or team using the workflow on a particular business process stage.

We can use the command buttons to **Add**, **Remove**, **Cut**, **Copy**, **Paste**, or **Delete** stages. Business process flows can now be displayed in floating mode, but this feature is only available in Unified Interface apps. Another good thing about the business process flow is that it's now an entity, which means we can refer to it just like other entities in views, charts, dashboards, and site map.

MultiSelect Option Set

This is another exciting feature that Dynamics 365 CE has introduced. Here, we can create a multi-select option field by setting the data type to **MultiSelect Option Set** in the new field creation window. Once a field has been created, we can see the multi-select options, as shown in the following screenshot:

After selecting each option, they will be displayed in the text field, as shown in the preceding screenshot. When you close the tab, the values will be separated by a semicolon. This field is available for both new Unified Interface apps and the web client. This field can be added to a variety of forms, such as the quick create form, main form, and quick view form, as well as on views.

Dynamics 365 app for Outlook

Although this app was introduced in an earlier version of Dynamic CRM, Dynamics 365 brought new changes to it. The new Dynamics 365 app for Outlook utilizes the UIA, which means it works seamlessly across different devices. While using this app in Outlook, you will find its existing features along with the new Unified Interface design. Now, it allows us to check tracked emails and appointments within Outlook, which is a great feature to include.

You can find out more about deploying a Dynamics 365 app for Outlook at https://docs.microsoft.com/en-us/dynamics365/customer-engagement/outlook-app/deploy-dynamics-365-app-for-outlook.

Dynamics 365 app for phone

Dynamics 365 app for phone has also been updated with the Unified Interface design to provide a user-responsive design experience. Navigation for Dynamics 365 app for phone has changed, as shown in the following screenshot:

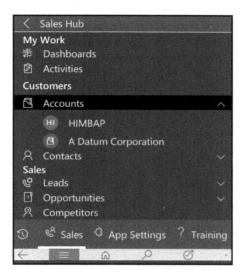

Let's look at another great feature that's been introduced by Dynamics 365.

Virtual entities

Virtual entities allow you to render data in Dynamics 365 that isn't part of the Dynamics 365 database. Previously, if we wanted to show data from outside of Dynamics CRM, we had to develop complex custom integration, but now we can easily display custom data in Dynamics 365 using data providers. Data that's available under virtual entities is read-only and for display purposes. Virtual entities have limitations; for example, they can only be used for organization entities, which means you can't utilize the user-owned entities' security features in virtual entities. However, you can utilize an existing calculated field for any calculation. This must be done in external data sources, but this is still a great feature from an integration point of view.

You can find out more about virtual entities at `https://docs.microsoft.com/en-us/dynamics365/customer-engagement/developer/virtual-entities/get-started-ve`.

Relevance Search

Another new feature that's been added to Dynamics 365 CE is Relevance Search, which allows you to search records across multiple entities. This search utilizes the Azure search index. When Relevance Search is enabled in Dynamics 365 CE, we can select an entity that we want to include in the search. After that, the enabled entities data is synced to the Azure search index. Later on, while you are searching for data, your search is performed against the Azure search index.

The great thing about this search is that it can look for the search text in the documents attached to notes, emails, and appointments. Using Relevance Search can provide faster results as it is using Azure technology, but while selecting entities for Relevance Search, keep the sensitivity of the data in mind as your data will go out of your Dynamics 365 CE organization.

In the following screenshot, you can see the **Relevance Search** result for the text HIMBAP. Here, we can see all the record types where it found the **HIMBAP** text from the sample data:

This search is only available for Dynamics 365 CE online: it's not available for on-premise use. Relevance Search only works with text information, which means you can't search for data on numeric or date fields.

Microsoft also announced that users will be getting a Dynamics 365 CE online release twice a year, during April and October.

So far, we have learned about the top new features of Dynamics 365 CE that can help our customers improve their business efficiency and implement a better customer experience. All these new features can increase a user's productivity in their day-to-day work.

Now that we are well aware of Dynamics 365 CE and its features, we'll discuss the deployment options for implementing Dynamics 365 CE. In the next section, we are going to discuss all the possible options for implementing Dynamics 365 CE for our customers.

Understanding deployment options

Dynamics 365 CE is for everyone, whether you want to utilize a cloud infrastructure, or you want to reuse your existing infrastructure for Dynamics 365 CE. In a broad way, we can deploy Dynamics 365 CE using the following options.

Cloud

This is the easiest and simplest option if you wish to utilize Dynamics 365 CE capabilities by taking out a Dynamics 365 subscription from Microsoft. Dynamics 365 CE online is hosted on Microsoft Azure datacenters, which are located across the globe. Microsoft has datacenter regions in the United States, Canada, Germany, India, Japan, and Oceania.

 Refer to `http://o365datacentermap.azurewebsites.net/` for a complete list of datacenters.

When you buy a subscription for Dynamics 365, you select your country region and, based on the region, your Dynamics 365 CE organization is hosted on the nearest datacenter. For example, if I buy a Dynamics 365 CE organization, my organization will be hosted on the India datacenter. Selecting Dynamics 365 CE cloud means you don't need to do any infrastructure investment. You don't need to bother installing software or patches for Dynamics 365 CE. All the required infrastructure and software will be hosted on Azure, and Microsoft will take care of Dynamics 365 CE for you.

All the maintenance work is carried out by Microsoft itself, whether that's making daily backups of your Dynamics 365 CE organization or installing patches. You only need to set up the client's machine to access Dynamics 365 CE cloud. It can be accessed using any of the popular browsers and from anywhere in the world by just connecting to the internet. This is very useful when your organization or users are scattered around the world. You don't need to configure something extra to make your Dynamics 365 CE organization available to them. Microsoft provides SLA with 99.9% uptime for your organization so that you don't have to worry about your organization's downtime.

Although you can't access Dynamics 365 CE Azure SQL database, we can use the Dynamics 365 Data Export Service by Microsoft to synchronize the Dynamics 365 CE database to our own Azure subscription. This service is a free service that is available in Microsoft AppSource. In some cases, we have limited control over troubleshooting in Dynamics 365 CE online and we need to work with Microsoft support to resolve issues, especially if it is related to the SQL server.

 Microsoft AppSource is a marketplace for business applications that have been developed by Microsoft and other Microsoft vendors. It can be accessed from `https://appsource.microsoft.com/en-US/`.

Some of the Dynamics 365 CE services are only available to Dynamics 365 CE cloud, which is another bonus of going with the cloud option. Services such as Data Export Service, Customer Insights, Field Service app, Marketing app and Project Service, Relevance Search, and Advanced Service Analytics are not available for on-premise users.

On-premise

In the case of on-premise Dynamics 365 CE, since the deployment is done on your own premises, you need to take care of the infrastructure and software requirements for Dynamics 365 CE. You can reuse your existing infrastructure if it is compatible with Dynamics 365 CE. Depending on the number of users and workloads, it can be deployed on a single application server, a SQL server, or it can be installed on multiple servers. The following diagram represents a typical medium-size deployment:

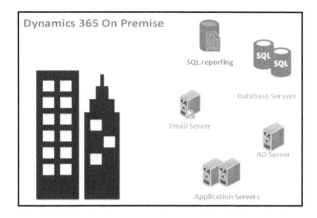

On-premise deployment is best suited for organizations that don't want their data to leave the premises because of data sensitivity. In the case of on-premise deployment, you are responsible for any maintenance activities, such as patch installation and daily backups, which means you need to have an IT team to take care of these activities. You also have full access to your SQL Server and **SQL Server Reporting Services** (**SSRS**) reporting servers. On-premise deployment is only accessible from your premises, which means that if a user wants to access Dynamics 365 CE from outside of your premises, they won't be able to unless they have a VPN set up that will reach your network or you have set up an **Internet Facing Deployment** (**IFD**) that implements claim-based authentication.

Hybrid deployment

Hybrid deployment utilizes both Cloud and on-premise features. In the case of hybrid deployment, Dynamics 365 CE is hosted by Microsoft vendors and they are responsible for all the maintenance tasks and patch upgrades. You don't need an IT support team to handle your Dynamics 365 CE organization. Vendors may provide you with access to the SQL server based on the subscription.

Dynamics 365 CE clients

Dynamics 365 CE clients allow users to access the Dynamics 365 CE organization. Users can access the Dynamics 365 CE using the following clients.

Web client

The web client allows users to access the Dynamics 365 CE organization using a browser and a specific organization URL. Dynamics 365 CE supports all popular browsers, including Internet Explorer, Microsoft Edge, Firefox, Chrome, and Safari. It is the most popular client for accessing Dynamics 365 CE because we don't need to install any programs. You can access different apps that have been installed for your Dynamics 365 CE organization from here. Sitemap navigation allows you to access various areas of Dynamics 365 CE in the web client easily. Web client is deprecated now, so all the customers who are using Web Client currently need to move the Unified Interface before 1 October 2020.

In the following screenshot, you can see what the top navigation bar of the web client looks like:

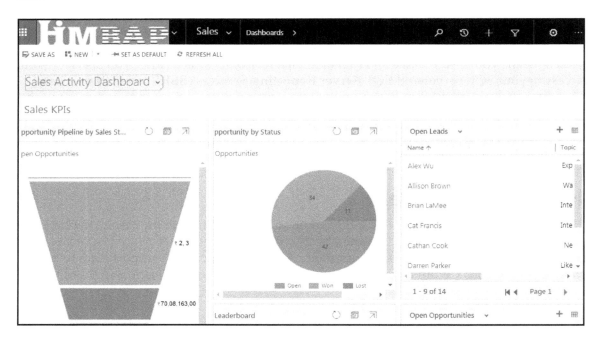

The navigation bar shows the organization's logo, along with the currently selected module. This navigation bar is primarily used to handle the navigation of a web client.

Unified Interface client

The Unified Interface client allows users to access Dynamics 365 CE using their browser, just like the web client, but it also provides a user-responsive design experience. Users will have the same experience of using Dynamics 365 CE across devices of different screen sizes.

The following screenshot is of Unified Interface. Here, you can see the difference between the web client and the Unified Client layout:

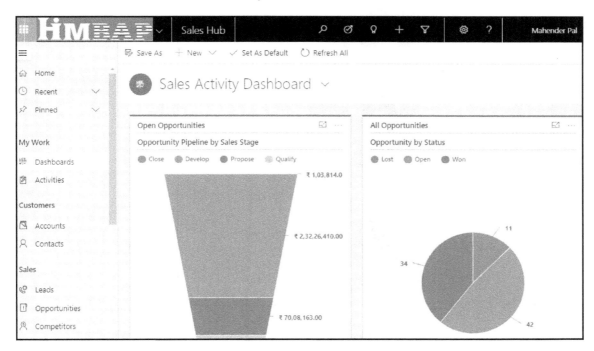

The Unified Interface is based on Power Apps model-driven apps, where users can bond to specific Dynamics 365 apps based on their job profile. All the new apps of Dynamics 365 use the Unified Interface client.

Mobile client

The number of mobile users is increasing in the world every day. Keeping this in mind, every business application that's built today is accessible from mobile devices. Users can also access Dynamics 365 using mobile or tablet clients. Dynamics 365 CE for phone can be downloaded from iOS and Android stores. Once the organization's URL has been configured, you can access all of your apps from your mobile using a responsive design.

The following screenshot is of Dynamics 365 CE for phone showing all our Dynamics 365 CE apps:

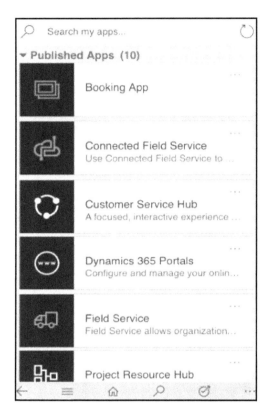

The Dynamics 365 CE for phone app now supports offline capability. It's no longer necessary for mobile users to be online to connect to the Dynamics 365 CE server since they can access their data in offline mode as well.

Users can work with different entities based on their security permissions. Although the business process flow is supported in offline mode, it is limited to single-entity business processes only (business process flows for multiple entities is not supported). All the work that's done in offline mode is synchronized back to the Dynamics 365 CE server when the user has connected to the server again.

Dynamics 365 CE for Outlook

Another way of accessing Dynamics 365 CE is by using the Outlook client. This client can be installed on top of the Office Outlook client. Once installed, it allows us to access Dynamics 365 CE functionalities within Outlook without needing to navigate to any other window. Using the Outlook client, we can track different entities records, such as appointments, emails, tasks, and contacts. This means you can access a tracked record if and when required from Dynamics 365 CE applications.

The following screenshot is of a Dynamics 365 CE Outlook client that has been synced with our Dynamics 365 organization. You can see what navigation options are available on the left-hand side:

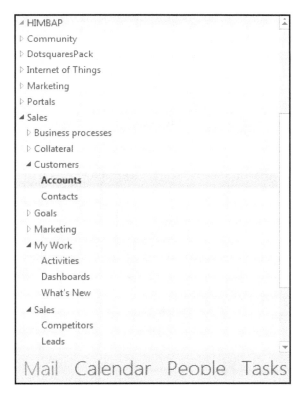

You can download Dynamics 365 CE for Outlook from `https://www.` `microsoft.com/en-us/download/details.aspx?id=56972`.

The Dynamics 365 CE Outlook client also supports offline capabilities for users who are not connected to the Dynamics 365 CE server. This is useful for sales or marketing professionals. All the entities data based on the Outlook filters configuration is available for updates. Once connected to the server, all the data will be synchronized.

 Outlook filters are configured in Office Outlook applications. Here, you can configure the entity list in order to synchronize an entity's data between Dynamics 365 for CE server and Dynamics 365 for Outlook.

Dynamics 365 CE app for Outlook

The Dynamics 365 CE app for Outlook is lightweight and is used for accessing records from Outlook for desktop and the web.

The following screenshot shows what the new Dynamics 365 CE app will look like in Outlook:

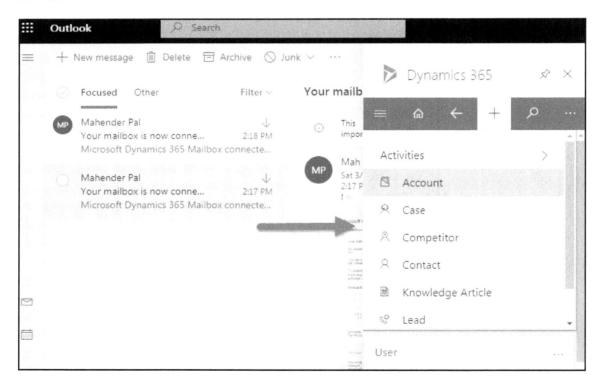

The navigation options in the Dynamics 365 CE app are similar to what we have in the Dynamics 365 CE mobile client.

Users don't need to install anything to access the Dynamics 365 CE app for Outlook; they just need to configure the Dynamics 365 CE app for Outlook from the settings in their Dynamics 365 CE organization. Access to Dynamics 365 CE records is fast compared to the Outlook client because it utilizes web APIs to retrieve data in real time.

USD client

The **Unified Service Desk (USD)** client is mainly used by the service department so that they can work with different applications under a single interface. It provides many out-of-the-box features that are required by the service industry. For example, call centers require telephonic integration and call script support. Users can configure the USD easily based on their requirements, and custom controls can be developed if required. Users can easily access all the data for their customers from associated applications, instead of switching over to different applications. This helps call center employees answer customer queries quickly and easily.

Custom client

Apart from the clients we discussed earlier, custom clients can be built for Dynamics 365 CE using Dynamics 365 CE web services or web APIs. Custom web apps or Windows apps can be built using the .NET framework that cater to specific requirements of the business.

Now, we have discussed all the client applications that can be used to access Dynamics 365 CE applications. Customers can select which client application they want to use based on their requirements. They can use some of them or all of them, if desired. We can suggest client applications to our customers during requirement gathering sessions. Now that you know about Dynamics 365 CE client applications, we'll discuss the different subscription options that are available for Dynamics 365 CE and which applications are included in those plans.

Understanding subscription options

Microsoft also simplified the licensing model for Dynamics 365 CE. **Dynamics 365 Subscription** can be purchased based on the user subscriptions shown in the following diagram:

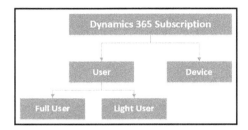

Light User are normal users, known as team members. They have read-only access to all the apps, with read and write access to limited entities. This type of license is best suited for users who perform light tasks, such as accessing data for read-only purposes, running reports, and using the dashboard. **Full User** are basically Dynamics 365 CE power users, and they have full access to all the features.

Device subscription is suited for call centers where multiple users share the same devices but use their own logins. With different user subscriptions, organizations can select the Dynamics 365 subscription plan that provides the best and the most flexible options. Based on the subscription plan that is selected, users can access Dynamics 365 applications.

Based on the new licensing guide that was released on October 1, 2019, customers can purchase individual apps based on their requirements. Microsoft has divided Dynamics 365 CE apps into two categories:

- **Base**: This is the main app that users need to use based on their day-to-day work. For example, for a salesperson, the Dynamics 365 CE Sales app will be a base app.
- **Attach**: This is an additional app that a user requires in addition to their base app.

The following diagram provides details about the various Dynamics 365 apps categories. Here, you can see all the apps that come under the **Base Apps** category, as well as the apps that come under the **Attach Apps** category. **Project Service Automation** is only available as a base app and can't be purchased as an attach app:

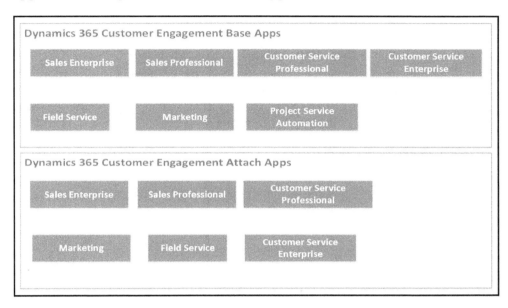

Let's understand this using an example of a customer who wants to use Dynamics 365 CE in their two departments: sales and customer support. Here, they need to buy a Sales app for their sales department as a base app, and a Customer Service app for their customer support department as a base app. But let's say the customer support person also needs a Sales apps for some of the additional tasks they perform. In this case, they can buy a Sales app as an additional app for less. Here, the Sales app will be an attach app.

For more details about Dynamics 365 pricing, please go to `https://mbs.microsoft.com/Files/public/365/Dynamics365LicensingGuide.pdf`.

Setting up a Dynamics 365 online trial

To experience Dynamics 365 CE capabilities and test its features, we can set up a quick 30-day trial. To set up the trial, follow these steps:

1. Open your browser and go to the following link: `https://signup.microsoft.com/Signup?OfferId=bd569279-37f5-4f5c-99d0-425873bb9a4bdl=DYN365_ENTERPRISE_PLAN1Culture=en-usCountry=usali=1`.

2. On the page that opens, select your country. Based on this information, your Dynamics 365 CE organization will be hosted on the nearest Azure datacenter. For this example, I have selected `India`. Fill out the rest of the details that are required, as shown in the following screenshot, and click **Next**:

3. On the next screen, enter your admin user and organization details. Your Dynamics 365 CE organization will use this user as the admin. You can add other users that. After that, click on the **Create my account** button.

4. Next, provide your mobile number in order to receive an OTP. This will prove you are not a robot or a malware program. Once you have entered the OTP, Dynamics will start creating a user. Once the user has been created, click on the **Setup** button.
5. After this, you need to select your default language, which apps you want to use in your trial, and the currency you will be using.
6. Click on **Complete Setup** to finish setting up your account:

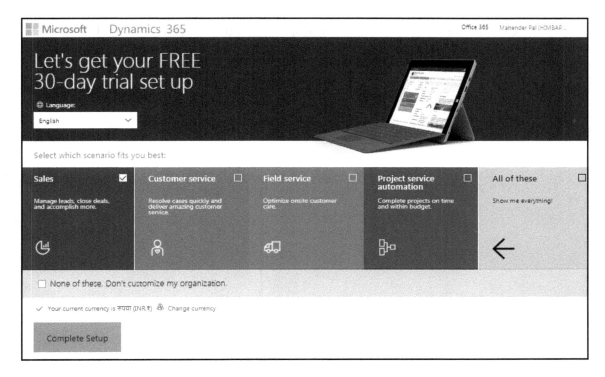

Once you've done this, you will be navigated to the Dynamics 365 CE trial.

Summary

In this chapter, we learned about Dynamics 365 and Dynamics 365 CE. We discussed the various apps that are available under the Dynamics 365 Hub. We also learned about the different ways we can deploy Dynamics 365 CE applications, along with the available client options that can be used to access Dynamics 365 CE. Finally, we discussed the different subscription options that are available in Dynamics 365 for customers and learned how to set up a 30-day trial.

In the next chapter, we are going to discuss project management and different methodologies that can be used for better project management. Then, we will discuss the methodologies that are used the most when implementing Dynamics 365 CE.

Implementation Methodology 2

This chapter will help you to understand what a project is and how we can manage one. Here, you will learn high-level project management activities. In addition to this, we will discuss project management methodologies and why we need them. We will also learn about different, commonly used project management methodologies such as Waterfall, Agile, Scrum, Feature Driven Development, DevOps, and Microsoft Sure Step and their phases. Once you have an idea about project management methodology, we will discuss the main questions that you need to consider when deciding which methodology is best suited for your Dynamics 365 CE implementation.

The main topics that we are going to discuss in this chapter are as follows:

- Understanding project management
- Understanding project management methodologies
- Choosing a methodology for Dynamics 365 CE

Understanding project management

Before discussing project management methodology, let's first establish what a project is. A project is a collection of temporary activities—commonly known as **tasks** in the software industry—that should be completed within a specific timeframe and budget to achieve a specific goal. Tasks must be initiated and completed in a specific time slot. Your project duration and the budget of the project is dependent on many factors, including how many activities we are going to include in our project and how many resources are required to complete that set of activities. For example, a maintenance project of any software will have a smaller duration and budget compared to developing a new software product.

Defining project activities are also referred to as **project scoping**. Project scoping is responsible for defining what is required and how we can achieve our requirements. The best practice is to define a project scope properly before starting to work on any of the project's activities. Adding activities after a project has started can impact a project's timeline and budget. You can see, in the following diagram, that the project is divided into three high-level steps where we start by defining our project activities, then we start working on these activities, and finally complete all of the activities to finish our project:

Project activities are performed in different stages for better management and to give more control over the quality of output. These stages are also known as **project phases**. A project phase is normally dependent on the output of the previous phase, so the next phase can take the output of the previous phase as input.

Let's take a simple example of assembling a bike, where one phase is to get all bike parts and the next phase is to assemble them together to form a complete bike. Project phases are progressive in nature, which means that every phase of the project needs to add some improvements to achieve the overall project target. Now that we have a good understanding of the project, let's discuss project management.

Project management is a process and it is very important for any project to successfully achieve its goal. The project management process controls all of the phases of a project and connects them together toward achieving a project goal. A project management process can be primarily divided into five phases, as shown in the following diagram:

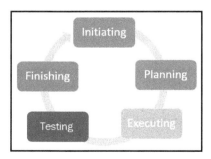

Let's take a closer look at each of these phases:

- **Initiating**: This phase is responsible for identifying all of the requirements of a project and it is also considered the start of the project activities. In this phase, all of the project requirements are documented so that the documentation can build the foundation of the project. We can also say that this phase is responsible for scoping the project and setting its target output. Before going to the next phase, every project activity should be defined clearly. Documents generated in this phase are commonly known as **requirement documents**.

- **Planning**: This phase is responsible for planning the strategy to work on all of the project requirements listed in the previous phase. This phase is very critical in any project because poor project planning can cause project failure, so we should always put a good amount of effort into project planning. This phase is also responsible for defining a project's timeline and resource allocation. Resources are selected for respective tasks based on their skillset.

- **Executing**: In this phase, all project activities are carried out by the respective project team members based on the documentation generated in earlier phases. While working on the activities, every team member is responsible for completing their assigned activities within the timeframe of the activity itself.

- **Testing**: Once all of the project activities are completed, they are tested against the project requirement to ensure that they are fulfilling customer expectations. Requirements documented in the first phase are used as a base for testing activities. If activities do not fulfill requirements, they are sent back to the respective team for reworking.

- **Finishing**: This is the final phase of any project. Here, all project activities are complete and the project is ready for closure. Before releasing the output of the project, a final review is done against the project requirement to see whether the project's final output meets all of the requirements. This final review also helps the team to make a note of the challenges that they faced during this project so that the same challenges can be managed properly in all future projects.

Project management is responsible for carrying out all of the preceding phases to ensure that the project target is achieved based on the client project expectation. To implement project management effectively, different project management methodologies are available, which we will be discussing in the next topic.

Understanding project management methodologies

While working on a project, project managers use different techniques and tools to keep their project organized and to get them delivered on time. One of the most critical decisions a project manager takes is selecting an appropriate project management methodology. We learned about common project management phases in the last topic. While implementing those phases, project managers need to follow specific practices to plan, manage, and execute the project, and this is what we call the **project management methodology**.

We can also call it a model that can be applied to project management to achieve a project goal within the set project timeline and budget. Project management methodology helps managers to manage their projects from the initial stage to delivery of the project. It helps the manager to set up a protocol for different activities. For example, how the project team will communicate, how tasks will be assigned to team members, setting up quality control, managing the project timeline, and delivering project output.

No doubt using project management methodology provides many advantages to an organization by standardizing its business processes, setting up communication rules, setting up guidelines, and reducing the risk of project failure. Companies can follow different methodologies for project implementation, but which project management methodology will be used for a project depends on the project manager. Project managers use project methodologies based on their past experiences and industry requirements because not all methodologies can be used in every project. For example, while working on the construction project, a particular project methodology may be more helpful than one that is common for software projects.

The various project management methodologies that we will be looking at are listed here:

- Waterfall
- Spiral
- Agile
- Scrum
- RAD
- Microsoft Sure Step
- Kanban
- Feature Driven Development
- DevOps

We will be studying each of these methodologies in the following subsections.

The Waterfall methodology

This is one of the most popular and simplest methodologies used for project management. In this approach, a project is divided into sequential tasks that are then carried out one by one until all tasks are completed. This is similar to a waterfall, where water flows from top to bottom, hence the name. In this methodology, you can't move back to the previous phase. Instead, the only possible option is to go back to the initial phase and start again. The output generated from one stage becomes the input of the next stage.

In the Waterfall methodology, comprehensive documentation is done in every phase, which is very helpful when carrying out maintenance or when a new member joins during a project. They can easily refer to the documentation to learn about project details. The Waterfall model divides a complete project into six different stages. We can understand how these stages are implemented one by one by using the following diagram:

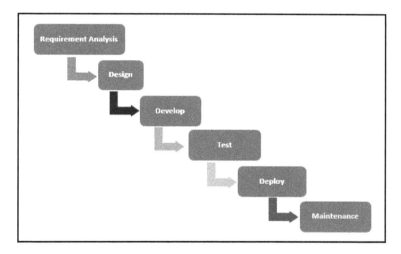

Let's discuss these stages in detail:

1. **Requirement Analysis**: This is the first phase of the Waterfall model. In this phase, we find out what is required. This phase needs a lot of interaction with the client to understand their requirements in detail. Various techniques are used to identify requirements, and we will be discussing these techniques in later chapters. All of the requirements are recorded properly in the necessary documents. Once project requirements are known, the feasibility of the solutions is discussed. All of the requirements are analyzed properly and different possibilities are considered for developing a potential system. In this phase, any existing infrastructure that clients have, such as existing servers, are also analyzed for potential use in the new system.

2. **Designing**: In this phase, the blueprint of the final output is prepared based on the project requirements generated in the first steps and then an appropriate technology is selected. All of the functional and technical design documents are prepared in this phase along with the system architecture. Once all of the design documents are ready, the project moves to the next phase.

3. **Coding**: In this phase, code is developed by team members based on design documents. Team members work on the individual modules, which are integrated with other modules once completed. Team members also perform unit testing of their code to avoid any design time or runtime errors.

4. **Testing**: Once all of the modules are developed, they are tested against the requirement document generated in the first phase by the quality team members. The quality team first prepares test cases using requirements, and then manual or automated testing is performed later on. Manual testing is done by a QA team member manually without using any testing tools or script, whereas automated testing is done using tools and scripts. Automated testing is useful for retesting test cases after code changes or any upgrades.

5. **Deployment**: In this phase, the final output is verified by clients and this involves user acceptance testing involving end users. An end user performs function testing to make sure that the project output is based on their expectations. End user training sessions are also conducted in this phase.

6. **Maintenance**: In this phase, post-deployed changes are implemented. This includes fixing any client-side issues, adding more functionality to a project, or upgrading software patches, if required.

Waterfall is a common method of the software and construction industries. This methodology emphasizes further collection of all of the requirements in the initial phase and documenting them properly to use them in later phases. This model is easy to understand as projects progress through easily understandable phases, one by one. However, this model can't be used for projects where it is difficult to find out all requirements at the initial stage. This is because it is very difficult to add new requirements once a project is initiated.

The Spiral methodology

This is another very old model for project management that can be considered as a combination of the Waterfall and iteration models. In the Spiral model, a list of requirements is identified for each iteration, which is known as a **spiral**. The output of every spiral is a small prototype of the project. The client can review this prototype and provide feedback. Similarly, requirements are identified for the next spiral. This process is followed until the project is complete and ready for delivery. As we can see in the following Spiral model diagram, a small prototype is developed in each spiral:

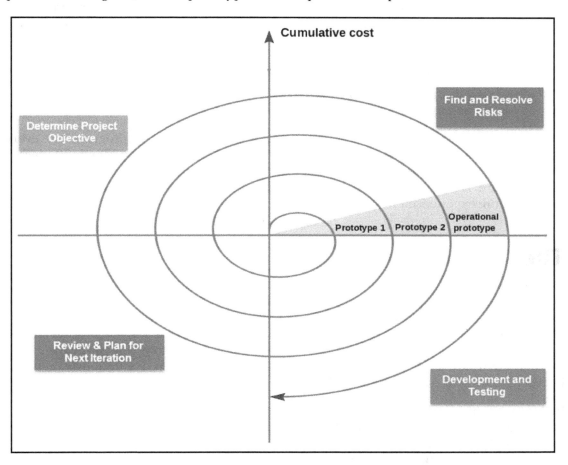

There are four phases in the Spiral model. Let's discuss these next:

- **Determine Project Objective**: In this phase, requirements are gathered from the client and a feasibility study is carried out against those requirements. Any existing infrastructure is also analyzed for use in a potential system. All of the planning is done in this phase which includes preparing a project schedule and resource allocations for each spiral.
- **Find and Resolve Risks**: In this phase, as the name suggests, all requirements are visited to identify any potential project risks. Proper documentation is done for all of the risks and these risks are resolved using the best possible options.
- **Development and Testing**: All of the development and testing is done in this phase. A small prototype of the system is developed and tested before delivering it to the client.
- **Review and Plan for Next Iteration**: In this phase, customers review the prototype and provide their feedback. After the review, the next spiral requirements are planned.

This model is suited for large projects where clients can review project progress after every iteration and provide feedback about a prototype. It also allows for requirement changes after the project is initiated. Project risks are identified at early stages and fixed to avoid project failure. However, this model can't be applied to small projects and risk analysis requires more experienced resources.

The Agile methodology

This is a very common project management methodology used nowadays, especially for managing software development projects. This model is best suited when complete requirements are not clear when initiating a project but project stakeholders have an overall idea of what they are looking for. The Agile methodology basically implements the idea of developing software in many iterations; every iteration uses the complete **Software Development Life Cycle** (**SDLC**) process and stakeholders are also continuously involved in every iteration to provide their feedback.

In this model, the project moves to the next level in iterations and project tasks are performed based on their priorities. The project tasks' priority list is known as the product backlog in Agile. Team members work collectively on the product backlog and provide estimations for the tasks based on their priorities.

SDLC is a process used by software development companies to develop software. It is divided into many phases, beginning with requirement gathering and ending at the maintenance phase.

We can define an Agile methodology using the following diagram, which explains the high-level Agile methodology process:

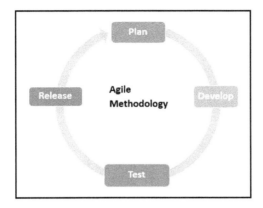

Agile methodology helps teams to deliver a much better product quickly using small iterations compared to other methodologies. The Agile methodology uses the following main principle:

1. Continuous team interaction
2. Working module with documentation
3. Continuous collaboration with stakeholders
4. Responding to changes quickly

Agile methodology maintains continuous team communication that involves every team member from developer to customer. An Agile team is not managed by just a project manager; instead, the team management is the responsibility of every team member. Daily calls, known as **Scrum calls**, are held to discuss project progress and any roadblock. After every sprint—which normally ranges from one week to four weeks—a working model is released with complete documentation.

End users perform user acceptance testing after every sprint and continuous interaction with stakeholders also ensures that the project is going in the right direction. The working model that is released after a sprint is always based on customer expectations. Agile project management addresses the response to change quickly. Using this principle, project teams respond quickly to customers, end users, stakeholders, and market trends, ensuring that the final product is helpful to the end users and that it is something that they really want to use.

Today, Agile is used as a framework for other methodologies such as Scrum and Kanban, where the whole project is managed by continuous iteration and collaboration. There is no doubt in saying that Agile can help teams to increase flexibility and collaboration, which ultimately results in a more successful project where the end goal is not clearly defined during project initiation.

The Scrum methodology

Scrum is basically used to implement the Agile methodology, so we can also call it as a subset of Agile. Using Scrum, we deliver incremented products to customers after every sprint of one to two weeks. Once the sprint is over, every team member meets to plan for the next sprint. Some high-level activities involved in Scrum are sprint planning, daily stand-up calls, sprint reviews, and build releases after every sprint. Scrum is normally used when requirements are changing very rapidly. The following diagram represents the complete common steps performed in the Scrum methodology:

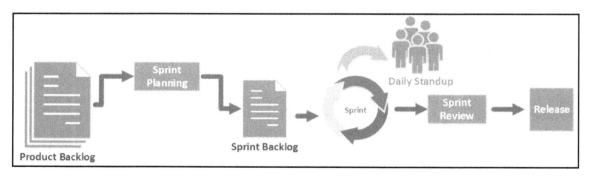

Let's now discuss common phases included in the Scrum methodology.

Product backlog

The first phase is to collect customer high-level requirements and prepare product backlog. Customer requirements are ordered based on their priority in a product backlog. These requirements are prioritized by the product owner. The product backlog includes all of the features that the customer expects in the final product. These requirements are termed **user stories.**

A user story provides details about the requirement from an end user perspective, focusing on what they want to do or what feature they want to have in a product. These user stories do not include the complete set of requirements—instead, they only include features that customers have in their mind at the time of starting a project. The customer expected feature list can be changed during implementation, but the product backlog still acts as a requirement document for the Scrum process for implementation. This document is used as a base document for sprint planning.

Sprint planning

After the product backlog is prepared, the next step is planning a sprint. Sprint planning is done after every sprint is over. In sprint planning, the Scrum team selects a list of requirements that will be included in the current sprint. Some of the following questions are answered in sprint planning:

- What is the goal of this sprint?
- Which product backlog items will be included in this sprint?
- What will be the time estimation for the user stories to include in this sprint?
- Who is available for this sprint?
- How we are going to deliver incremental builds after the sprint?

The output of sprint planning is sprint backlog and time estimation. Selected requirements from product backlogs are included in the sprint backlog based on their priority, effort estimation, and team capability. Scrum methodology gives flexibility to the team regarding the user stories implemented within the current sprint as sprint backlog items can move from one sprint to another. If any sprint backlog items are not completed during the current sprint, they are moved to the next sprint.

Daily standup

During the sprint, team members meet over daily Scrum meetings, which should not go over 15 minutes. These Scrum meetings are managed by Scrum team members. The Scrum Master acts as a team coach who motivates every team member to give their best performance. In daily meetings, team members update the team on the status of their tasks, the next task that they are going to work on, and they discuss roadblocks if there are any. Daily calls help teams to get updates about the status of user stories. Any potential issues can be identified in advance and the team works collectively to resolve them.

During daily standup calls, a burndown chart is updated based on the team's status. A burndown chart can be considered an output of daily Scrum calls, which helps every team member to understand how many tasks are remaining.

Sprint review

The sprint review is done at the end of every sprint. In the sprint review process, a demo of the completed user stories is presented to the Scrum team, stakeholders, and end users. Stakeholders and end users provide their feedback after the demo and the Scrum team acts on the feedback accordingly.

Backlog refinement

Once the sprint is over, the next step is to refine the product backlog. During this process, new user stories are added to the product backlog and unnecessary user stories are removed from it. User stories' priorities can be changed by the product owner if required.

There is no doubt that the Scrum methodology helps us to implement projects quickly. Larger projects can be divided into multiple sprints. It is very flexible in terms of how easily it accommodates new changes. For example, if stakeholders request a new feature, a product owner can easily add them to the product backlog. But sometimes, this becomes a risk for the project when stakeholders keep requesting new functionalities.

RAD

Rapid Application Development (RAD) is another methodology that is used to implement Agile. RAD is very popular nowadays where the main reason to use this methodology is to build a working prototype of the system quickly and efficiently. This methodology is also very flexible in terms of accepting changes during the development process. Here, less time is spent on planning and the main concentration is on developing a prototype using iterative steps, which helps project managers and stakeholders to accurately measure project progress.

They can provide their feedback after using a prototype and teams incorporate them quickly. The following diagram explains how RAD methodology is used for projects:

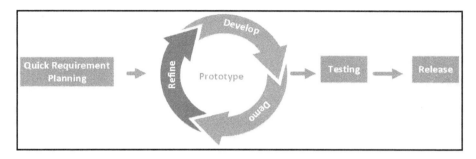

Let's discuss the common phases used in RAD.

Requirement planning

In this phase, requirement gathering and planning is done for the project. In RAD methodology, the planning phase is shorter compared to other project methodologies. Requirements are gathered to understand what customers are looking for in the final product. Current business processes are also analyzed in this phase. Once requirements are gathered, the project moves to the next phase after taking approval from the customer against requirements.

Developing a prototype

In this phase, the design and development of the prototype start. A team works on the requirements gathered in an earlier phase to prepare the UI and data model. Then, they customize the UI based on customer feedback. It is very important to take the approval of the customer for UI before jumping to the development of the code. Once the design and data model is completed, the team starts writing code for requirements.

After unit testing, a prototype is demonstrated to all team members including stakeholders. Stakeholders provide their feedback, and they then communicate to the team which functionality works well and which failed. Then, the team works on the refinement in the prototype based on the feedback provided. This phase is implemented in many iterations depending on the requirements. After incorporating all of the feedback and requested changes, the project moves to the next phase.

Testing

In this phase, the QA team performs system and integration testing to make sure this new prototype will work well with the existing system. Most of the issues are already fixed in an earlier phase based on customer feedback. In RAD, each prototype is tested independently, which reduces the overall testing time. In this phase, the development strategy is also tested to make sure that deployment goes smoothly.

Release

This is the final phase of RAD, where the final product is released for end users. This phase includes end user testing, data migration, and the changeover to the new system. Customers can log any issues faced after release.

RAD helps to achieve more in less time. Quick iteration can accommodate new changes requested, so the final product is always based on customer expectations. As integration testing is already performed, it is less common to face any integration issue during project release. However, this methodology can only be used for product development where a module can be developed independently and it requires shorter development cycles.

Microsoft Sure Step

The Microsoft Sure Step methodology is developed by Microsoft to implement Dynamics products for customers. The Microsoft Sure Step methodology has built-in processes and the disciplines necessary to implement Dynamics solutions. It also includes built-in document templates required for various tasks during Dynamics implementation with a set of guidelines and best practices for successfully implementing Dynamics. Microsoft Sure Step classifies projects into categories that we will discuss in the following subsections.

Microsoft Sure Step – projects

This provides information about different users involved in Sure Step projects, including the customer as well as the consulting side. We can understand the Sure Step methodology project using the following diagram, as well as see details regarding the different phases and the project:

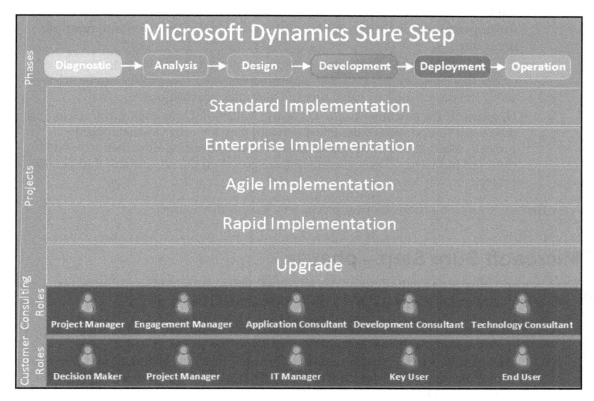

In the preceding diagram, we can see that we have different project categories in the Microsoft Sure Step methodology, so let's discuss these projects one by one to understand more about them:

- **Standard**: Microsoft Dynamics implementation for a single customer site comes under this category. This project requires moderate-to-complex customization on Dynamics applications.

- **Enterprise**: Microsoft Dynamics complex implementation for a single site or multiple sites comes under this project category. As these are complex implementations, it requires a decent amount of effort to develop Dynamics solutions. This project is larger in terms of scope compared to other project types.
- **Agile**: Projects under this category use iterative approaches for implementing Microsoft Dynamics applications. In these types of projects, not all requirements are known when the project begins, so new requirements can be added during the implementation process. The whole Agile project is divided into multiple iterations.
- **Rapid**: Microsoft Dynamics implementation projects with limited scope come under this category. Most of the requirements under this project can be achieved using the out-of-the-box capability of Dynamics applications.
- **Upgrade**: If the customer is already using Microsoft Dynamics applications and they want to update it to the latest version, they are regarded as upgrade projects. Microsoft Sure Step provides project supporting documents based on different industries. These documents are based on the selection of the specific project.

Now that we know a bit more about projects, let's look at the phases.

Microsoft Sure Step – phases

The Microsoft Sure Step methodology also implemented a series of phases. Every phase has its own importance. Let's have a closer look at these phases one by one:

- **Diagnostic**: The main objective of this phase is to find out what is required. Customer requirements are gathered and appropriate Microsoft Dynamics applications are demonstrated to the customer based on their key requirements. Sometimes, a small **Proof Of Concept** (**POC**) is also built to show the capability of Microsoft Dynamics products. All of the requirements are collected in a requirement specification document. Once requirements are captured, the project moves to the next phase.

- **Analysis**: In this phase, the requirement documents produced in an earlier phase are analyzed properly and a feasibility study is done for customer requirements. Fit gap analysis is done to compare customer requirements with Microsoft Dynamics functionality and gaps are identified where customization and development are required. This phase also sets up a change control plan, which identifies how new requirements will be added to the project scope if required.
- **Design**: This phase is used to prepare the design and configure Microsoft Dynamics applications based on the requirements. The team works on both the function and technical design of the application. The screen layout of the application is prepared and approval is taken from the customer. The technical design document is prepared in this phase, which has details of any customization and development required.
- **Development**: In this phase, code development is done and the system is built based on the technical design document. If the system requires integration with a third-party system, that is also built in this phase. Once development is done, all of the system modules are tested by QA team members. If the current system requires any data migration scripts or procedure, this is also developed in this phase.
- **Deployment**: In this phase, a Microsoft Dynamics solution installed on the customer location QA servers and UAT is performed against all of the requirements to make sure the final product is based on customer expectations. Key users are trained in this phase to use the new system. A go-live checklist is prepared, which includes critical configuration for production deployment. Finally, after the UAT is completed, production cutover is performed based on the previously decided cutover timings to release the project for end users who will be using the systems in their day-to-day work.
- **Operation**: This phase is the last phase of the project, where the final review of the system is done and the post-deployment support strategy is decided.

The Microsoft Sure Step methodology takes less time to implement Microsoft Dynamics for the customer as it includes a set of tools, required templates, and best practices.

Kanban

This is another popular project management methodology that follows Agile methods for managing projects. It uses a visual method of managing projects as it moves through the process. In this methodology, work items are represented with the help of a Kanban board, as shown in the following diagram, which allows team members to see the state of every piece of work at any time:

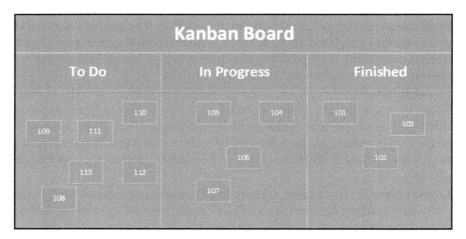

Work items denoted by numbers in the preceding diagram are displayed using Kanban cards. In the preceding Kanban board, we can see the current status of all work items. **To Do** is a list of pending items that are not started yet, whereas **In Progress** items are those that are under development. The **Finished** queue shows all of the items that are completed. Kanban uses the following basic principles:

- A visual board for project activities
- Work on limited project activities at a time
- Flow management for activities
- Implementing feedback
- Implementing collaboration between teams

Work items in this methodology can be re-prioritized based on the stakeholders' requirements. Kanban work items are never bound to a specific iteration, so this provides flexibility to developers. Team members collaborate with each other to improve the flow of work in the Kanban board throughout the project. This methodology is best suited for projects with small teams.

Feature Driven Development

Feature Driven Development is another project management methodology that comes under the Agile family, which means it also follows an iterative and incremental development process. In this methodology, client requirements are presented as features that become the basis of product development. We can consider features such as user stories in the Scrum.

The following diagram explains the phases of the Feature Driven Development methodology:

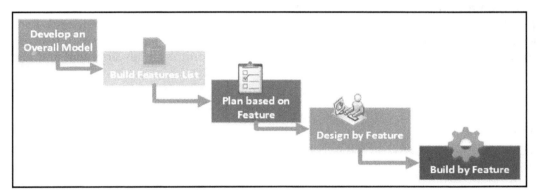

Let's discuss these phases in more detail:

- **Develop an Overall Model**: In this phase, an overall model of the solution is prepared, which explains the high-level functionality of the solution. It does not provide all project details at this stage. This phase helps the team to understand the overall goal of the project.
- **Build a Features' List**: Once the overall model is ready and team members have an understanding of the project goal, all customer requirements are divided into features. In this phase, a features list is prepared, which is used as a basis for the whole project. Big features are divided into small manageable features that should not take more than 2 weeks to develop.
- **Plan based on Feature**: After having a complete features' list ready, planning for features, implementation starts. Planning is done for every feature, which involves different activities such as setting their priority, identifying risks, resource allocation, and identifying dependencies if there are any.

- **Design by Feature**: In this phase, the team starts working on the design of the features assigned to them. Design documents are created for features. Once the design is ready for the features, a property inspection is done to avoid any confusion during the development of these features.
- **Build by Feature**: Once the design phase is complete, teams start developing code based on the design documents. After this, code is tested for the feature. Once testing is completed, it is verified by the chief architect. After the approval of the chief architect, this feature is added to the mail build.

Following the preceding five simple phases, the Feature Driven Development methodology can be used for rapid product development. Not much time is spent initially discussing requirement details. Instead, the overall model is prepared to understand the high-level objectives of the project. However, this methodology can't be used with a small team as it requires an expert chief architect to lead the team and monitor all development and testing processes.

DevOps

DevOps fills the gap between the development and operation teams. The word DevOps is a combination of the words, *development* and *operations*. This helps to automate the process to develop and deploy projects faster and more efficiently. DevOps basically uses Agile to create a value-driven environment for quick deployment of software products and features.

The following diagram provides us with the basic idea regarding the DevOps methodology:

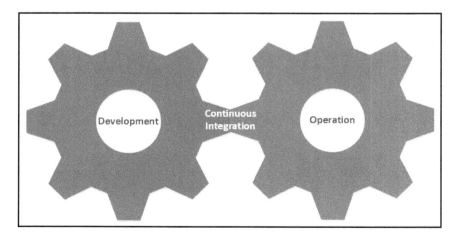

Let's discuss the common phases of DevOps:

- **Development**: In this phase, software development takes place continuously. The development process is divided into small development cycles.
- **Testing**: In this phase, automated testing is done for the code developed in an earlier phase. This involves writing an automated testing script. These automated testing scripts are used by automation testing tools for testing functionality developed by the team.
- **Integration**: In this phase, new functionality is integrated with the existing functionality and integration testing is executed. Continuous development supports continuous integration as well.
- **Deployment**: In this phase, continuous deployment takes place. Deployment is done in such a way that it should not impact any of the existing functionality.

The main advantage of using DevOps is to make the whole development and release process faster. As a result, a product can be released to a user in a much faster way as all of the tasks are automated and do not require any manual efforts. This is very useful when we need a project release very frequently. The use of automated tools ensures high-quality products with efficiency. Products can, therefore, be released to the market in a much faster way. Release automation also minimizes any risk of deployment failure, which significantly reduces the number of bugs.

Apart from the preceding methodologies, sometimes, companies create their own hybrid project management methodologies, which include template, tools, and processes from various project management methodologies. Now, we have discussed the most popular project management methodologies and learned that every methodology has its own merits and demerits. While planning for project implementation, the first task is to pick a project management approach that is right for your project to make implementation smoother and more efficient. Now, in the next section, we are going to discuss which of the preceding methodologies can be used for implementing Dynamics 365 CE.

Choosing a methodology for Dynamics 365 CE

Microsoft Dynamics 365 CE can be implemented using different project management methodologies such as Sure Step, Agile, Scrum, Waterfall, and DevOps, which we discussed in the project management methodology section. The project manager plays a key role in selecting the right implementation methodology for your organization. Which methodology the project manager picks depends on their past project experience and sometimes it is a decision for the Microsoft Partner Company that implements Dynamics 365 CE for you. But before selecting the right methodology for your company, let's first understand why it is very important to use project management methodology while implementing Dynamics 365 CE for your organization.

The most common reasons for using project management methodologies for implementing Dynamics 365 CE include the following:

- For managing project timelines efficiently
- For better project management
- For using predefined tools and templates
- For reducing project failure risks
- For team collaboration and skills development
- To ensure stakeholders for return on investments

Now that we know the main reasons for using project management methodology, the next question comes to mind: which methodology is best suited for Dynamics 365 CE implementation? Before discussing a suitable methodology, we should try to get answers to the following questions:

- **Is the project objective clear?** This question is important for selecting methodologies. For example, we can use the Waterfall model if the project goal is clearly defined; otherwise, using Agile methodologies will be helpful for Dynamics 365 CE implementation.
- **Are all of the requirements known?** Requirements play a critical role in the selection of methodologies because some methodologies require all project requirements to be clearly defined before starting implementation planning. On the other hand, some methodologies only require that the high-level goal of the project should be known and detailed requirements can be captured once the project begins.

- **Are requirements complex or simple?** This is another important question. Simple requirements will take less time and can be mostly achieved using out-of-the-box Dynamics 365 CE features or with minimal customization. On the other hand, if requirements are complex, they require a good amount of development efforts, which can increase project release timelines.

- **Can the requirements be changed?** Some methodologies, such as the Waterfall model, do not allow changing requirements once Dynamics 365 CE implementation is initiated. In contrast, other methodologies, such as Spiral, Agile, and Scrum, accept changes in every iteration.

- **Will the customer be available for project meetings?** During Dynamics 365 CE, customer involvement plays a critical role. Some methodologies require minimal interaction with the customer during the initial phases of the implementation. However, some methodologies require continuous interaction with the customer to get their feedback after every iteration. Client feedback plays a crucial role in Dynamics 365 CE, ensuring minimal risk of project failure.

- **What are project release timelines?** Some customers require Dynamics 365 CE implementation to be completed in a short timeframe depending on their business requirements. Customers want to provide a new system to their end users as soon as possible, especially when end users are waiting for a long time to access new functionality. This is also the case when they want a resolution for issues in an existing system. We can use methodologies such as DevOps to allow quick production release, allowing for the automating of the release process with efficiency.

- **Can a project be divided into modules?** Some Dynamics 365 CE project requirements can be divided into multiple individual modules that can be developed independently without any dependency. Sometimes, a team can work on modules in parallel, whereas sometimes it's not possible to break down requirements into multiple modules.

- **Is the customer expecting a single release for their project?** Sometimes, a Dynamics 365 CE customer requires a single production release for all departments. They want a new system to be applied in one go. However, some clients want to implement Dynamics 365 CE department by department, which requires multiple releases of the project. The Waterfall model is best suited for the single production release, whereas Agile family methodologies can be used for multiple releases. Every sprint can release specific functionality to a specific department.

- **How many resources are required for implementation?** The project member team size for Dynamics 365 CE implementation is based on the project requirements, whether these are simple or complex. Some project management methodologies are best suited for small team sizes because it is difficult to handle a large team. For example, in a Scrum, team size is always recommended as being from 3 to 9 for better management. In contrast, the Waterfall model can comfortably support large team sizes.

- **Is the project documentation required?** Documentation is very important for any project for later referral. It is very helpful when a new resource is added to the Dynamics 365 CE implementation team or any resource is replaced with existing resources based on their availability. Some project management methodologies put less stress on maintaining project documentation. However, some methodologies produce documentation after every implementation phase. Some methodologies, such as Microsoft Sure Steps, provide out-of-the-box templates to prepare project documentation.

Once we have answers to all of the preceding questions, it is easy to select the appropriate Dynamics 365 CE implementation methodology. In conclusion, the Waterfall model can be selected for your Dynamics 365 CE implementation if all of the project requirements are known, the client is not available for day-to-day communication, and they are looking for a single release for the organization. But keep in mind that the Waterfall model adds a high risk of project failure as the client needs to wait to see the product only after all of the phases are over for the Waterfall methodology. While using the Waterfall model, there are chances that the final solution is not based on client expectations as a client has minimal involvement in the Waterfall model.

Agile family methodologies are best suited based on current market trends. Customers want to bring their product into the market as soon as possible with high efficiency. In Agile, it is also normal practice to not change the whole system at once, which can also introduce integration issues, especially if a customer is using multiple software applications.

Using DevOps methodology can help release automation, and integration can be performed easily. Nowadays, Scrum is also very popular for Dynamics 365 CE implementation where everyone has clear visibility of the ongoing process throughout sprints. New change requests from clients can be easily and quickly adjusted. Scrum adds a high success rate in Dynamics 365 CE implementation as a customer is involved from the initial start to the release of every sprint. Daily standups can help us to identify any potential future issues with ease and they can be resolved in time.

Summary

In this chapter, we learned about the project and how to manage the project efficiently. We also discussed the importance of the project management methodology and the different popular methodologies used for project management. We also discussed the main questions whose answers you need to find to select the best-suited project methodology for your Dynamics 365 CE implementation. Now, we have a good understanding of project management and project management methodology.

In the next chapter, we will discuss how to perform requirement gathering and analysis for your Dynamics 365 CE implementation.

Requirement Gathering and Analysis

3

This chapter will help you to understand the requirements of project management methodology and the importance of project management tools to deliver any project successfully. We will also discuss various methodologies that are used for implementing Dynamics 365 CE.

This chapter will help you to select a project methodology that's suitable for your Dynamics 365 CE project.

The main topics that we are going to discuss in this chapter are as follows:

- Understanding requirements
- Requirement gathering and analysis
- Fit-Gap analysis for Dynamics 365 CE
- Preparing a project plan

Technical requirements

This chapter does not have any technical requirements, but while undertaking requirement gathering for your customer, it's recommended to have the following tools (or similar) in order to document customer requirements:

- Microsoft Office or Office 365 subscription to document project activities
- Microsoft Visio, or a similar tool
- Microsoft Project management, or a similar project management tool

Understanding requirements

Before understanding the requirement gathering process, let's first understand what a requirement is. A requirement is basically a request from a customer or an end user. This request may be for adding new functionality in the system or to modify the existing functionality of the system. Different terminologies are used to refer to requirements such as user stories, use cases, features, and so on, based on the project management methodology used.

We need requirements in order to design, develop, and test a Dynamics 365 CE implementation or any product. There is no doubt about the fact that requirements set up a foundation on which a new system is implemented or built. If requirements are not correct, it increases the risk of a Dynamics 365 CE implementation failure.

Requirements can be divided into the following different categories:

- Business requirements
- Functional requirements
- Non-functional requirements

Let's discuss these different categories of requirements.

Business requirements

Business requirements represent a high-level idea of business automation processes for Dynamics 365 CE implementation, enhancements to the existing Dynamics 365 CE implementation, or developing new Dynamics 365 CE solutions.

We will be discussing Dynamics 365 CE customization and configuration details in later chapters. These requirements are gathered by business analysts and are documented in the **Business Requirement Document** (**BRD**). This document explains what the proposed system will look like from the business's perspective.

Business requirements consist of both functional and non-functional requirements, and also the needs of the organization. Business requirements should be gathered because they provide a foundation for the complete project. The following are the main objectives of the BRD:

- To provide background details about the existing system and reasons for changes, along with business context and vision

- To list the high-level business requirements and explain what is in the scope of the project and what is out of scope
- To provide details about business processes, infrastructure, and technologies used within the organization
- To provide metrics for successful Dynamics 365 CE implementation
- To provide expected timelines to change the current system
- To provide details about the Dynamics 365 CE implementation plan, including whether a customer wants to implement a department-by-department release or a single release for all the departments

The BRD also includes approval from the business.

To understand further what business requirements look like, let's take an example of a bike service company, HIMBAP Auto Service Center, who wants to implement Dynamics 365 CE in their organization and all of their service centers. Their business requirements for the new system are as follows:

- An operational tool to improve customer service, automating and standardizing our customer service management.
- It should support customer segmentation.
- An analytical tool for improving client relationship management and analyzing client information using a 360-degree view, and reports on customer service performance by customer service centers.
- Allow real-time capturing of client information and communication across multiple devices.
- The system will immediately be accessible to all staff when they log in, and will highlight key relationship management tasks and reminders by customer.
- The system must provide a customer activity summary, including existing service history, current service plan, communication history, and other relevant customer contact information to allow sales priorities and strategies to be developed.
- A view of services purchased by the customer provides the ability to identify all customers, whether they are a business or an individual, and ascertain their geographic location.
- The system should be able to capture basic competitor information.

All of the preceding requirements explain what the customer is looking for. We can also say that business requirements basically talk about the pain points of the customers. Once we know all of the business requirements, they are captured in the BRD.

Functional requirements

Once we have the business requirement, which gives us a high-level idea of the proposed system, another requirement category (known as a functional requirement) comes into the picture. These requirements come from the end users or business users who actually use the system in their day-to-day jobs, so these requirements are basically about how the system will function. It describes what the main functions are that can be performed using the proposed system, what the capabilities of the new system will be, how it will behave when specific data is entered into the system, and so on.

Functional requirements are documented in the **Functional Requirement Document (FRD)**. A functional requirement also contains information about the business process automation that the new system should have. It specifies how the data will flow between different components of the system, and what the security requirements are going to be in order to use it. Functional requirements commonly focus on the following requirements:

- Application interface
- Security requirements of the new system
- Data input and output methods
- Reporting requirements
- Business processes and rules
- Reporting requirements

If we take the example of our HIMBAP Auto Service Center, we can describe some of the functional requirements, such as the following:

ID	Category	Description
1	User management	Admin user should be able to create and update users.
2	User management	Admin user should be able to create different profiles for users such as executive members, office staff, and service engineers.
3	User management	User should be able to access data based on their permissions.
4	Data management	User should be able to feed data manually as well as be able to import data.
5	Data management	Application should allow users to migrate existing data for customers, service history, and service plan purchase history.
6	Customer management	User should be able to set up a multi-relationship structure for customers.
7	Customer management	System should allow customer segmentation as business or individual.
8	Customer management	User should be able to communicate with the customer using the application.
9	Customer management	All of the communication with the customer should be available for reporting purposes.
10	Lead management	Application must be able to automatically route a lead record to a service center based on the geographic territory.

We can see how all of the preceding requirements focus on the system behavior and actions that should be available in the new application or solution.

Non-functional requirements

Another type of critical requirement is non-functional requirements, which mainly focus on the operation of the new solution or application. Any customer requirement that talks about how the new application *should be* comes into this category. Non-functional requirements talk about the following characteristics of the application:

- **Application availability**: This requirement talks about application availability during any downtime or failure. For example, any application maintenance mustn't take longer than 1 hour. We can also define which specific functionalities are critical and should be available as soon as possible.

- **Security**: This requirement talks about what security features an application should have. This is a critical requirement as it has a direct impact on the customer data stored in the application. Security requirements of the application ensure that customer data is protected from any unauthorized access. Users can also access application data based on their security permissions.

- **Reliability**: This requirement deals with the ability of an application to work without any failure. The failure may be because of code bugs, patch updates, or any hardware failure. Every new application or upgrade to an existing application is expected to work for a long time without any problems.

- **Usability**: This is a critical requirement for any application. Most business applications fail because users are unable to easily learn and use them. The usability requirement includes simplicity of the application, simplicity of its user interface, and availability of help within the application.

- **Performance**: This requirement talks about the responsiveness of the system based on different user actions, and how quickly an application should respond to user actions. The poor performance of an application leads to a negative user experience, therefore application response time should be quick.

- **Scalability**: This requirement talks about increasing an application's capacity to support more workload if and when required. This may involve supporting more users, supporting more requests during a specific time, or processing more transactions without much impact on the application.

  Most of the time, the scalability of an application is increased using hardware. For example, we may increase scalability by adding more hardware resources such as memory, servers, or disk space.

- **Maintenance**: This requirement talks about an application's ability to be maintained. This mainly includes fixing any existing bugs, restoring application data in case of failure, adding patches, and upgrading the application to the latest version.

Based on these characteristics, we can define non-functional requirements for our HIMBAP Auto Service Center as the following:

ID	Category	Description
1	Accessibility	Application should be available 24/7 for users.
2	Accessibility	Application should be accessible via popular web browsers as well as mobile devices.
3	Usability	The new system should be easy to use with or without minimal user training.
4	Usability	Application should have inbuilt help instructions.
5	Maintenance	Any application upgrade or maintenance should be done after office hours.
6	Security	Office staff should be forced to change their application password every month.
7	Security	Only Service Center Head should be able to add or modify application users.
8	Security	Only Service Center Head should be able to change user permissions.
9	Scalability	Application should be able to support more transactions if and when required during festival season.
10	Reliability	Any account update should be rolled back if any payment transaction fails.

Now that we have understood what a requirement is and learned the three categories of requirement, let's look at how we can gather these requirements and analyze them.

Requirement gathering and analysis

Requirement gathering is a critical part of any Dynamics 365 CE implementation or any other project. All of the other phases depend heavily on requirement gathering and analysis, so if requirement gathering and analysis are not correct, it leads to a significant impact on the Dynamics 365 CE implementation.

Let's discuss the two steps of requirement gathering and analysis process in detail.

Requirement gathering

Requirement gathering is a process designed to capture different types of requirements to implement Dynamics 365 CE or for solving issues in the existing Dynamics 365 CE implementation. Requirement gathering is done by a **Business Analyst (BA)**. Before requirement gathering, it is critical to identify stakeholders and key users. It is important to involve stakeholders and key users from the start of requirement gathering, to avoid any kind of confusion or misunderstanding.

Requirement gathering involves multiple activities such as open discussions, storyboards, building prototypes, and discussing different scenarios. These techniques can be different from one implementation to another. While using these techniques, we should always first understand the requirements clearly and confirm with the team before suggesting any solution to them. Based on the experience of the BA in a specific domain, some assumptions can be made related to customer requirements, but it is always recommended to discuss those assumptions with the relevant teams and gain their approval to avoid any confusion. You can see this process in the following diagram:

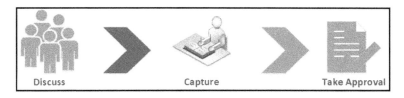

Requirement gathering can be done using the following different techniques:

- Interview
- Questionnaire
- Workshops
- Brainstorming
- Prototype

Let's discuss these techniques one by one, in detail.

Interview

This is the most common and effective method for requirement gathering. Using this technique, we can directly communicate with the stakeholders and key users to understand their requirements and objectives for implementing a Dynamics 365 CE application. Interviews are done by having face-to-face interaction; this can either be one-to-one or it can be in groups. The interview should always be pre-planned, based on the availability of the respective teams. While preparing interview questions, we can include the following types of questions in our interview:

- Open-ended questions
- Closed-ended questions

Open-ended questions

Open-ended questions are an important way to get a team's view about the current system, how they use it, and what goal they want to achieve through Dynamics 365 CE implementation. These questions can't be answered in one word—for example, *yes* or *no*. The answers to these questions can be provided in one or two lines. These questions are dependent on the Dynamics 365 CE apps that they are going to use. The following are some examples of open-ended questions for Dynamics 365 CE implementation for the HIMBAP Auto Service Center:

- What is your objective for implementing Dynamics 365 CE?
- What are the main business processes?
- What are your day-to-day activities?
- What is your pain point in the current system?
- How many users will be using Dynamics 365 CE?
- What is your sales life cycle?
- What activities do you perform for marketing?
- What actions do you take to resolve customer issues?
- What Microsoft technologies are you using currently?
- Do you want to integrate Dynamics 365 CE with another application?

Closed-ended questions

Interview questions that require specific answers come into the closed-ended question category. Answers for these questions can be short. Teams can provide an answer to these questions in single or multiple words. Answers to closed-ended questions can be designed as simply having *yes/no* or multiple-options answers. Here are some examples of closed-ended questions for the HIMBAP Auto Service Center Dynamics 365 CE implementation:

- Which Dynamics 365 CE deployment do you want to use (Cloud/On-Premises)?
- Do you use Microsoft Office 365?
- How do your customers communicate with you normally (email/phone/fax/personally)?
- How are service requests generated currently (using emails/phone/trade shows)?
- Do you provide service contracts?
- Are contracts based on your services category?
- Do you provide service 24/7?
- Do you schedule services on holidays or weekends?
- How do you distribute service requests (based on territory/ZIP code/customers)?
- Do you have existing data to migrate into Dynamics 365 CE?

It is always recommended to send your interview questions to respective teams in advance so that they can prepare for the interview. Teams may provide more details to you if questions are sent in advance, compared to directly conducting an interview. You can also record team interviews using recording software, which is always a good idea to ensure nothing is missed out.

Questionnaire

This is another type of requirement-gathering technique in which a list of questions is prepared based on the requirements. This technique is very useful to get more information in less time compared to the interview technique. For this technique, face-to-face interaction is not required, and this technique is used when we need to get requirements from large groups.

A questionnaire document is prepared with a list of questions and sent to the respective teams. Sometimes, online surveys are also created to get answers to feature-specific questions. This list of questions is prepared based on the specific module or feature sets.

Two types of questionnaires are the following:

1. Open-ended questionnaire
2. Closed-ended questionnaire

Let's discuss these two types of questionnaires in detail.

Open-ended questionnaire

As the name suggests, these questions provide teams with flexibility to express their thoughts freely. Open-ended questions are prepared with spaces for the answer. The following is an example of an open-ended questionnaire for our HIMBAP Auto Service Center Dynamics 365 CE implementation:

- What improvement are you looking for in the new system? Please provide details. _____
- What are the different types of users who will be using Dynamics 365 CE? Please provide details. _____
- How are your territories defined? Please provide details. _____
- What type of service do you provide to your customers? Please provide details. _____
- Do you outsource any of your services? If yes, provide details. _____
- Do you set goals for teams? If yes, how are those goals defined? Please explain. _____
- What types of reports are used and why they are generated? Please provide details. _____
- Do you categorize customers? If yes, please explain. _____
- Do you create competitor details in your system? If yes, how do you maintain them? _____
- Do you maintain a price list for auto services? If yes, please provide details. _____

Closed-ended questionnaire

In this type of questionnaire, we have multiple options available for answering a question. Users can select available options based on their requirement, but they can't freely provide their opinion or answers as compared to an open-ended questionnaire. The following are some examples of questions that we can use for our HIMBAP Auto Service Center Dynamics 365 CE implementation:

- How will the user be accessing the Dynamics 365 CE application? Please select appropriate options:
    1. Browser
    2. Mobile
    3. Outlook
    4. Tablet
    5. All

- Please select all of the apps of Dynamics 365 CE that you are planning to use:
    1. Sales
    2. Marketing
    3. Service
    4. Field Service
    5. Voice of the Customer
    6. Project Service Automation

- Do you have a knowledge base?
    1. Yes
    2. No

- Do you follow any processes to approve articles before they are published in the knowledge base?
    1. Yes
    2. No

- Do you provide roadside assistance?
    1. Yes
    2. No

- Do service engineers work in shifts?
    1. Yes
    2. No

- How do you communicate with your customers?
    1. Using emails
    2. Using phone call
    3. Using letter
    4. Using fax
    5. Any other option _____
- What are your sales channels?
    1. Company website
    2. Emails
    3. Phone call
    4. Resellers
    5. Retailers
    6. Other _____
- How do you capture customer feedback?
    1. Using feedback form
    2. Using online survey
    3. Through social media
    4. Through phone call
    5. Other _____
- Are you using any loyalty management programs?
    1. Yes
    2. No

Once questionnaire responses are gathered, they can be compiled to look at requirements. This is a very useful technique to gather more information quickly.

Workshops

Another technique to gather requirements from a large number of people is by conducting workshops. Workshops can be conducted based on the divisions of the organization wherein the team can provide their views, and we can get quality information after a group discussion. In some requirement-gathering techniques, we deal with individual people who may provide their personal ideas that may not match with the object of implementing Dynamics 365 CE. In the case of workshops, as multiple people are involved, we will only get requirements that match the organization's objective. While conducting workshops, we need to make sure to involve the right people.

Compared to other methods, it is an expensive way to gather requirements as a large number of people are involved, but it definitely helps to get correct information in a limited time. Proper planning should be done before conducting workshops; for example, workshop discussion topics should be planned in advance, and the workshop location and duration should be finalized before the scheduled event.

Brainstorming

Sometimes, while gathering business requirements, it is critical to listen to the subject matter expert's idea to solve a specific business problem. Brainstorming is the process of subject matter experts contributing their ideas to solve a specific business issue, problem, or requirement. During brainstorming, people can express their ideas about the topics, without any hesitation. We can use brainstorming for one or more topics and prepare ideas for the solution. Different ideas can be prioritized depending on the discussion with the group and, finally, we can come to a conclusion by selecting the best-suited solution for the business.

Prototype

This is another very important technique and is the most common for requirement gathering nowadays. In this technique, a proof of concept is built based on the initial requirement gathering. This prototype includes basic functionalities of the final proposed solution, and it is normally built to provide a sense of the actual system. Prototyping is built by following the iterative process, where every iteration enhances the prototype based on the customer feedback until it reaches the final stage.

Analysis

After getting the answer to *What* is required, the next step is to find out *How* to achieve requirements. All the documents are analyzed to check for the quality of the information provided, to make sure there is no confusion or misunderstanding about the requirements. In the case of any incomplete information, this is corrected before moving to the next step. The following activities can be performed for requirement analysis.

Analyzing documentation

In this activity, all of the existing documentation is analyzed to know more about the current business processes and business rules. It also helps to provide more clarity on the user requirements. We can identify stakeholders based on the requirements or features. Sometimes, users are not very clear on what is present in the current system, so in that case, analyzing the existing document can be very helpful. However, sometimes it can be a waste of time if the documents are not synced with the current system because they are outdated.

Analyzing existing application

This is another activity that is required when analyzing the existing application. In this activity, for any existing servers, the legacy application is analyzed based on the requirements collected. For example, let's say we are working on upgrading a project where we need to upgrade the earlier **customer relationship management** (**CRM**) version to Dynamics 365 CE. Upgrading from an earlier Microsoft CRM version requires a code upgrade as well as a customization upgrade. We need to analyze the existing Microsoft CRM code to check if it is using the 2011 service endpoint in both server-side code and client-side code. Customer may have developed custom solutions for some of the features that are now available out of the box, so we can remove the old solution and use out-of-the-box features instead.

It's common to prepare assessment reports where all of the information are documents related to the custom components developed, existing client-side code, server-side code, any integration, and any legacy application details. Similarly, if a customer is using the legacy application and now wants to use Dynamics 365 CE, we need to review the legacy system database and its tables to plan for migrating its data to Dynamics 365 CE.

Fit-Gap analysis

Another important activity performed once all the requirements are gathered is Fit-Gap analysis. A Fit-Gap analysis is basically used to understand the gap between business requirements and the proposed system. Based on the requirements collected, it validates whether or not the proposed system fits or does not fit the business requirements. All the gaps are documented, and an appropriate action plan is prepared to fill the gap. The Fit-Gap analysis process can be understood with the following diagram:

We will be discussing more on Fit-Gap analysis in the next section, in which we will understand the Fit-Gap analysis activities in more detail.

Fit-Gap analysis for Dynamics 365 CE

While implementing Dynamics 365 CE, Fit-Gap analysis is done at various levels. In each level, we compare the features to see if it fits best with the Dynamics 365 CE functionality or not. If Dynamics 365 CE does not fit into the requirement, proper estimation is provided for the customization and development that we need to do to fill the gap. The following is a sample Fit-Gap analysis sheet prepared for the HIMBAP Auto Service Center. You can see how requirements are mapped with different Dynamics 365 CE categories:

Microsoft Dynamics 365 CE Implementation Fit Gap Analysis						
Req Area: Business Requirements Customer: HIMBAP Auto Service						
#	Description	Important	Category	Originated by	Phase	Est. Hrs
BR1	Send support ticket number to customer after service request generated	Medium	Workflow	Requirements Document	Phase 1	
BR2	Ability to create and update customer and related object data.	Medium	Customization	Requirements Document	Phase 1	
BR3	Ability to set critical information as required. Users should not be allowed to save without entering this information.		Std Feature	Workshop	Phase 1	
BR4	Ability to search for a customer using different information available on the customer.	High	Std Feature	Workshop	Phase 1	
BR5	Auto populate data based on parent lookups.	High	Std Feature	Workshop	Phase 1	
BR6	Ability to define user schedules and business.	High	Configuration	Workshop	POC	
BR7	Integrating with Service Portal hosted on Azure.	High	Other	Interview	Phase 1	
BR8	Ability to store customer documents in SharePoint.	High	Configuration	Workshop	Phase 1	

Let's discuss in detail the list of activities performed for Fit-Gap analysis.

Out-of-the-box features – Fit-Gap analysis

In this activity, all the requirements are compared with the vanilla Dynamics 365 CE features. Dynamics 365 CE provides a variety of out-of-the-box features that can be used to fulfill many business requirements. For example, simple business requirements of creating records for customers, contacts, leads, products, and activities can be achieved using vanilla features.

Similarly, Dynamics 365 CE provides support for searching entity data using different options like **Quick Find View**, **Global Search**, **Relevance Search**, and **Advanced Find Search**. But if customers need to search for data in a legacy database, it will be considered as a gap, and we need to have a custom solution to allow the customer to search for data in a custom database.

Configuring Fit-Gap analysis

This Fit-Gap analysis activity involves identifying requirements that can be accomplished using configuration options in Dynamics 365 CE. The most common requirement from a business is to handle different user permissions based on the job role and position. Dynamics 365 CE provides out-of-the-box security features to protect its data from unauthorized access.

Dynamics 365 CE has many out-of-the-box security roles that can be assigned to users based on their job profile. We can identify gaps in the out-of-the-box security roles and document configuration requirements for the security roles, to fill the gap based on the business-specific requirements.

While working on a new security role, it is best practice to copy the most suited existing security role and then modify it based on requirements, instead of creating a new security role with empty permissions.

Another common requirement is that every business has to communicate with its customers using different digital communication channels such as emails, SMS. Dynamics 365 CE provides out-of-the-box support for communicating with the customer using emails.

Dynamics 365 CE does not provide out-of-the-box features for SMS integration, but we can easily set up SMS integration using other tools such as Microsoft Flow or by using other **Independent Software Vendor (ISV)** solutions from Microsoft AppSource. Similarly, we have different configuration options in Dynamics 365 CE that we can utilize to cater to business requirements. We will be discussing more on Dynamics 365 CE configuration in later chapters.

Customizing Fit-Gap analysis

Through this activity, we identify requirements that can't be achieved using configuration and that require the customizing of Dynamics 365 CE. This may be related to relabeling entity display names in Dynamics 365 CE or creating a workflow to apply business logic. For example, end customers can be referred to using different terminology such as customer, vendors, suppliers, advertiser, agency, client, and so on. We simply relabel the account entity in Dynamics 365 CE based on the business requirement.

Dynamics 365 CE's vanilla version comes with many business entities that can be used to store data. But if our customers want to store specific data that does not match any of the existing entities, we can create a custom entity and add a field to that entity accordingly. Similarly, we can customize Dynamics 365 CE at various levels. We will be discussing the customization features further in a later chapter. Based on the requirements, we can find out the gap in which we need to do customization, in order to fill the functionality gap. Proper estimation is provided for the customization efforts required to accomplish a specific requirement.

Extending Dynamics 365 CE – Fit-Gap analysis

Microsoft Dynamics 365 CE gives us an extensive extendable platform that provides support for writing custom extensions for Dynamics 365 CE. After completing earlier Fit-Gap analysis activities, we may find some of the requirements can't be achieved using configuration or customization. To implement those requirements, we may need to write custom extensions using Dynamics 365 CE **software development kit (SDK)**.

 Microsoft Dynamics 365 CE SDK provides a setup for tools that we can use to write custom extensions for Microsoft Dynamics 365 CE.

Your customers may be looking to apply specific business logic that they want to trigger on specific events—for example, creating service tasks as soon as a new service request is generated, or perhaps they want to integrate Dynamics 365 CE with a custom application hosted on Azure. These kinds of requirements can't be achieved using customization or configuration. We need to use code for this.

ISV solution – Fit-Gap analysis

Another analysis activity is performed to check if there are any requirements that can be fulfilled using an ISV solution developed by Microsoft vendors that is compatible with Dynamics 365 CE.

 ISV solutions are the solutions developed by ISVs. You can find ISV solutions developed by Microsoft and Microsoft partners in Microsoft AppSource at `https://appsource.microsoft.com/en-US/`.

Most of the time, it is a better option to use an existing ISV solution that has already been used and tested by other customers, instead of putting development time and effort into building functionality from scratch. This is how we can use Fit-Gap analysis and make sure Dynamics 365 CE fits business requirements. If we see any gap, we can fill the gap by using the different options that we discussed previously.

Preparing a project plan

Once the requirement is gathered and analysis is done, the next step is to start preparing for the Dynamics 365 CE implementation plan. The main objective of project planning is to define the project scope and how to achieve it. Therefore, before creating the project plan, we need to define the project scope.

Defining the project scope

Another critical activity that is required before starting any project is to clearly define your project scope. Project scoping is the process to define all the work needed for Dynamics 365 CE implementation. We need to keep the project objective in mind while defining project activities. The main objective of the project scope is to have a clear idea about the project for the parties, the business, and the consulting team. In order to define the project scope document, we need to make sure that we have identified the following things:

- Project objectives
- Project requirements
- Phases
- Project activities

- Respective teams
- Project cost
- Schedule

Let's discuss these in more detail.

Project objectives

This is the main element required for the project scoping document. We need to have a clear idea of the project objectives because they are going to be the decision-makers for the whole project implementation life cycle. All of the defined project objectives should be measurable as they determine the project's success. They should be used to measure the success of every Dynamics 365 CE implementation phase.

Let's say one objective of implementing Dynamics 365 CE is to automate the customer approval process. These business processes, as well as the success criteria, should be defined clearly to validate the success of the automation. While providing details about project objective, we need to keep in mind that the overall project objective should clearly define customer's vision for using Dynamics 365 CE well.

Project requirements

Project requirements should be captured and documented properly using the methods discussed in the earlier section, *Requirement gathering and analysis*.

Acceptance criteria

Acceptance criteria should also be included in the scope document. These criteria clearly define whether the Dynamics 365 CE implementation has been successful and has met business requirements. These criteria are evaluated during **User Acceptance Testing (UAT)**.

Exclusions

It is very important to mention what is inside the scope of Dynamics 365 CE implementation and what is outside of the scope of implementation. Business and consulting teams should mutually agree on these items.

Phases

If Dynamics 365 CE implementation is going to happen in multiple phases, it should be clearly defined. The project scope should define the timings of deliveries of every phase, as well as the success measures.

Project activities

The project scoping document should have details about all of the project's activities and their duration based on the phases. Every project task should have details such as task ID, description, task estimations, and resources.

Respective teams

The team should be identified and documented on the project scoping document for both parties. It should clearly specify members from business teams, as well as consulting teams. This involves identifying different project resources, such as who will be project manager from the customer side and who will be managing projects from within the consulting team, stakeholders, development team, and the QA team.

Project cost

Project cost is a critical decision-maker for the project. Sometimes, customers will decide whether they want to go with a Dynamics 365 CE implementation or not based on the project cost. The project scoping document should clearly detail the cost of the project. The following is an example of a high-level project cost estimation:

Microsoft Dynamics 365 CE Implementation		
Estimated Hrs	**Details**	**Total**
138	Project Management	$28,980.00
40	Requirement Gathering and Analysis	$7,600.00
40	Setup and Configuration	$7,600.00
80	Data Migration	$15,200.00
32	Reports Modification	$6,080.00
150	Customization & Development	$28,500.00
100	Integration	$19,000.00
40	Training	$7,600.00
140	UAT	$26,600.00
80	Go-Live Support	$15,200.00
890	**Total Services Investment**	**$162,360.00**

You can see in the preceding screenshot that each activity has details on the estimated hours and cost.

Schedule

The project scope document should also have details for the project delivery schedule. It should clearly define the project task start date and end date. The following is an example of a Dynamics 365 CE implementation schedule sheet:

PROJECT TASK	START DATE	END DATE
Project Management		
Requirement Gathering and Analysis		
Setup and Configuration		
Data Migration		
Reports Modification		
Customization & Development		
Integration		
Training		
UAT		
Go-Live Support		

Project tasks may differ based on the project. For example, project tasks will be different depending on whether we're performing an implementation or an upgrade. Complete details about the project schedule and responsibilities of the task should be provided in the project plan. These details include each activity in the Dynamics 365 CE implementation as well as the resource information, such as who will be working on these activities.

Assumptions

If any assumptions are made for Dynamics 365 CE, it should be mentioned in the scope document as well. This ensures that the stakeholders and other team members are fully aware of any assumptions made.

Risks

Another piece of key information that is required for a Dynamics 365 CE implementation scope is risks. A risk is an event that may or may not occur, but we need to identify and document any risks involved. This is because it can impact a Dynamics 365 CE implementation significantly. A proper risk management plan should be created, to ensure how teams will communicate and respond in the case of risk events.

Once we have identified all of the items that are required, we prepare a Dynamics 365 CE implementation scope document that describes all of the deliverable elements, the work required to achieve them, and acceptance criteria, with other details.

Identifying roles and responsibilities

Another piece of information that you should have when preparing a project plan is to identify the roles and responsibilities of the respective team members. Roles and responsibility details, provided in the project plan, includes any responsibility of the business and stakeholders—for example, approving documentation; the responsibility of the project managers, such as how they will be executing the whole Dynamics 365 CE implementation; and so on. It also includes the responsibility of the development team, resources who will be working on a user story or task, who will be executing test cases, who will report bugs back to the development team, and so on. Alongside this information, we also need to provide details about the UAT, such as who the key users that will perform the UAT are and who will be providing training to the key users.

Details schedule

The project plan also requires detailed activity schedules. We will need to provide details such as when a particular task is going to start, who will be working on it, and when they will be delivering it. The detailed schedule includes every single activity that is going to happen during the Dynamics 365 CE implementation. This schedule helps all of the project team to understand timelines for different project phases and plan their activities accordingly.

Identifying milestones

Another thing that can help the project manager and the whole project team to determine whether or not a project is on track is to divide the project into different milestones. Project managers divide project tasks into these milestones and they should be updated regularly to keep the status up to date.

Once all of the information is ready, the project manager can create a project plan for the Dynamics 365 CE implementation. Project managers can use simple Excel sheets to prepare project plans, or they can use project planning tools. Microsoft Project is the most common tool used to prepare project plans, and it can be used to track a project's progress.

You can view details on Microsoft Project at `https://products.office.com/en-in/project/project-and-portfolio-management-software`.

While preparing the project plan, it is also recommended to prepare a draft of the project plan first. You should keep your project plan simple and easy to understand. The following are the key points that you need to keep in mind while preparing the project plan:

- Provide Dynamics 365 CE implementation details and customer details.
- Maintain the version number for your project plan as it helps you to track revisions.
- Include all Dynamics 365 CE phases in your project plan.
- Include milestones and related tasks within these milestones.
- Assign every task to the respective team member.
- Include timelines for tasks.
- Include different statuses for tasks, such as **Not Started**, **In Progress**, **Ready for Test**, **Completed**, and **On Hold**.
- Keep a comments section, to include additional information for the tasks.

This way, we can prepare our project plan and present it to all of the team members, to give them a complete picture of Dynamics 365 CE implementations.

Summary

In this chapter, we learned about project requirements and how to capture them using different techniques. We learned about analysis techniques and their requirements. Later, we discussed how to perform a Fit-Gap analysis and work on the project plan. Finally, we learned about the main points you need to keep in mind while preparing the project plan.

In the next chapter, we are going to discuss how to prepare functional and technical design documents that can be used in the later phases of a Dynamics 365 CE implementation.

4
Preparing Functional and Technical Design Documents

This chapter will help you to understand how to prepare **Functional Design Documents** (**FDDs**) and **Technical Design Documents** (**TDDs**). We will cover what FDDs are and how they are used. We will also cover the information that is commonly included in an FDD. This chapter will help you to know more about the features of a good FDD.

Next, you will learn about TDDs and the information commonly included in a TDD. You will also learn about infrastructure diagrams for a mid-sized Dynamics 365 CE deployment. Later, you will understand the Dynamics 365 CE application architecture and its extension points.

The main topics that we are going to discuss in this chapter are as follows:

- Understanding functional and technical design
- Preparing an FDD
- Preparing a TDD

Technical requirements

This chapter does not have any technical requirements, but when preparing documentation for your customer, it's recommended that you have the following tools (or similar) to document customer requirements:

- Microsoft Office or an Office 365 subscription for preparing documents
- Microsoft Visio or a similar tool
- A tool to generate an **entity-relationship** (**ER**) diagram

Understanding functional and technical design

Design documents are critical to any software project, whether it is a matter of developing new software or upgrading any existing software. These documents are also called **specs documents**. They play a critical role during the upgrade or maintenance phase, so it is recommended to create such a document. We will be discussing how to prepare these documents. However, before looking at what it is we need to prepare these documents, let's first understand what FDDs and TDDs are, and what the difference is between functional and technical design. We will also learn why it is that we need these documents, and what purpose they serve.

Functional design documents

An FDD helps the business stakeholders and all of the team members to understand a Dynamics 365 CE implementation and how it will function. It does not include any detail on how the system will work internally or what the internal components of the system are. Instead, it provides information on how the system is going to behave based on specific inputs. We can see all the features that are going to be implemented in Dynamics 365 CE in this document. This document mainly answers the following question: *What functionalities will be implemented using Dynamics 365 CE?*

An FDD is required to make sure that the consulting team and business stakeholders are on the same page. During the approval process of an FDD, many revisions are prepared. Stakeholders and key users can provide their feedback about the FDD, such as whether the information is presented correctly, or if there is something that does not match their expectations. The consulting team confirms whether or not the functionalities mentioned in the FDD are feasible, and if they can be implemented using Dynamics 365 CE. A business analyst or functional consultant takes their feedback and updates the FDD. The document is then sent to the respective team members and stakeholders. This process continues until all of the team members are in agreement on the FDD. Once this document is approved or signed off, it can be used as a foundation for a Dynamics 365 CE implementation and updates at later stages.

The following are features of a good Dynamics 365 CE FDD:

- Provides a business objective for implementing Dynamics 365 CE
- Defines Dynamics 365 CE implementation vision and scope
- Provides details about approvers

- Explores any assumptions that are made for FDD
- Provides a required specification for Dynamics 365 CE configuration
- Provides a Common Data Model for Dynamics 365 CE
- Provides details about business units and their hierarchy
- Provides a list of security roles required
- Provides all of the customization required for a Dynamics 365 CE implementation
- Provides a screen layout for all the required entities
- Provides data validation on different entities' screens
- Provides details about the business process and business logic that will be implemented
- Provides details about any custom extensions and integrations that will be developed
- Provides details about reports and dashboards required by the customer

Technical design documents

Another design document that is especially important for the technical team is the TDD. The TDD covers the technical details of the FDD. This document mainly answers the following question: *How will the functionality be implemented in the new system?*

A TDD provides solutions to technical issues, so it not only provides guidance on what needs to be developed but also on how it will be developed. This document is prepared for the technical team, who are responsible for customizing, extending, and integrating Dynamics 365 CE with other systems. These details are hidden from stakeholders and key users while using Dynamics 365 CE. A TDD also provides details on the architecture of a Dynamics 365 CE implementation.

The following are features of a good Dynamics 365 CE TDD:

- Provides details about the Dynamics 365 CE implementation infrastructure architecture
- Helps to understand the overall customer application architecture
- Lists all of the possible integration required
- Lists all of the custom logic required to write using scripting or server-side code
- Explains the workflow required to automate day-to-day business activities
- Provides details about the development environment and release management

Now that we understand what FDDs and TDDs are, let's look at how we can prepare them. We'll start with how to prepare an FDD.

Preparing an FDD

Now that we know what FDDs and TDDs are, let's discuss how to prepare these documents and what information is available in an FDD. The contents of an FDD can differ from project to project and requirement to requirement. However, there are common sections that every FDD requires. We will be discussing these in detail, based on our HIMBAP Auto Service Center Dynamics 365 CE implementation. Let's discuss these sections, one by one.

Introduction

Every FDD document should contain an introductory section that will have many subsections for project details such as Dynamics 365 CE implementation details, requirements, audience, and so on. Let's discuss them in detail.

Document purpose

This is a formal introduction to the FDD. We need to provide details such as what information is presented in this document.

Project details

In this section, we need to provide details about the Dynamics 365 CE implementation and its high-level objective. We can include these details here, or simply mention them in another document that was generated earlier to refer to project details.

Target audience

This information is required to inform team members about the audience for this document. We can provide a list of all the roles that come under our target audience category, similar to the following:

- Project managers
- Business analysts
- Consultants

- Developers
- Testers
- Architects

Terminology

In this section, we need to include any special words or abbreviations used in the document.

Assumptions

This section includes any assumptions about this Dynamics 365 CE implementation. For example, we can include the following examples for the HIMBAP Auto Service Center implementation:

Assumptions	Description
1	Microsoft Dynamics 365 CE Online implementation will be done for HIMBAP Auto Service Center.
2	Microsoft Dynamics 365 CE will be accessed using the latest versions of popular browsers and mobile devices.
3	Microsoft Dynamics 365 implementation does not include any hardware and software installation at customer location.
4	Data migration will be done for initial data load on accounts, contacts, services, service history, brand, and cases.
5	HIMBAP Auto Service Center will be responsible for maintaining a code base and solutions for Dynamics 365 CE.

Risks

In this section, any risks involved in the Dynamics 365 CE implementation should be mentioned. For example, we can have the following common risks for a Dynamics 365 CE Online implementation:

Risk	Description
1	Dynamics 365 CE Online performance depends on the internet speed.
2	Access to Dynamics 365 CE databases is not possible.
3	Dynamics 365 CE Online availability is not guaranteed.
4	The number of custom entities is limited in Dynamics 365 CE Online, but the customer can contact Microsoft to adjust that limit.
5	Reports for Dynamics 365 CE Online can be built using FetchXML only.

Dynamics 365 CE setup and configuration

In this section, Dynamics 365 CE setup information is provided so that admin users can configure Dynamics 365 CE settings based on the requirements. We need to provide details of all the main areas of Dynamics 365 CE that require configuration.

Administration settings

The administration settings area can be accessed by selecting **Settings** | **System** | **Administration**. Here, all the administration settings for Dynamics 365 CE can be configured. The following screenshot shows the administration settings options in Dynamics 365 CE:

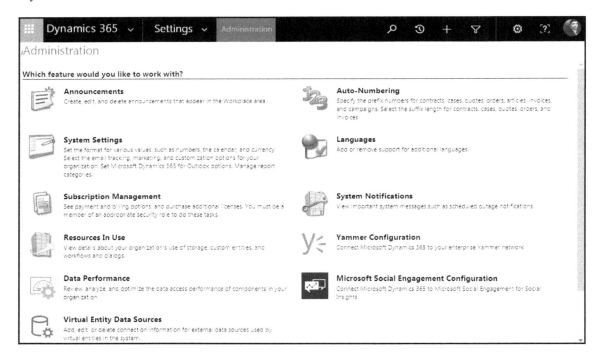

Any configuration options related to administration should be listed here. We will be discussing all of these options in `Chapter 5`, *Configuring Your Dynamics 365 CE Organization,* while discussing configuration options for Dynamics 365 CE.

System settings

The system settings area is used to configure global application settings such as formatting options, data auditing, email configuration, outlook filters, and calendar settings. The following screenshot represents the Dynamics 365 **System Settings** options:

Any organization-specific setting should be mentioned here. We will be discussing how to use these options in `Chapter 5`, *Configuring Your Dynamics 365 CE Organization.*

Data management settings

In this section, we need to provide any data management-related configuration information required by the business. For example, if customers want to implement duplicate detection while creating or updating entity records, or they want to delete historical data that is not required after a specific time interval, they can do so using bulk delete options. All of the data-related settings can be done through the data management settings. The following is a screenshot of the Dynamics 365 CE **Data Management** settings:

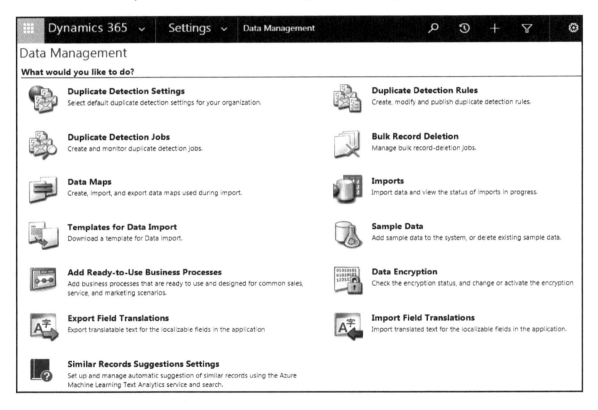

We will be discussing how to configure these options in detail in `Chapter 5`, *Configuring Your Dynamics 365 CE Organization*.

Business unit hierarchy

A business unit in Dynamics 365 CE is the logical grouping of users and teams. Dynamics 365 CE security is implemented based on business units. We can consider business units as various departments of a business. Every Dynamics 365 CE organization contains a default business unit, with the same name as the Dynamics 365 CE organization. This business unit is known as the root business unit. This section is very important for a Dynamics 365 CE FDD. In this section, we need to provide details about the business unit's structure that we are going to implement for customers. For HIMBAP Auto Service Center, we are going to implement the following business unit hierarchy:

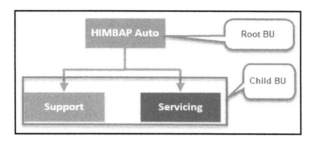

Field-level security profiles

Field-level security is used to implement security for sensitive fields. Customers may want to control the create and update operations on sensitive fields. For example, your customer may want to only allow service managers to create and update the Service Cost field. Field-level security is maintained using field-level security profiles. In this section, all the field-level security profiles should be mentioned, as this is required for our Dynamics 365 CE implementation.

User	Description
Service Manager	Only the service manager can apply a discount to the total service amount.

We will be discussing more on field-level security in `Chapter 6`, *Customizing Dynamics 365 CE*.

Security roles

The security of Dynamics 365 CE entities and their data is implemented using security roles. These are a group of permissions that define which operations a Dynamics 365 CE user can perform on an entity. Dynamics 365 CE contains many out-of-the-box security roles that can be modified based on customer requirements.

In this section, we provide details about the security roles that will be used for the customer. We will be discussing more on security roles in `Chapter 6`, *Customizing Dynamics 365 CE*.

For HIMBAP Auto Service Center, we are going to use the following out-of-the-box security roles:

Business unit	Security roles	Changed name
HIMBAP Auto	System Administrator	HIMBAP Admin
HIMBAP Auto	System Customizer	HIMBAP Customizer
Support	Customer Service Representative	HIMBAP Support
Servicing	CSR Manager	HIMBAP Service Manager
Servicing	Salesperson	HIMBAP Technician

ER diagram

This section provides information about the entities and their relationships to each other. The number of entities may change as they are created, so a consultant can introduce or reuse entities after discussing this with their team. An FDD must include an updated ER diagram; so, if there are any changes in the structure, the business analyst or functional consultant needs to update the FDD. The following diagram shows an example of an ER diagram:

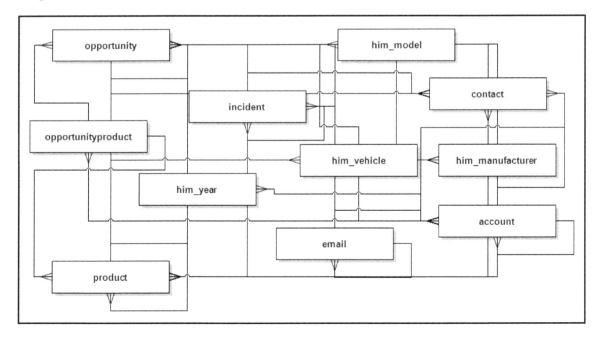

This ER diagram represents out-of-the-box entities and custom entities that we are going to mainly use for our HIMBAP Auto Service Center customer. As you can see, we are going to reuse some of the existing entities, as well as creating some custom entities.

Dynamics 365 CE entity design

This section provides details about the entities and their relationships. Different types of information about the entity—such as forms, views, attributes, and relationship details—are provided here, which helps the consultant to customize out-of-the-box entities or to create new entities based on this document.

We are going to use the following entities for the HIMBAP Auto Service Center:

Customer

We are going to use the existing account entity to store customer information. The display name of this entity will be changed to the customer.

Customer form

We will be customizing an out-of-the-box account form to look like the following:

Attributes

Please refer to the `Appendix1` folder on the GitHub repository for this book, at `https://github.com/PacktPublishing/Implementing-Microsoft-Dynamics-365-Customer-Engagement/blob/master/Appendix1.xlsx`.

Views

We will be using the following views for our customer entity:

Default view	Change to	Sorting	Filter condition
Active Accounts	Active Customers	Name	Status Equals Active
Inactive Accounts	Inactive Customers	Name	Status Equals Inactive
Account Lookup View	Customer Lookup View	Name	Status Equals Active
Account Associated View	Customer Associated View	Name	Status Equals Active
Account Advanced Find View	Customer Advanced Find View	Name	Status Equals Active

All of the views will have the following fields:

- Customer Name
- Customer Number
- Main Phone
- Address 1: City
- Primary Contact
- Email

Relationship

You can refer to the following details to set up a custom N: 1 relationship in the customer entity:

Primary entity	Secondary entity	Type of behavior	Relationship name	Lookup field name
User	Customer	Referential	`him_systemuser_account_Manager`	Manager

Duplicate detection rules

The following duplicate detection rule will be enabled on the customer entity:

- Accounts with the same account name

Contact

We are going to use the existing contact entity to store contacts associated with the customer.

Contact form

We will be customizing an out-of-the-box **Contact** form, to look like the following:

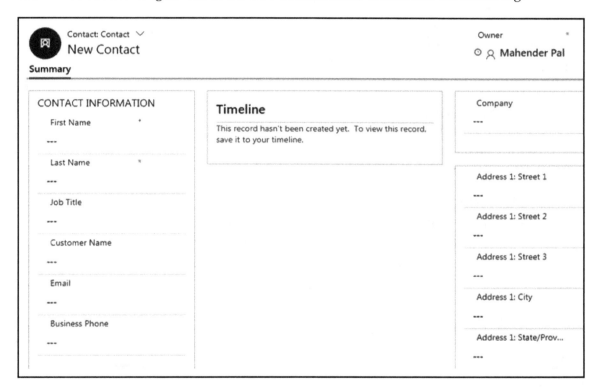

Attributes

Please refer to the `Appendix1` folder on the GitHub repository for this book, at `https://github.com/PacktPublishing/Implementing-Microsoft-Dynamics-365-Customer-Engagement/blob/master/Appendix1.xlsx`.

Views

We will be using the following views for our customer entity:

Default view	Sorting	Filter condition
Active Contacts	Name	Status Equals Active
Inactive Contacts	Name	Status Equals Inactive
Contact Lookup View	Name	Status Equals Active
Contact Associated View	Name	Status Equals Active
Contact Advanced Find View	Name	Status Equals Active

All of the views will have the following fields:

- Full name
- Customer name
- Email
- Mobile phone

Auto service

If we are going to reuse the opportunity entity to store service information, we need to customize the opportunity entity form, as we have in the following example:

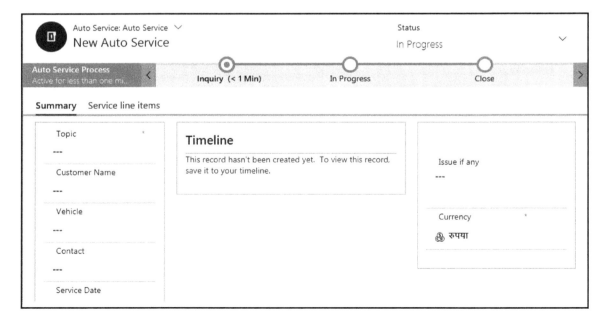

Attributes

Please refer to the `Appendix1` folder on the GitHub repository for this book, at `https://github.com/PacktPublishing/Implementing-Microsoft-Dynamics-365-Customer-Engagement/blob/master/Appendix1.xlsx`.

Views

We will be using the following views for our auto service entity:

Default view	Change to	Sorting	Filter condition
Open Opportunities	Open Auto Services	Topic	Status Equals Active
Closed Opportunities	Closed Auto Services	Topic	Status Equals Inactive
Opportunity Lookup View	Auto Service Lookup View	Topic	Status Equals Active
Opportunity Associated View	Auto Service Associated View	Topic	Status Equals Active
Opportunity Advanced Find View	Auto Service Advanced Find View	Topic	Status Equals Active

All the views will have the following fields:

- Vehicle
- Topic
- Customer
- Contact
- Service Date

Relationship

Set up the following custom N:1 relationship in the auto service entity:

Primary entity	Secondary entity	Type of behavior	Relationship name	Lookup field name
Vehicle	Auto Service	Referential	`him_vehicle_opportunity_Vehicle`	Vehicle

Auto service line

We are going to reuse the opportunity product entity to store auto service line items, and we are going to use this form as it is.

Case

We are going to use a **Case** form to store service support information for the auto service. We need to customize the **Case** entity form, as shown in the following screenshot:

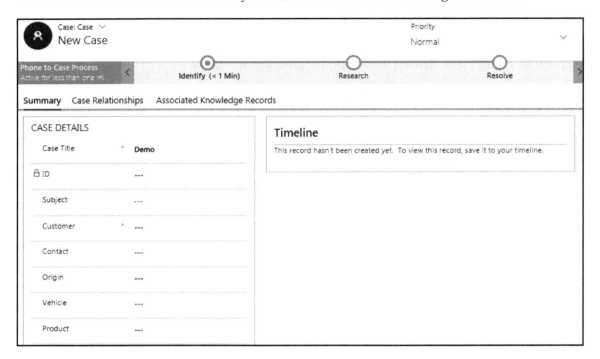

Attributes

Please refer to the `Appendix1` folder on the GitHub repository for this book, at `https://github.com/PacktPublishing/Implementing-Microsoft-Dynamics-365-Customer-Engagement/blob/master/Appendix1.xlsx`.

Views

We will be using the following views for the customer entity:

Default view	Sorting	Filter condition
Active Cases	Case Title	Status Equals Active
Resolved Cases	Case Title	Status Equals Resolved
Case Lookup View	Case Title	Status Equals Active
Associative Cases	Case Title	Status Equals Active
Case Advanced Find View	Case Title	Status Equals Active

All the views will have the following fields:

- Case Title
- Case Number
- Customer
- Vehicle
- Status Reason
- Created On

Relationship

Set up the following custom N:1 relationship in our auto case entity:

Primary entity	Secondary entity	Type of behavior	Relationship name	Lookup field name
Vehicle	Case	Referential	`him_vehicle_incident_Vehicle`	Vehicle

Vehicle

This is a custom entity used to hold vehicle information such as vehicle registration number, manufacture, build year, and so on. We will be using the following design for this entity form:

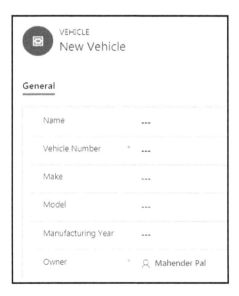

Attributes

Please refer to the `Appendix1` folder on the GitHub repository for this book, at `https://github.com/PacktPublishing/Implementing-Microsoft-Dynamics-365-Customer-Engagement/blob/master/Appendix1.xlsx`.

Views

Change all the views to have the following columns:

- Vehicle Number
- Customer
- Make
- Model
- Year

Relationship

Set up the following custom N:1 relationship in the vehicle entity:

Primary entity	Secondary entity	Type of behavior	Relationship name	Lookup field name
Customer	Vehicle	Referential	`him_account_him_vehicle`	Customer
Model	Vehicle	Referential	`him_model_him_vehicle`	Model
Manufacturer	Vehicle	Referential	`him_manufacturer_him_vehicle`	Make
Year	Vehicle	Referential	`him_year_him_vehicle_Year`	Year

Manufacturer

This is a custom entity used to hold manufacturer information relating to the vehicle. We will be using the following design for this entity form:

Attributes

Please refer to the `Appendix1` folder on the GitHub repository for this book, at `https://github.com/PacktPublishing/Implementing-Microsoft-Dynamics-365-Customer-Engagement/blob/master/Appendix1.xlsx`.

Model

This is a custom entity used to record model details of the vehicle. We will be using the following design for this entity form:

Attributes

Please refer to the `Appendix1` folder on the GitHub repository for this book, at `https://github.com/PacktPublishing/Implementing-Microsoft-Dynamics-365-Customer-Engagement/blob/master/Appendix1.xlsx`.

Year

This is a custom entity used for year details. We are going to use the default form, without making any changes for this entity. There are no additional attributes created for this entity apart from the primary field, which is used to store the year name.

We are going to use all the other out-of-the-box entities that are present on the ER diagram as is, without making any changes.

User reports

This section contains information about the records required. Dynamics 365 CE has many default records that can be used as they are, or they can be customized based on the requirements. We are going to discuss more details on the reporting options in later chapters.

We have now looked at how we can include these sections in our FDD, which can help the technical team to design an application. Now, we are going to discuss the sections commonly found in a TDD.

Preparing a TDD

As we discussed earlier, a TDD provides technical solutions for the proposed system, and its main objective is to provide technical details of the work that needs to be done. This information is presented to the project team members. A TDD includes details on how solutions will be implemented for the business's requirements. Similar to an FDD, elements of a TDD also can vary from project to project and requirement to requirement, but there are common sections that are required in TDD. Let's discuss these sections, one by one.

Introduction

Every TDD should contain this section, as an introduction provides general details about the document. Similar to an FDD, the introduction section includes some high-level details about the project, such as Dynamics 365 CE implementation details, requirements, and audience. We are not going to discuss this section again, but you can refer back to the FDD section for more details on a design document's introduction section.

Proposed technical design

In this section, we provide technical design details of the project, such as the proposed system server details, infrastructure architecture, and integration architecture. Let's discuss these sections in detail.

Infrastructure architecture

This section contains the Dynamics 365 CE infrastructure architecture. This is very much required if the client is using an on-premises deployment. In cases where the customer is using an online deployment, there is no need to provide these details, as no infrastructure is required for the Dynamics 365 CE cloud implementation. A Dynamics 365 CE on-premises deployment can be done on a single server or on multiple servers. The following is a typical infrastructure architecture for an on-premises Dynamics 365 CE deployment for a mid-sized organization:

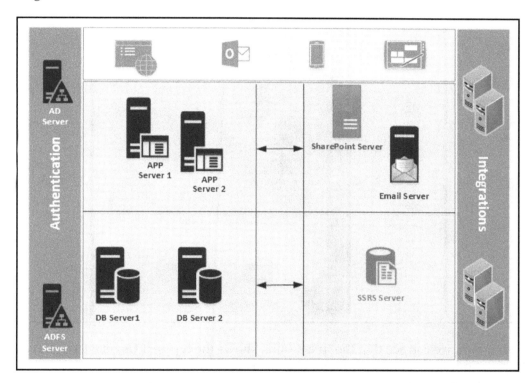

We can see in the preceding diagram that authentication can be implemented using **Active Directory** (**AD**) authentication, and we can also implement an **internet-facing deployment** (**IFD**) using an **Active Directory Federation Services** (**ADFS**) server. We can use different clients for accessing Dynamics 365, based on the requirements. We can also use dedicated servers for other things such as applications, databases, reporting, SharePoint, and email integration (as is shown in the preceding diagram). Based on the requirement and scope of the project, all the infrastructure details should be provided in this section.

Solution architecture

In this section, we provide details of the solution architecture that we are going to build for the customer. The main objective of this architecture is to provide all project team members with an understanding of the proposed system. This solution architecture should include all of the major components and integration details. For example, the following is a sample solution architecture diagram for HIMBAP Auto Service Center:

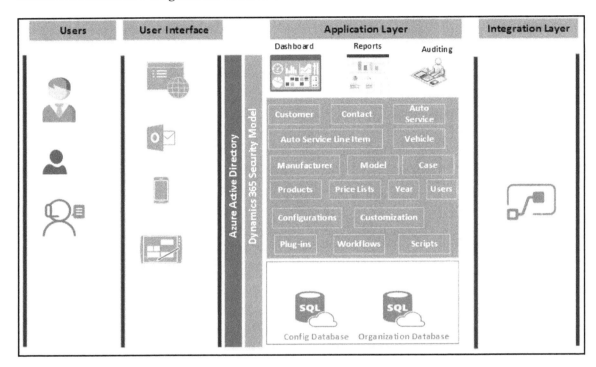

In the diagram, we can see that the first section shows the types of **Users** we can have for our application. They can use different clients to access Dynamics 365 CE applications, such as a web browser, Outlook, mobile, and tablet applications. There will be an authentication layer that will use **Azure Active Directory** (**Azure AD**), as we are using online deployment. We will also have the **Dynamics 365 CE Security Model**, which will control the visibility of the data based on the user security roles. The **Application Layer** will contain the **user interface** (**UI**) components and Dynamics 365 configurations. It will also contain business entities with their customization and extensions, as well as Dynamics 365 CE databases. The **Integration Layer** contains integration logic, and we will be using Microsoft Flow for integration in our case.

Users

In this section, we can include user details based on the customer requirement. For example, the HIMBAP Auto Service Center Dynamics 365 CE implementation can be accessed by different types of users, such as technicians, support users, admin users, and business users. These users will be accessing Dynamics 365 CE for their day-to-day jobs.

User interface

In this section, we can provide details of all of the possible Dynamics 365 CE clients that the customer wants to use. For example, a new system for HIMBAP Auto Service Center will be accessed using different clients such as a web browser, Outlook, mobile, and tablet clients. When the user tries to access Dynamics 365 CE using these options, they will be authenticated using Azure AD. After authentication, a Dynamics 365 CE security model will be applied, which allows the user to access only areas to which they are authorized. They can only access an entity for which they have required permissions.

Application layer

In this section, we can provide all of the components that will be included in the application layer. For example, the solution for HIMBAP Auto Service Center will have a dashboard, reports, out-of-the-box business entities, custom entities, and other system configurations such as auditing, data management, and emails. A complete list of the entities can be found at `https://github.com/PacktPublishing/Implementing-Microsoft-Dynamics-365-Customer-Engagement/blob/master/Appendix1.xlsx`.

All of the custom logic implemented using scripting, plugins, and custom workflows are part of the application layer.

Integration layer

In this layer, we can provide details for all of the integration that will be done for the customer. For example, we have planned a solution in a Microsoft Flow integration for HIMBAP Auto Service Center to send SMS notifications to vehicle owners.

Integration architecture

In this section, we provide more details about Dynamics 365 CE integration architecture, such as if we are going to integrate Dynamics 365 CE with any other Microsoft or non-Microsoft products. For example, in our case, we are going to integrate Dynamics 365 CE with Microsoft Flow to update vehicle owners about their vehicle service status.

You can see the example in the following diagram:

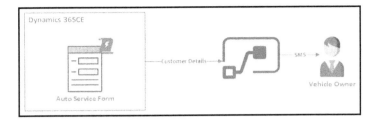

When an auto service record is updated, it will trigger a Microsoft Flow integration and will send an SMS notification to the customer. We will be discussing this further in later chapters when we come to discuss integration options for Dynamics 365 CE.

Application architecture

In this section, we will provide details about the Dynamics 365 CE application architecture, along with all of the possible extension points that can be used for extending the capabilities of Dynamics 365 CE. The following screenshot shows the application architecture of Dynamics 365 CE:

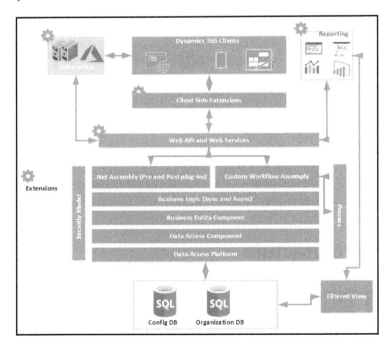

As discussed previously, we can use different clients to access a Dynamics 365 CE application. We can write different client-side extensions such as a JavaScript library, HTML web resources, custom apps, and SiteMap extensions. We can use the Dynamics 365 CE Web API and web service to integrate both on-premises and Azure applications. We can use the Web API and web service out of the box, or we can write our own extensions for integration.

We can write different server-side extensions using plugins and custom workflows that extend the capabilities of out-of-the-box workflows. We can write sync or async plugins in Dynamics 365 CE that can interact with both custom and system business entities. We will be discussing these in more detail in `Chapter 7`, *Extending Dynamics 365 CE*.

Dynamics 365 CE has two databases: config and organization databases. The config database is used to store configuration information about Dynamics 365 CE, whereas the organization database is used to store customer data for entities such as accounts, contacts, and so on. Dynamics 365 CE contains a special type of view that is known as filtered views; we use these to develop reports for Dynamics 365 CE. Filtered views allow the user to access data based on their security roles. We will be discussing these reports in more detail in `Chapter 9`, *Business Intelligence and Reporting*. If we are working with Dynamics 365 CE on-premises, two SQL Server databases are created; but if we are using Dynamics 365 CE Online, an Azure database will be used for our Dynamics 365 CE subscription.

Development environment and release strategy

This is another piece of critical information that we need to include in our TDD. Based on the project complexity, the solution architect provides development environment setup details. A simple setup can be used for less complex projects, in which one or two developers are working on the same development instance and their own set of entities. Later, these changes can be promoted to a **quality assurance** (**QA**) environment after unit testing. In this approach, developers need to be careful when selecting their entities, to ensure that the other developer is not working on the same entities.

On the other hand, there can be multiple development instances for developers, based on project complexity. All of the changes that are from the individual developer instances can be merged into a master development instance, and from there, it can be promoted to a QA or a **system integration environment** (**SIT**) environment. Microsoft **Knowledge Base** (**KB**) for solution life cycle management can be used as a reference document to set up development environments.

You can download Solution Lifecycle Management KB from `https://www.microsoft.com/en-us/download/details.aspx?id=57777`.

Keeping the HIMBAP Auto Service Center implementation, we can use the following simple development environment approach:

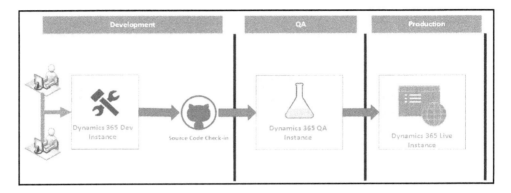

Developers can work on a single development instance and, from there, the solution will be released to a QA environment after unit testing. Once QA and **user acceptance testing** (**UAT**) are complete, the solution will be released to the production environment. All of the code and customization will be included in the development solution and can be promoted as an unmanaged solution to all the environments. We are going to discuss unmanaged versus managed solutions in `Chapter 6`, *Customizing Dynamics 365 CE*. We can understand solution release management with the following flow chart:

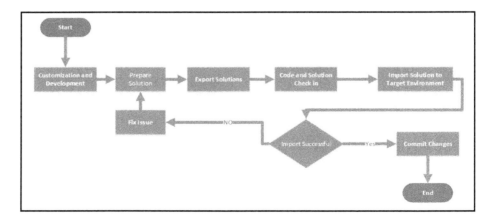

A development solution will include all of the components such as entities, workflows, and plugin assemblies (we will be discussing solution components in detail in Chapter 6, *Customizing Dynamics 365 CE*). Once development is over, we will export the unmanaged solutions and check the solutions, as well as our code, in source control. The exported unmanaged solution will be imported to the target environment. If the import is successful, changes can be committed to source control. If it is not, any solution issues can be fixed, and the deployment process can be restarted.

Data migration

If a business wants to bring its historical data into Dynamics 365 CE, a proper data migration plan should be included in the TDD. We will be discussing the data migration options of Dynamics 365 CE in Chapter 11, *Migration and Upgrade*.

Dynamics 365 CE extensions

In this section, we need to provide details of the extensions required for Dynamics 365 CE. These extensions can be implemented using customization or by writing the client-side/server-side code. We can include sections for each extension that needs to be developed for the customer, with details of the screen.

Scripting

Dynamics 365 CE allows us to implement custom logic by using client-side scripting. We use JavaScript code to implement our custom logic—for example, adding form field validation, or getting data from another entity. We can perform custom logic on entity form and field events. We will be discussing this further in Chapter 7, *Extending Dynamics 365 CE*.

This section includes all of the scripting requirements for a Dynamics 365 CE implementation.

Plugins

Plugins are another way to apply our custom business logic to extend Dynamics 365 CE capabilities. We can write .NET assemblies that we can bind to specific events to trigger and run our custom logic written in assembly. We will be discussing more on Dynamics 365 CE plugins in Chapter 7, *Extending Dynamics 365 CE*.

In our document, we should include all the custom plugin requirements for a Dynamics 365 CE implementation.

Workflow tasks

In Dynamics 365, we can use two options out of the box to automate Dynamics 365 CE tasks: Workflow and Power Automate. Using Workflow can be very useful, especially for business users, and no technical knowledge is required to write workflows. Dynamics 365 CE provides an out-of-the-box workflow designer that we can use to create different workflow processes based on our requirements. Workflows are also associated with a specific event to trigger their logic. Similarly, we can create a Power Automate workflow from Dynamics 365 CE. We can use different connectors and work with multiple applications in a single Power Automate workflow. We will be discussing more on Dynamics 365 CE Workflow and Power Automate capabilities in `Chapter 8`, *Integrating Dynamics 365 CE with Other Applications*.

In this section in our document, we need to provide all of the possible workflow requirements for our Dynamics 365 CE implementation.

The sections are applicable to every Dynamics 365 CE implementation, but depending on the project, we can include some more details. For example, if we are going to use an automated solution release process, it should be included in this document. We can also include some details about the QA testing process.

Summary

In this chapter, we learned about FDDs and TDDs, and why these documents are required for a Dynamics 365 CE implementation. We also learned what information can be included in FDDs and TDDs.

In the next chapter, we are going to discuss how we can configure a Dynamics 365 CE organization.

5
Configuring Your Dynamics 365 CE Organization

This chapter will help you learn about the Dynamics 365 configuration options available in Dynamics 365 CE for individuals and administrators. You will learn which of the options can be configured for individual users, and which are the configurations that can be done by the admin user. You will learn the different configuration options available under the business management and service management settings. You will also learn about the data management capabilities of Dynamics 365 CE. Finally, you will learn how to set up SharePoint integration for Dynamics 365 CE.

The main topics that we are going to discuss in this chapter are as follows:

- Understanding Dynamics 365 CE configuration
- Configuring personal settings options
- Configuring administration settings
- Configuring business management settings
- Configuring service management settings
- Configuring data management settings
- Configuring document management settings
- Setting up email configuration

Technical requirements

This chapter has the following technical requirements:

- Access to Microsoft Dynamics 365 CE Online or an on-premises instance to configure
- A Microsoft Exchange Online trial
- A Microsoft Office 365 plan that includes Outlook

Understanding Dynamics 365 CE configuration

Once you have bought your Dynamics 365 CE subscription or set up a 30-day trial, you need to change the behavior of Dynamics 365 CE based on your requirements. Dynamics 365 configuration refers to the settings that can be changed using the Dynamics 365 CE application itself. We don't need to use any external tools to configure these settings. All of the system-level configurations are done from the **Settings** area. If you are using the classical web client interface, then you can navigate to **Settings** from the top navigation bar; but if you are using the Unified Interface client, then you can navigate to the **Settings** area using the **Advanced Settings** options, as shown in the following screenshot:

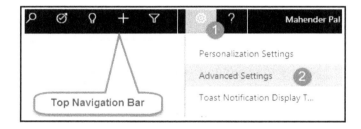

Keep in mind you can only configure settings if you have the required permissions. You need to have a System Customizer or System Administrator role to configure Dynamics 365 CE. There are some specific settings that you can only configure if you have a System Administrator role.

Now we have an idea about configuration, let's discuss different configuration options in Dynamics 365 CE.

Configuring personal settings options

Dynamics 365 CE lets users configure Dynamics 365 CE, to give them a personalized experience. They can set up their personal settings based on their individual requirements. These settings are applicable to the current user only. If we want to change these settings for the whole organization, we can change them from the **System Settings**. We will be discussing **System Settings** in the *Configuring administration settings* section. If you are using the classical web client interface, you can access personal settings via the settings gear on the navigation bar and select **Options** from the dropdown. If you are using the Unified Interface client, then you can use the **Personalization Settings** option from the dropdown.

Let's discuss in detail the options available under the **Personalization Settings** option.

General

In this section, we can set up our day-to-day activity settings. For example, we can set up which sections should be opened by default when a Dynamics 365 CE application is opened; how many records we want to see in the grid view; and so on. We have the following settings available in this section:

Settings	Description
Select your home page	This section allows us to set up a **Default Pane** and **Default Tab**, which should open daily when we open a Dynamics 365 CE application.
Set the number of record for List	This setting allows us to set up a default number of records that we want to see in any list. We can see a minimum of 50 records and a maximum of 250 records in the view.
Select the default mode in Advanced Find	We can select **Detailed** options here to see query details by default. We can add new query filters but when this option is set as **Simple**, query filters are hidden by default. To see them, we need to click on the **Details** button under the Query tab.
Set the time zone	Users can select their time zone under this setting. By default, it is set based on the organization's region.
Select default currency	Users can select their default currency if they have configured the **multi-currency** option in their Dynamics 365 CE organization.
Support high contrast settings	We can enable/disable high contrast levels for a Dynamics 365 CE application.
Set the default country/region code	This option lets users select their default country/region code for phone numbers.

Now, let's look at the next personal setting.

Synchronization

This configuration can be used to set up our synchronization if we are using Dynamics 365 CE for an Outlook client or Exchange Online. It can create our Outlook field, which decides which data will be synchronized from the Dynamics 365 CE application. We can also set up offline filters, which help us to synchronize data from a server to an Outlook offline client. This is useful for users who work with an Outlook offline client. Apart from this, we can also set up common synchronization rules for appointments, contacts, and tasks for our organization.

Activities

We can use this configuration to set up our calendar view with start and end times for our work hours. Once this is configured, our Dynamics 365 CE calendar will be rendered based on these configurations.

Formats

Under this tab, we can set up number, currency, and data time format options based on the country selected. We can click on the **Customize** button if we want to change the formatting options. For numbers, we can select a decimal symbol, a grouping symbol, digit group, and negative number formatting. We can also configure currency format options. For example, we can choose whether we want to use the currency symbol at the beginning or at the end. Similarly, we can set up the date and time options. Any changes to the format can be displayed under the **Format Preview** section.

Email Templates

This option allows us to create/delete email templates that we can use to send email notifications to our customers. We can create two types of email template: an entity-specific email template, or a global template. A template is created specific to an entity; for example, we can create an email template for an account entity, and this template can be only used for sending emails to our customers. It can't be used to send emails to another entity, for example. Global templates are not associated with any specific entity.

Email Signatures

Here, we can create signatures, just as with other commonly used email clients such as Outlook and Gmail. We can insert these signatures manually, or we can define multiple signatures if required. We can set up default signatures that will be inserted automatically when a new email message is created, like so:

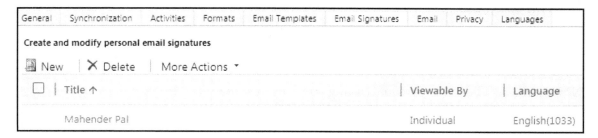

In the preceding screenshot, you can see that I have created a signature for myself that will be inserted in new email messages automatically.

Email

In this section, we have the option to configure whether or not someone else can send email notifications on our behalf. As shown in the following screenshot, if this option is not set, no other users can send emails on your behalf:

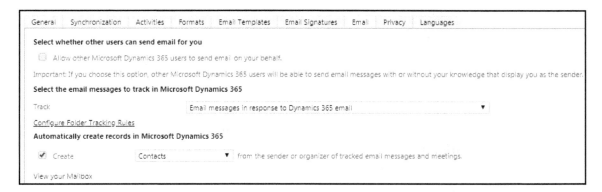

The **Track** option allows us to select the types of messages we want to track in the Dynamics 365 CE app. Further to this, we can also configure the **Create** option to create a contact or lead record when someone sends an email to us. The **Unified Interface only** option allows us to show email conversations on the Timeline control on the entity form.

Privacy

Sometimes when working with Dynamics 365 CE, we will have exceptions, and if we want to send these exception details to Microsoft, we can configure these options.

Languages

This option allows us to select our default language. If multiple languages are enabled for the organization, we can change it here. Otherwise, the default language is selected based on the region, for every user.

Now we know about the personal settings options in Dynamics 365 CE, so let's discuss other configurations that can be done by the admin users.

Configuring administration settings

The administration settings area is used to configure common settings for a Dynamics 365 CE organization. We can use this area to configure different settings—for example, sharing updates to all Dynamics 365 CE users; setting auto-numbering for some of the out-of-the-box entities; configuring system-level settings; and setting up languages.

Let's discuss different settings options under the **Administration** area. We can navigate to the administration area from **Settings** | **Administration**.

Announcements

As the name suggests, we can use this setting to share updates with our Dynamics 365 CE users. While adding new announcements, we can add the following details:

- **Title**: This is the name of the announcement; it is a required field.
- **Body**: Details of our announcement; it is a required field.
- **More Information URL**: Any external URL that we want to use for more details—for example, your company website or your SharePoint portal page URL.
- **Expiration Date**: Date of announcement expiration. Once this date is over, announcements will not be visible to Dynamics 365 CE users.

By default, there is no navigation area to access announcements in Dynamics 365, but it can be added easily by customizing Dynamics 365 CE Sitemap. We will be learning how to customize Sitemap in the next chapter. We can access announcements by appending the `/home/homepage/home_news.aspx` URL to our Dynamics 365 CE organization URL. So, for example, I can access my announcements using the following URL:

`https://himbap.crm8.dynamics.com/home/homepage/home_news.aspx`

Here, `himbap.crm8.dynamics.com` is our Dynamics 365 CE trial organization URL.

Auto-Numbering

This setting allows us to configure an auto-incremental numbering feature for some of the out-of-the-box entities. We can change the prefix text and suffix length, as we can see in the following screenshot. Only these two fields are editable. We can use up to three characters in the **Prefix** dropdown, and we can select different length options from the **Suffix Length** dropdown. The following screenshot shows how the settings look:

We can also see a preview of the changes after modification. Once these settings are changed for a particular entity, the system will generate an auto-number for the entity, based on the new settings. When a new record is created, for example, in the preceding screenshot, the configured auto-number prefix and numbers will be used to generate new contract record auto-numbers.

System Settings

The **System Settings** option is used to configure system-level settings. The **System Settings** dialog has different tabs that allow us to configure settings for the different areas. Let's discuss these tabs, one by one.

General

As the name suggests, this tab allows us to configure general settings for a Dynamics 365 CE organization. Let's discuss the options available in this tab.

Enable Auto-Save

This option allows us to enable the auto-save option for the main entity form. The auto-save option saves your record 30 seconds after the update, so it is useful if you have created an account entity record and now want to make some more changes on the account record. You can open a record and make the required changes, and if you don't manually save your account record, the system will save your record automatically after 30 seconds, because this option is enabled by default.

 If the **Auto-Save** option is enabled, Dynamics 365 CE users won't see the **Save** button on the entity command bar once the record is created. If you want to see the **Save** and **Save & Close** buttons, you need to disable this option.

Set the full-name format

This option allows us to set up a **Full Name Format** for a contact and lead entity. We can select different options from the list, as shown in the following screenshot:

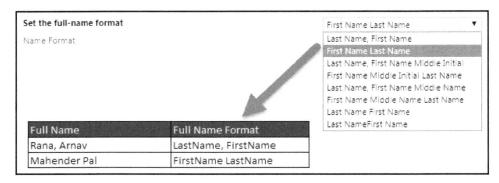

Changes to this format are only applicable to new records created. It does not change the **Full Name Format** for existing records.

Set whether reassigned records are shared with the original owner

This setting is used to share records with the original owners after they are assigned to another user. For example, let's say you are working with one lead record, and now this lead is passed to another salesperson. By default, you won't be able to see this lead anymore if you have user-level permissions (which means you can only access records that are created by you, assigned to you, or shared with you). You can only access this lead when it is shared with you. This option allows us to share records automatically with the original user when the records are assigned to another user. By default, this option is disabled. The following screenshot explains different options available under **Set up Search**. Follow the steps shown in the screenshot:

The first option that we can see in the preceding screenshot allows us to set up a global **Relevance Search**. **Relevance Search** can be used to search data in different places such as entities, notes attachment, and email attachments, and it returns the results in a single list, sorted by relevance. It can search for data in different formats such as HTML, XML, ZIP, TXT, EMP, and JSON. It searches the data only from text; we can't search data on numeric or date type fields using **Relevance Search**. Basically, it uses the external search service of Microsoft Azure to implement **Relevance Search**.

The following is a screenshot of the search text **HIMBAP**, and we can see how it is showing all of the record types in which the system found the text **HIMBAP**:

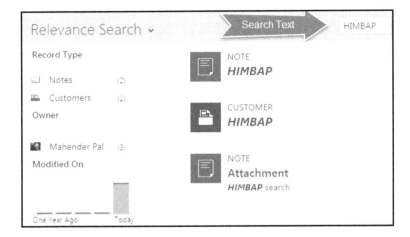

 If **Relevance Search** is enabled, it becomes the default search for your Dynamics 365 CE organization. Currently, Relevance Search is only supported for Dynamics 365 CE Online.

Once we have enabled **Relevance Search**, we can configure a list of the entities using solutions, as shown in the following screenshot:

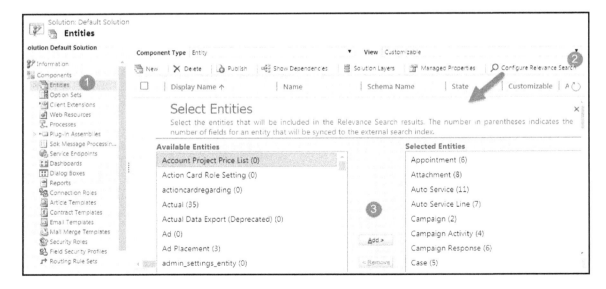

We can navigate to **Settings ǀ Customization ǀ Customize the system** and select a list of the entities from this dialog. By default, some out-of-the-box entities are enabled for **Relevance Search**, but we can add or remove entities based on our requirements. **Relevance Search** is performed based on the find columns in a Quick Find view, so we can add required fields using the **Add Find Column** button on the Quick Find view editor.

The second option, **Enable Quick Find record limits**, allows us to set up a Quick Find view result record limit. The Quick Find view is used to search for data on a single entity. When this option is set to **Yes**, it will show an error message when the Quick Find result is more than 10,000. If this option is set to **No**, it will throw an error when the Quick Find result is more than 50,000.

The third option allows us to set up another global search called **Categorized Search** that can be used to search within multiple entities. We can click on the **Select** button and select a list of the entities that we want to include in the **Categorized Search**. We can search a maximum of 10 entities in the category search.

Set custom Help URL

Dynamics 365 CE now allows us to set up our custom help system for Dynamics 365 CE, which means when the user clicks the Help icon available on the Dynamics 365 CE top navigation bar, as in the following screenshot:

The user will be redirected to the custom help system. This section allows us to set up a URL for our custom help system.

Use the new Unified Interface only (recommended)

Currently, when you set up Dynamics 365 CE, you are redirected to the Unified Interface client directly, as this option is enabled by default. So, if you want to always use the classical web client, you can disable this option. If you wish to go to the web client only sometimes, you can also make changes in your Dynamics 365 CE URL. For example, let's say the following is the URL for my Dynamics 365 CE organization:

```
https://himbap.crm8.dynamics.com/main.aspx?forceUCI=1&pagetype=apps
```

In this URL, you can see we have two parameters, `forceUCI` and `pagetype=apps`. We can remove the last parameter and change the `forceUCI` parameter to `forceClassic`. So, our URL to open the classical web client will be as follows:

```
https://himbap.crm8.dynamics.com/main.aspx?forceClassic=1
```

Timeout settings

We can set up timeout settings in Dynamics 365 CE. By default, the session timeout setting is set to **1,440** minutes (24 hours), which means if you have a Dynamics 365 CE browser session open for 24 hours, it will ask you to re-enter your Dynamics 365 CE credentials. We can keep the default settings or we can use our custom settings, as shown in the following screenshot:

We also have the option to show a warning before the session expires. Apart from timeout settings, we can also set up a timeout for inactive sessions. For example, if a user has left the Dynamics 354 CE browser session inactive, we can set it to time out after a certain amount of minutes. Similarly, we can set up the timing of the warning message as well.

Enable embedding of certain legacy dialogs in a Unified Interface browser client

This option is used to enable/disable some of the legacy command buttons to Unified Interface. When this option is enabled, we can see command buttons such as **Edit**, **Merge**, and **Share**.

The following are the other settings available in this tab:

Setting	Description
Allow text wrapping in form field labels and values	This option allows us to configure text wrapping for entity field labels and values. This setting is helpful for longer field labels and values.
Set Skype for Business Options	If you want to call your customer using Skype for Business from Dynamics 365, this option should be enabled.
Microsoft Teams Integration	This option allows us to set up Microsoft Teams integration. If you are already using Microsoft Teams to collaborate with your team, you can enable this option.
Set the currency precision that is used for pricing throughout the system	This option allows us to set up decimal places for the currency field. We can set this up to 4 decimal places.
Set whether reassigned records are shared with the original owner	When we reassign records to another user, the original user won't have access to a record if they have user-level access, but we can use this option to share the record with the original user after reassignment.
Set blocked file extensions for attachments	We provide file extensions that we want to block from attaching to Dynamics 365 CE records.
Set the currency display option	We can use this option to set currency display options with a currency symbol or currency code.
Enable Bing Maps	This option is used to enable the Bing Maps control on the entities that have address composite control such as account, contact, and lead.
Set the default country/region code	We provide our county/region code here as a prefix to phone numbers.
Set the telephony provider	Here, we can set up a default click-to-call application if we want to use Skype or Skype for Business.
Set whether users see Microsoft Dynamics 365 message	When this option is enabled, it displays a user to download apps for Dynamics 365 CE.
Disable social engagement	We can use this option to enable/disable social engagement.
Set whether users see welcome screen	We can use this option to show/hide the welcome message to Dynamics 365 CE users.
Show legacy Dynamics 365 – custom app	We can use this option to show/hide the Dynamics 365 CE legacy app that contains all out-of-the-box modules.
Use legacy form rendering	This option is available for the backward code compatibility. This will be removed in a future release.

Set the default card state for Interactive Dashboards	We can use this option to expand or collapse contact cards by default in an interactive dashboard.
Enable embedding of certain legacy dialogs in Unified Interface browser client	This option is used to show legacy command buttons on the Dynamics 365 CE command bar—for example, **Edit**, **Merge**, and **Share**.
Enable users to view contact cards	We can use this option if we want to view additional details about a contact from the contact lookup.

Now we know the common settings in the **General** tab, let's move to the next tab, where we can configure auditing-related settings.

Auditing

This section is used to configure auditing for our Dynamics 365 CE organization. The **Auditing** feature in Dynamics 365 CE allows us to track changes in the entity field. **Auditing** is enabled at three levels. Organization-level auditing setting is configured using the following screen:

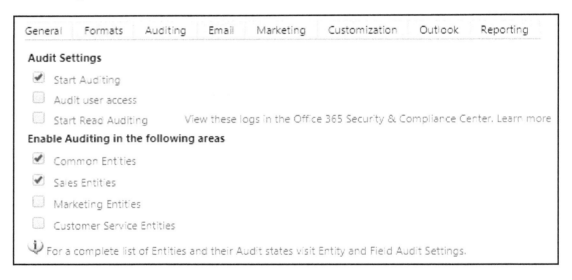

We can enable **Auditing** using the **Start Auditing** option. We can also enable **Audit user access**, which will track user access to Dynamics 365 CE organization data. The **Start Read Auditing** option allows us to access audit information from the Office 365 portal.

Once auditing is enabled at organization level, we can configure it for entities and fields. Proper consideration should be taken when selecting fields for auditing; otherwise, it can increase database size. We can navigate to **Settings** | **Auditing** to manage auditing configuration and to see auditing logs. We can click on **Entity and Field Audit Settings** to configure it for entities and fields. By default, most of the fields for out-of-the-box entities are enabled for auditing, so we can disable auditing for the fields we don't require to be audited. Keep in mind that even though you have enabled auditing for the field, it will only work if the entity is enabled for auditing. Similarly, the system will start auditing only when you have enabled auditing at the organization level, as shown in the following screenshot:

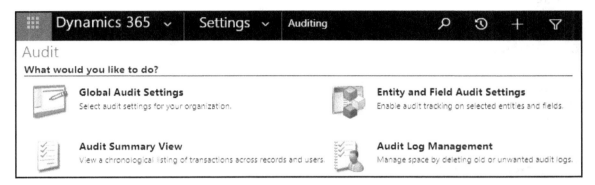

We can use **Audit Summary View** to see all of the auditing captured for our Dynamics 365 CE organization. If we want to delete old logs, we can use the **Audit Log Management** option. Bear in mind that we can only delete old logs.

Email

This tab is used to set up email settings for a Dynamics 365 CE organization. We can set up options for how we want to integrate email, using server-side synchronization or an email router.

We can set up default synchronization methods for all the users from this tab. By using the email process for unapproved users and queues, we can configure whether we want to process emails for the users and queues whose email addresses are not approved by the system administrator. By default, these options are enabled. Using this tab, we can also set up email tracking options. We can use the following two options for email tracking:

- Using tracking token
- Using smart matching

These tracking token options are used by a Dynamics 365 CE organization for identifying and matching email messages. When a tracking token is used for email tracking, an alphanumeric number is generated and appended to the email subject line by Dynamics 365 CE. This alphanumeric character is used to relate incoming email messages to any existing email activity in Dynamics 365 CE.

While using smart matching, Dynamics 365 CE uses the email subject, sender, and recipient to compare it with the existing email, and if a similar match is found, incoming email is associated with the existing email activity. We can also set up email attachment limits in this tab. By default, the file limit is set to 5 MB, which can be increased up to 128 MB if required.

Marketing

We can set up Dynamics 365 CE legacy marketing module settings here. We have different options to set up, such as whether mail merge is enabled for campaigns or not, or whether we want to create campaign responses for the incoming emails based on email token tracking. We also have the option to set auto-unsubscribe for marketing emails.

Customization

This tab gives us the option to always open Dynamics 365 CE in Application mode, which does not include menu, navigation, or command buttons. Another important setting that we can configure from here is to enable logging for plugin trace. This is an important setting for technical resources while working on Dynamics 365 CE development. Plugin tracing helps to track any plugin issues and obtain details about them. There is another setting that we can use to show/hide Microsoft Flow buttons from the navigation bar.

Outlook

If you are using a Dynamics 365 CE Outlook client, then you can use this tab to configure settings related to Outlook integration. This tab contains settings for the email tracking interval, synchronization of the data between Outlook and Dynamics 365 CE apps, and configuration to allow users to update their local Outlook data and address books. We can also set up a time interval for the synchronization of these settings.

Reporting

This table is used to configure different categories for Dynamics 365 CE reports. We can modify existing categories and add new categories. This section contains important settings to enable Power BI dashboards and tiles, which we can use for Dynamics 365 CE reporting.

Calendar

This setting allows users to set the duration for an appointment in terms of the number of days. By default, it is set to **10**. We can also set up scheduling engines in this tab.

Goal

This tab is used to set up goal rollup settings. We can configure the number of days after which we don't want to include a goal in a rollup. Another setting we can configure is to set up intervals between rollups.

Sales

This tab allows us to configure sales-related settings for the product and pricing. We can configure the following settings in this tab:

Setting	Description
Select whether products should be created in the active state	This option allows us to configure whether products will be created in the active or draft state.
Set whether the default pricelist for an opportunity should be selected via an inbuilt rule	If this option is enabled, the pricelist defined in the territory is selected automatically in the opportunity record.
Set maximum number of products in a bundle	We can set the maximum number of products that we want to include in the product bundle.
Customize close opportunity form	If this option is enabled, we can customize the close opportunity form and add a custom field there.
Make price lists optional	If this option is enabled, the user can add a line item to sales entities such as opportunity, quote, order, and invoice without adding a price list.
Qualify lead experience	If this option is enabled, Account, Contact, and Opportunity records are created after lead qualification; but if this option is disabled, it will ask the user to select which entity record they want to create after the lead is qualified.

Set pricing calculation preference	We can use this option to configure whether we want to use a custom pricing calculation on the sales entity using a plugin or whether we want to use a default pricing calculation from the system.
Set whether a discount is applied as a line item or per unit	We can use this option for the discount. We can apply it based on the line item or per unit.
Set maximum number of properties allowed for a product or bundle	We can use this option to provide the maximum number of properties a product can have.

All the preceding settings help us to manage our sales products. These settings are useful for customers using Dynamics 365 CE product catalog features.

Service

This tab is used to configure service app-related settings. For example, we want to enable/disable a **service-level agreement** (**SLA**) for all of the entities where an SLA is enabled. We can also configure options here to decide if we want to apply an SLA on the entity records automatically or if we want to apply it when the SLA is selected manually on the entity record.

In this tab, we can also set up record status when we want to pause an SLA. For example, when the case is on hold, we may not wish to track the SLA. Lastly, we have the option to apply default entitlement to case records based on the customer when a case is created or updated.

Synchronization

This tab contains settings for the Outlook synchronization filters and fields that are going to synchronize with the Outlook client. The Outlook filter defines which data will be available in Dynamics 365 CE for the Outlook client.

Mobile Client

In this tab, we can configure whether we want to enable conflict detection for offline synchronization or not. It if is enabled, any changes that are done in Offline mode on the mobile client that create any conflict with Dynamics 365 CE server data will be detected and captured in the Sync Error entity.

Previews

Any new Dynamics 365 CE feature that is in preview will be available under this tab, and if we want to enable that preview feature for our Dynamics 365 CE organization, it can be done from this tab.

This is how we can configure different system-level settings using the **System Settings** options from **Administration Settings**.

Language

Dynamics 365 CE is a multilingual application. While setting up Dynamics 365 CE, we select our default language. If required, we can set up additional languages using this option. We can select an appropriate language option and click on **Apply** option. Once this language is enabled, the user will be able to change their display language using the personal settings options. Personal settings options are available next to the **Advanced Find** button on the top navigation bar. Keep in mind that after adding additional language support, we need to change translations and add localized text for any user interface items, as all the user items are available in the base language by default. We can export or import translations from solutions.

Subscription Management

Using this setting, we can manage our Dynamics 365 CE subscription. This option is available only in Dynamics 365 CE Online. This setting will open the Office 365 home page for us, where we can manage all of our Office 365 applications.

System Notification

Any notifications related to Dynamics 365 CE will be available here—for example, any notifications of scheduled outages planned by Microsoft.

Resources In Use

This setting helps us to understand how many resources we have used from available resources. For example, currently, Dynamics 365 CE Online supports 1,500 custom entities, but we can work with Microsoft if we want to create more custom entities than this number.

Yammer

Dynamics 365 CE can be connected to Yammer using this setting, as shown in the following screenshot:

Yammer is a social media tool that is used for communication within your organization. It provides a center to communicate, create, and edit documents, and share information with other colleagues.

Virtual Entity Data Sources

Virtual entities are used to display data in Dynamics 365 CE from different sources. To bring in data from outside of a Dynamics 365 CE virtual entity, data providers are used. We can use existing data providers or we can set up our own custom data provider using plugins. Virtual entity data sources are used to store details about the data providers, as well as their connection parameters.

Now that we have discussed administration settings, let's see which configurations can be done from the business management settings area.

Configuring business management settings

Business management settings are used to configure settings that are related directly to day-to-day business activities of Dynamics 365 CE users. Let's discuss configuration options available under this setting.

Fiscal Year Settings

We can use this configuration to set up fiscal year-related settings for our organization; for example, when we start our fiscal year. In India, the fiscal year starts from April 1, so we can set up our business start date as of April 1. The following screenshot shows how we can set up the display fiscal year information in Dynamics 365 CE:

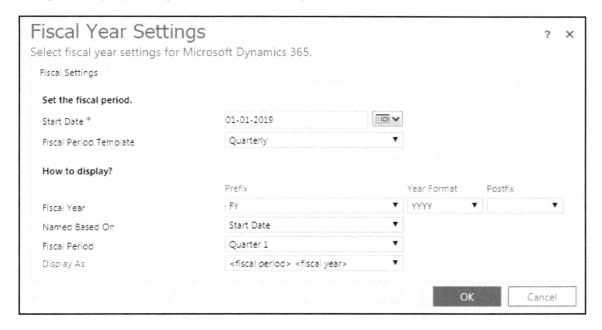

We can also set up how our fiscal year will be divided. For example, we may want to analyze our business performance annually or after 6 months, or quarterly, depending on our requirements. We can set it up under the fiscal year template.

Business Closures

Business Closures are used to capture all of the dates on which our business will be closed for operations. We can record all of the dates here for the complete year, as shown in the following screenshot:

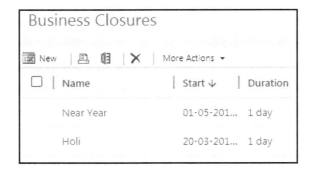

By configuring **Business Closures**, we can prevent any resource scheduling (the resource scheduling process is used to assign resources to services and tasks) during this time.

Queues

A queue in Dynamics 365 CE works as a container for different entity records such as cases and activities. Once we set up a Dynamics 365 CE organization system, we create default queues for the default team and for all of the users, but we can also set up our own custom view if required. While creating queues, we can fill in an email ID in the queue record. Later, we can use this email ID to send or receive emails for the queue. We can create the following two types of queues in Dynamics 365 CE:

- **Public**: This queue and its items are visible to every user in the organization. For example, we may want to set up a Contact US queue to hold all of the emails sent to contactus@ourcompany.com.
- **Private**: A private queue can be created for specific users or teams. These queues are not accessible by other users.

The following screenshot shows an example of our company **Contact US** queue:

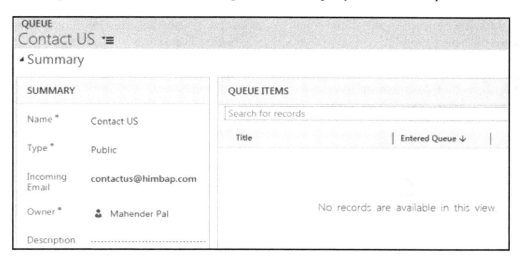

We can set up a mailbox for the queue, which will help collect all of the emails sent to the email ID under this queue.

Queues are heavily used by support resources. Depending on the requirement, we can set up queues for different support requirements. For example, we may set up a queue for high-priority cases, and a different queue for lower-priority cases.

Sales Territories

We can use this option to manage sales territories for our organization. Sales territories are used to manage our customers based on their geographical location. We can set up different territories based on customer locations and can assign appropriate teams to handle those territories. These territories may be related to our different offices.

 The same user can't be allocated to multiple territories.

Sites

We can use this option to set all the business locations. These sites may be related to our workshops where we work on customer support issues. For example, if we are a bike service company, we may have our workshops in different locations. We can capture all of the locations under sites and store the address of the location. These sites can further be used while scheduling resources for service appointments.

Currencies

We can use this configuration to manage additional currencies for our organization. While setting up Dynamics 365 CE, we set up our default currency that is used for business transactions, but we can also set up additional currencies using the option shown in the following screenshot:

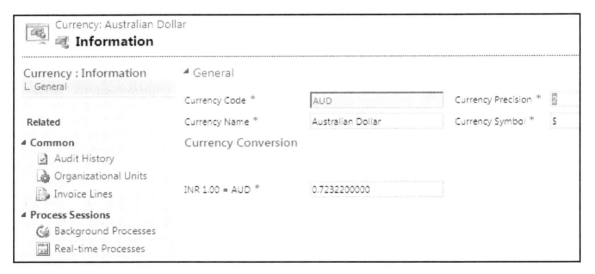

While setting up the currency, we can provide the **Currency Name**, **Currency Code**, **Currency Symbol**, and exchange rate. We may need to set up the integration or a process to update currency exchange rates regularly, based on the market.

Relationship Roles

Relationship roles are used to define associations between records. We can set up relationship roles for accounts, contacts, and opportunities.

Rollup Queries

We can use the **Rollup Query** option to query a group of related records. We can design our **Rollup Query** in the inbuilt query designer, inside a record, and can apply conditions for primary or related entities. Following is the screenshot of the **Rollup Query** screen created for the **Opportunity Line** entity:

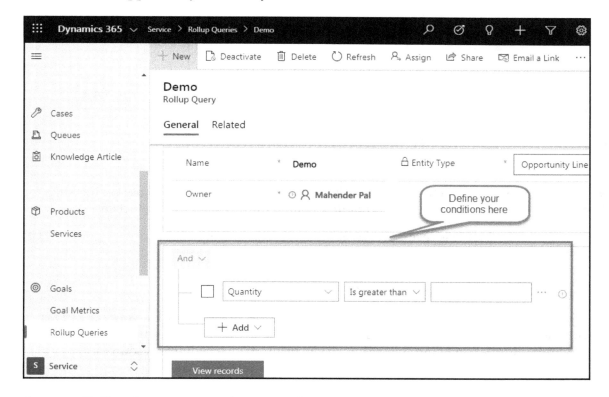

Once our **Rollup Query** is created we can refer it while creating goals.

Goal Metrics

A **Goal Metric** allows us to track our Dynamics 365 CE data against specific targets. For example, we may want to track our actual revenue for the fiscal period. To create a goal, first, we need to define goal metrics, which define how we are going to measure our goal. In goal metrics, we define the type of metric as to whether it is an amount or a count, and we define which fields will be part of the goal metrics. Following is the screenshot of **Goal Metric** which is available out of the box to track number of product unit sold:

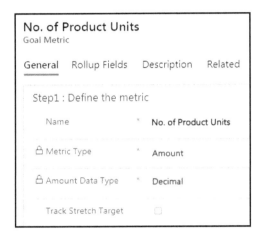

Under **Rollup Fields** section, we can define which field we are going to use for tracking, for example, this goal metric uses the **Quantity** field in the opportunity product entity.

Once our **Goal Metric** is ready, we can refer to it while creating goals.

Facilities/Equipment

You can configure these options if you use any facilities or equipment in your operations. For example, a training company may use a projector as equipment for training, so they can store this information under this setting. It can be used for scheduling resources.

Resource Groups

We can combine our organization's resources under groups using this option, and these can be used for scheduling resources.

Services

This setting can be used to capture all of the services we provide to our customers. While creating services, we can define which resources are required for this, and where the service is performed.

Subjects

Subjects are used to categorize cases, projects, sales literature, and **Knowledge Base** (**KB**) articles. We can define subjects under this setting, and then these subjects can be used while creating the preceding entity records, such as cases and projects.

Connection roles

Connection roles define a display name for the association between two entity records. By default, Dynamics 365 CE contains many connection roles. We can use this setting to modify existing records or to create new connection roles. For example, the following is a screenshot of the **Partner** connection role:

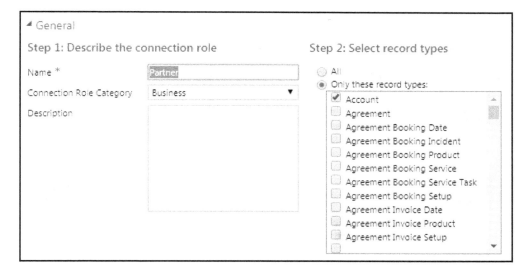

Here, we can select a list of the record types with which we want to use the connection role.

Automatic Record Creation and Update Rule

This is the most commonly used requirement in Dynamics 365 CE, where we can set up rules to create Dynamics 365 CE records based on different activity types. We can set up a rule record and define rules where we can specify an action to create and update entity records, as shown in the following screenshot:

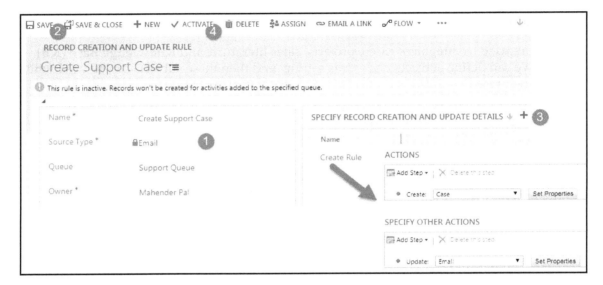

Once our rule is ready, we can activate it. We can also use these rules with queues. In such cases, this rule works when an email enters into the queue.

Now we know all of the configuration options that come under business management, let's discuss service management configuration.

Configuring service management settings

We can use service management settings to set up the administrative configuration for the service app or service module. We have already discussed some of the configurations available in this section, so we are going to discuss some important service configurations here.

Routing Rules Sets

We can use this option to create routing rules for cases that need to be routed to a specific queue, user, or team. Let's imagine we want to set up a routing rule to automatically transfer high-priority cases to a high-priority queue. The following screenshot shows us how we can do this:

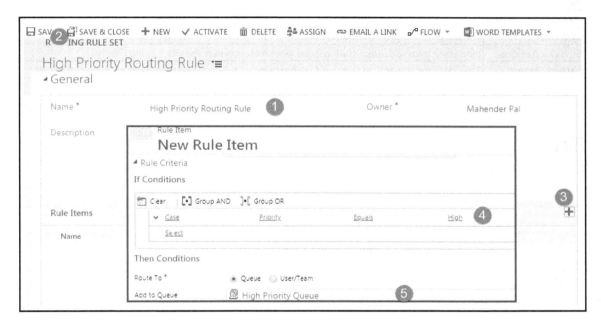

First, we need to create a routing rule record, and then, we can click on the + to create rule items. Under **Rule Items**, we can define the rule name and rule criteria. In the **Rule Criteria**, we can set up a rule that if a case priority field is set to **High**, then the case should be transferred automatically to the **High Priority Queue**.

SLAs

Dynamics 365 CE allows us to set up SLAs for our customers to provide them with a quality service. Setting up SLAs for our customers ensures that the customers are attended to in time. By default, an SLA is only enabled for case entities, but we can enable it for other entities by modifying the entity definition. We can create two types of SLA, as follows:

- **Standard**: This type of SLA can be only created for case entities, and it can't be paused.

- **Enhanced**: This type of SLA can be created for any entity. We can pause this type of SLA if required.

Once an SLA is created, we can set up SLA items. For SLA items, we can define the following properties:

Section	Description
Application When	Here, we provide conditions of when this SLA is applied to the entity record.
Success Criteria	Under this, we provide conditions of when the SLA is considered as successful.
Success Actions	Here, we provide steps that will be performed when the SLA is successful.
Failure Action	This defines the action that will be performed when the success criteria are not met.
Warning Actions	Here, we define a warning time; in other words, when it should start showing a warning message to the user before executing failure actions.

Entitlement

Entitlement defines service support facilities that we provide to our customers. For example, we may have different entitlements for our partners. Maybe our gold partners can raise up to 500 cases in a year, whereas our silver partners can only raise 200 cases in a year. While creating entitlements, we can select entitlement terms based on the entity. For example, the following entitlement created for a case entity shows how we can specify how many cases can be registered during the entitlement term (between **Start Date** and **End Date**). In the following entitlement example, we can see how we can use **ENTITLEMENT TERMS** and **ENTITLEMENT CHANNEL**:

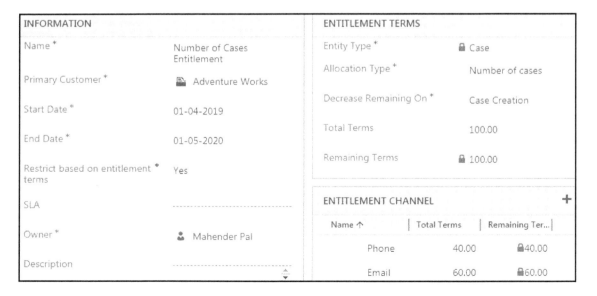

These entitlements can be associated with an SLA. We can also define entitlements for our organization, and create entitlements using these templates if similar entitlements are required to set up many customers.

Configuring data management settings

The data management section, as the name suggests, lets you manage your Dynamics 365 CE data. We have different options here that are used in our day-to-day activities. Let's see how we can configure them.

Duplicate Detection Settings

This option allows us to configure duplicate detection settings for our organization. We have the following options to enable duplicate detection:

Option	Description
When a record is created or updated	If this option is enabled, Dynamics 365 CE will detect duplicates based on the duplicate rules during the creation of or the updating of an entity record.
When Dynamics 365 CE goes from offline to online	If this option is enabled, duplicate detection is checked when the Outlook client is connected to the Dynamics 365 CE server.
During data import	It this option is selected, duplicate detection happens during data import in Dynamics 365 CE.

Duplicate Detection Rules

Duplicate Detection Rules lets you define rules to check for duplicate records based on the duplicate detection settings. We can select fields that we want to validate for duplicate detection. It is always recommended to use a unique field for duplicate detection checks, such as record ID or email address.

The following screenshot shows the example **Email** address field check rule, which will fire based on duplicate settings such as on record creation or on updating of an account entity:

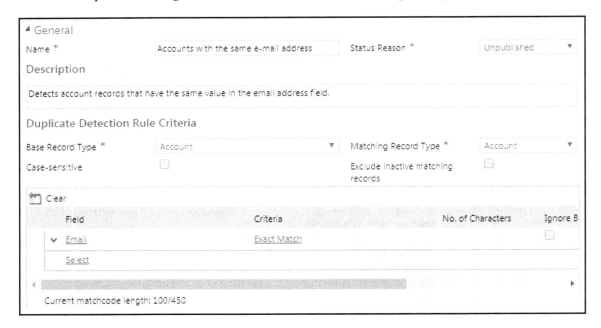

This will show a duplicate detection dialog if duplicates are found. Keep in mind that even though duplicate detection is set up, it does not stop users from creating duplicate records; so, Dynamics 365 CE users can still create account records with email records that match those from existing account records. If we want to prevent users from creating duplicate records, we can register custom logic in a Dynamics 365 CE organization. Once a duplicate detection rule is ready, we can publish it. Only published duplicate detection rules are used by Dynamics 365 CE for checking duplicate records.

 We can create multiple detection rules for the same entity type, but only five duplicate detection rules can be published for an entity at a time.

Duplicate Detection Job

We can use a duplicate detection job on existing records based on the duplicate detection rules set up for our entity in Dynamics 365 CE. We can select criteria for the targeted records, and the system will run duplicate detection rules on those records.

Bulk Record Deletion

This is a very commonly used feature in Dynamics 365 CE that lets you clear your old unused records. We can run the **Bulk Deletion Wizard** and define the criteria to delete records. Following is the screenshot from **Bulk Deletion Wizard** where we can define our source records:

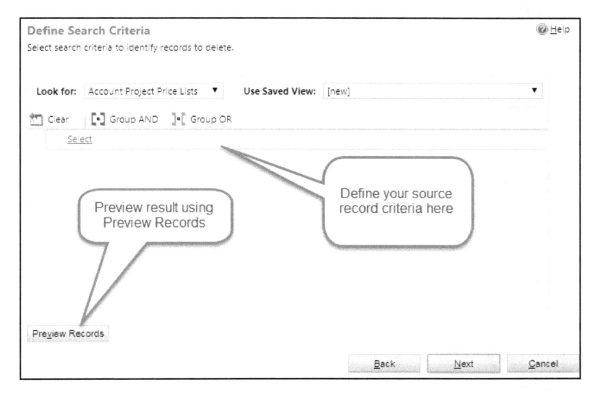

We can also schedule bulk deletion to run after a specified number of days. By default, this wizard lets you select a minimum of 7 days to schedule a bulk deletion job, but the dropdown lets you input a number, should you wish to run it before 7 days. We can also configure the wizard to send a notification once the bulk deletion job is completed. The bulk delete job uses an asynchronous service to run its operation and runs in the background without affecting Dynamics 365 CE user activity.

Data Import Options

Data management also contains different options to work with data import. We have the following Data Import options.

Data Maps

This option enables us to create data maps by importing XML files. We can create an XML file for either a single-entity or a multiple-entity record import.

 You can refer to `http://himbap.com/blog/?p=2357` for how to create multiple-entity data import maps.

Templates for Data Import

This option lets you generate source template files that can be used to feed data that we want to import. We can select our entity from the dropdown, and the system will let you download the data import file.

Make sure your entity does not contain more than one field with the same display name; otherwise, you will encounter an error while trying to download the data import file.

Import

This option enables you to import data using source files of different extensions such as `.xml`, `.csv`, `.txt`, `.xlsx`, and `.zip`. We are going to discuss how data can be imported in Dynamics 365 CE in a later chapter, in which we will also discuss different options for importing data.

Sample Data

This option allows you to set up Dynamics 365 CE sample data for demo purposes. Using this option, Dynamics 365 CE imports sample data to common entities such as account, contact, opportunity, product, and so on, which we can use to showcase Dynamics 365 CE capabilities to our customer. We can use this data for any customer demo. If sample data is installed, we can also remove it from here.

Configuring document management settings

The document management setting in Dynamics 365 CE allows us to manage our customer documents in related applications such as SharePoint, OneDrive for Business, and OneNote. Let's see how we can configure these settings.

Document Management Settings

This option allows us to set up entities for SharePoint integration. We can select a list of the entities from the following dialog, and can enter our SharePoint site where we want to store our documents:

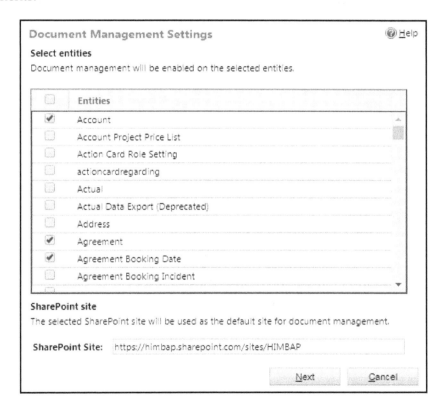

We can click on the **Next** button after selecting the entity, and on the next screen, we can select how we want to set up folders on the SharePoint site. We can select **Based on entity**, as shown here, or we can leave it unchecked:

If we check the **Based on entity** checkbox, we can add the **Account** or **Contact** entity to the root folder (main top folder in the folder hierarchy) in SharePoint. For example, if we select **Account**, the folder structure in SharePoint will be created similarly to the following:

In the preceding screenshot, we can see that we have an `Account` folder; and under `Account`, we have a demo GUID record; and under that, we will have all of the child entity record folders, such as `opportunity`, `orders`, and so on. This hierarchical structure is created based on a *1:N* relationship between the account and the child entity. In our case, we have selected **Account**. But if there is more than one relationship between the account and the child entity (apart from opportunity and contract) then Dynamics 365 CE won't set up this folder hierarchy.

And if we keep the **Based on entity** checkbox unchecked, individual entity folders are created in SharePoint without any hierarchy.

SharePoint Document Locations

The SharePoint document location record in Dynamics 365 CE points to the SharePoint document library record. It basically provides a mapping between Dynamics 365 CE records and SharePoint documents' libraries. These records are created automatically by Dynamics 365 CE when the first document is uploaded to an entity's record.

SharePoint Sites

This stores the SharePoint Sites address that we have used to store our document. This is set up during the document management setting integration wizard.

OneNote Integration

We can set up OneNote integration from this setting, wherein we can select a list of the entities for which we want to use OneNote to store notes. As soon as we enable **OneNote Integration**, we can see the **ONENOTE** tab under the social pane, as shown in the following screenshot:

OneNote integration will only appear when server-based SharePoint integration is set up.

OneDrive for Business

We can store our Dynamics 365 CE customer documents in SharePoint or in OneDrive. To store documents on OneDrive, we can enable integration with our Dynamics 365 CE. Once it is enabled, we can use OneDrive for Business folder settings to create folders under OneDrive where we can store our documents privately. While attaching documents to an entity record, we can select the location of our document, as shown in the following screenshot:

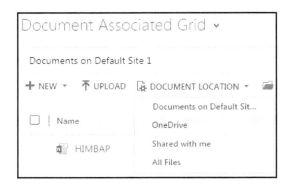

In the preceding screenshot, we can see we have the option to select our document location as SharePoint or OneDrive.

 OneDrive integration requires server-based integration for SharePoint.

Setting up email configuration

Emails can be used in Dynamics 365 CE to interact with customers. To send and receive emails in Dynamics 365 CE, we need to set up email integration. We have the option to use Outlook, server-side synchronization, or an external email tool for email integration. In our case, we are going to use server-side synchronization for email integration. To configure email integration for our organization, we can navigate to **Settings** | **Email Configuration**. We need to configure the following settings under **Email Configuration**.

Email Server Profile

Email server profiles are used to connect to **Exchange Server**. In Dynamics 365 CE, we can set up the following three types of email server profiles:

1. **Exchange Server (Hybrid)**: Using this option, we can connect our Dynamics 365 CE Online organization to an on-premises **Exchange Server**.
2. **Exchange Online**: This option allows us to connect with the **Exchange Online** server.
3. **POP3/SMTP Server**: We can use this option to connect Dynamics 365 CE with POP3 and SMTP servers.

In our scenario, we are going to use the **Exchange Online** server connection to set up our email integration. We will be using the default email server profile created for Dynamics 365 CE Online for email integration. This profile will connect to Exchange Online for email integration. In order to connect to the Exchange Online server, we are going to set up a trial for Exchange Online.

You can use the following steps to configure the trial for Exchange Online:

1. Navigate to **Microsoft 365 admin center** | **Subscription**.
2. Click on **Add Subscription**, and we can select the following option:

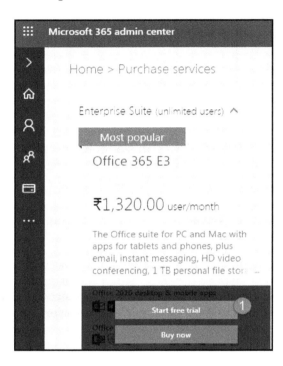

3. Complete the subscription setups, and assign the Office 365 license to the user. We can click on the **Edit User** link under the **User Management** option in Office 365 and assign an Office 365 license from the **Product licenses** option.

Mailboxes

When we add a new user or queue in Dynamics 365 CE, it automatically sets up a mailbox record for that user and queue. In order to set up a mailbox, we need to make sure that we approve the email of the user or queue, using the **Approve Email** button. We can see all the mailbox records created for all users under **Email Configuration | Mailboxes**. Navigate to **Mailboxes** and check **Mailbox Records**. Open **Mailbox Records** and click on **Test & Enable Mailbox** record. This process will connect to the Exchange Online server and will test the connection. If everything is working fine, we should see **Success** appear under **Incoming Email Status** and **Outgoing Email Status**, as shown in the following screenshot:

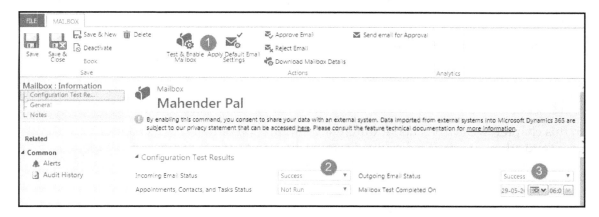

After this, we can send and receive emails in Dynamics 365 CE.

Migrate Email Router Data

We can use this option to migrate email router data to server-side synchronization. Email Router is another application that we can set up for email integration; so, if you were previously using an email router and now want to use server-side synchronization, we can use this option to migrate our organization email settings.

Email Configuration Settings

This option will open the **System Settings** dialog, where we can configure organization-level settings for email integration. We can configure options such as which email server profile we want to use for the organization, and which options we want to use for incoming and outgoing email, tracking appointments, and contacts and tasks.

Server-Side Synchronization Monitoring

This option will open the **Server-Side Synchronization Monitoring** dashboard to view a server-side synchronization summary.

This is how we can configure email integration for our organization.

Summary

In this chapter, we learned about different configuration options for Dynamics 365 CE end users and admin users. We discussed settings that give users a personalized experience. We also learned settings that can be configured by administrators for the Dynamics 365 CE organization.

In the next chapter, we are going to discuss customization options for Dynamics 365 CE.

Customizing Dynamics 365 CE 6

This chapter will help you learn about Dynamics 365 customization features. You will learn about the concept of customization and how to consider reusing existing components instead of creating new entities. You will learn about creating new entities and customizing entity forms, views, and data types. You will also learn about Dynamics 365 **Customer Engagement** (**CE**) security. Later, you will learn about customizing dashboards and charts, which will help you to set up business intelligence features for your customers.

The main topics that we are going to discuss in this chapter are:

- Understanding Dynamics 365 CE customization
- Understanding solutions
- Working with entities
- Setting up security options
- Changing navigation
- Customizing dashboards and charts

Technical requirements

This chapter requires you to have set up the Dynamics 365 CE trial, where you can perform customization. We have discussed how to set up the Dynamics 365 CE trial in the *Introduction to Dynamics 365 CE* chapter. You should also have a basic understanding of Dynamics 365 CE.

Understanding Dynamics 365 CE customization

All Dynamics 365 CE first-party apps (apps that are built by Microsoft and come with the Dynamics 365 CE vanilla setup) provide a generic business experience. For example, the Sales app provides us with a core set of features required to implement an end-to-end generic sales process. This involves commonly used business entities to store your customer data, business process flows to guide and complete your sales process, and generic business intelligence tools such as dashboards, charts, and reports. All of these processes can be modified—if required—based on our business-specific requirements, and also to provide end users with a personalized experience. Dynamics 365 CE Power Platform allows us to modify most of the existing components using the Dynamics 365 CE application itself. We don't require any additional tools to change the behavior of the components. The process of tailoring existing Dynamics 365 CE components based on our requirements is known as Dynamics 365 CE customization.

Even though we can use Dynamics 365 CE Power Platform to create new components, it is very important to consider existing components. Let's take a simple scenario of an Account entity. An Account entity is available in almost all of the Dynamics 365 CE first-party apps such as Sales, Marketing, Service, Field Service, and **Project Service Automation (PSA)**. This entity has all the possible attributes that we can use to store customer information. The term we use to describe a customer may vary from business to business. In some businesses, we may refer to our customers as Accounts, whereas other businesses may refer to them as a Company, Corporate, Advertiser, or Agency. Therefore, we can use the existing Account entity to capture different types of customer data. We don't need to create a new object to store customer details. For example, the following diagram shows different customer terms that can be mapped to an **Account** entity:

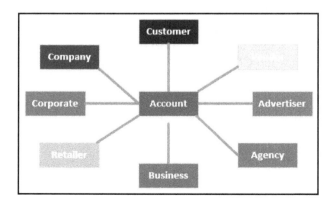

We can customize the Account entity based on these different profiles. Customization for Dynamics 365 CE can be very simple—for example, when relabeling an Account entity display name from Account to Customer. Or, it could be complex, such as when we need to add a set of new entities, set up a data model, and set up business processes as well. While working on complex requirements, it is worth checking in Microsoft AppSource in case any Microsoft **independent software vendors** (**ISVs**) have already developed a solution for a similar requirement, as this could save us time and money.

Now that we have a basic understanding of customization concepts for Dynamics 365 CE, let's discuss how to customize Dynamics 365 CE.

Understanding solutions

Before doing any customization for Dynamics 365 CE, it is very important to understand where we can keep our customized components. A solution acts as a container for Dynamics 365 CE components. All of the components that we see in Dynamics 365 CE are a part of the solution, which is known as a default or a base solution. When you are connected to your Dynamics 365 CE application, if you navigate to make.powerapps.com, which is a new way to access and modify your solutions, you can see the default solution for your organization, as shown in the following screenshot:

To customize the system, the language must match the base language. We cannot customize the system in another language.

You can double-click on **Default Solution** to see all the components it has. We can use the filter dropdown to see only a specific type of solution component, such as the following:

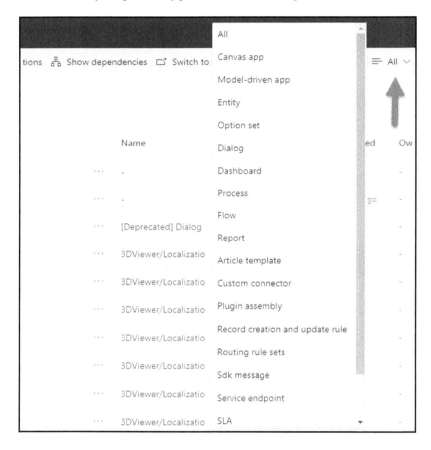

This solution holds all the out-of-the-box Dynamics 365 CE components, any components customized by us, and components that are developed by ISVs. In the preceding screenshot, you can see all of the components of the solution. The list of the components given in the screenshot represents which of the components can be included in the solution. Keep in mind that when adding the preceding solution components, only the components' metadata is added in the solution; it does not include any user data.

We can only include XML data in a solution by creating XML web resources.

In traditional applications, all of the components that are developed and changed are included in the package so that they can be moved from the development environment to other environments. In Dynamics 365 CE, we use solutions to package our changes so that our changes can be moved to other environments. When using solutions, we can segregate our customized components into custom solutions. Before starting any customization for Dynamics 365 CE, it is a best practice to create our own custom solution so that we can keep all of our new components as well as our customized components in this solution. This solution can be distributed to others after the testing process is over.

Now that we have a basic understanding of solutions, let's discuss some of the terms used for solutions.

Publisher

A publisher is basically the author of a solution. Every solution that we create must have a publisher, as this helps us to identify who has developed or customized components that are part of this solution. Every organization has a default publisher that is created by Dynamics 365 CE Power Platform during the setup of the organization. When you set up a new Dynamics 365 CE cloud instance or install Dynamics 365 CE on-premises, a new publisher with the name of **Default Publisher for <<Organization>>** s created. For example, let's imagine that my organization's name is HIMBAP. Dynamics 365 CE Power Platform will set up a publisher with the name of **Default Publisher for HIMBAP**. We will discuss more about publishers in the *Creating a custom entity* section.

Version

Every solution requires a version. We can specify the version number of the solution using four intervals. For example, we can use the format of **major.minor.build.revision**. We can use the version information based on our organization's requirements. Sometimes, vendors use the Dynamics 365 CE release version within their solution version to identify the version of Dynamics 365 CE that their solution supports.

Import

The import process is used to install solutions in our Dynamics 365 CE organization. During import, Dynamics 365 CE Power Platform checks for any solution component dependencies. If dependencies are not present in our organization, it will show as an error. If the solution contains any workflow or plugin steps, it will ask you to enable them.

Export

The export option is used to distribute our solution to other environments. While exporting solutions, we can select whether we want to export our solution as managed or unmanaged. These two categories will form our next topic of discussion. We can also include configuration as part of the solution. During export, Dynamics 365 CE will indicate whether a solution is missing in any dependent component.

Unmanaged solutions

Every solution that is in the development stage is in an unmanaged category. The default solution that we discussed earlier is also in an unmanaged stage. We can modify the existing components of the unmanaged solution and can also add new components to it. Let's create an example for our HIMBAP Auto Service Center. We can create a solution in which we can add all of the required out-of-the-box entities, and we can also create any new entities that are required. While exporting the solution, Dynamics 365 CE will ask whether we want to export our solution as a managed or an unmanaged solution. If we select an unmanaged solution, it will export an unmanaged solution using the following name format:

```
<<SolutionName>> _SolutionVersion.zip
```

Here, `SolutionName` is the display name of our solution, and `SolutionVersion` is the version information of the solution. When an unmanaged solution is imported into an organization, it overwrites any customization done using earlier solutions. We can also create or delete existing components of the unmanaged solution after importing into our Dynamics 365 CE organization. There is no direct way to uninstall an unmanaged solution in a single step, so we have to remove components one by one.

Managed solutions

When we don't want our solution to be editable in the target system, we export our solution as a managed solution. Managed solutions can be installed and uninstalled easily. We don't need to remove individual components the way that we do in unmanaged solutions. When a managed solution is installed in the target system, it does not overwrite the existing customization of the system. Whether our managed solution will be available for editing or not depends on the managed properties of the component under the solution. As you can see in the following screenshot, we can select different options for our components, to indicate whether the solution can be modified in the target system if it is installed as a managed solution:

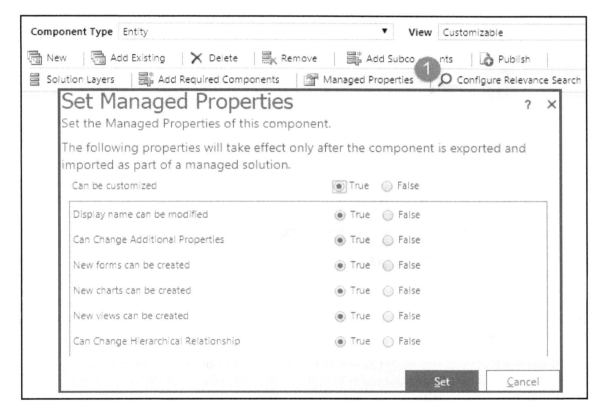

We can install an update of the managed solution in the target system as long as it has the same publisher that was used for the earlier version of the managed solution. For example, we can first install a managed solution with version 1.0.0.0, and later, we can install an updated version 1.1.0.0 in the target system. The publisher of both of the solutions should match; otherwise, we won't be able to import the updated solution to the target system.

We can understand the behavior of the system when both managed and unmanaged solutions are installed, using the following screenshot. We have an Account entity form, and let's imagine we have installed a managed solution that has also made some changes to the Account entity form. The user will be able to see the Account entity form version that has an out-of-the-box Account entity form design, as well as changes from the managed solution, like so:

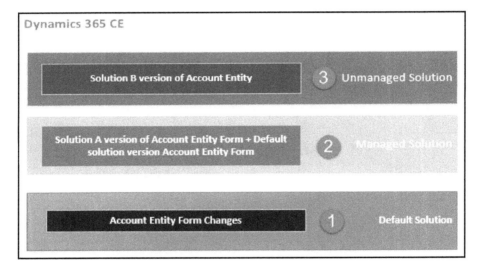

Now, let's imagine that on top of that, we have also installed an unmanaged solution B. Because it is unmanaged, it will overwrite changes in the earlier solution. Now, the user will only see the changes implemented in solution B.

If you are not an ISV and doing customization for your own organization, it is recommended to use an unmanaged solution to distribute your changes to your other environments. But if you are an ISV, you should use a managed solution to distribute to your customer.

While exporting a solution, it is recommended to include only your customized components in your solution. For example, let's say we have completed our changes, and now we want to deploy our custom solution to test the organization. We can include all the custom as well as the system components that we have modified in our solution. Another important thing we need to keep in mind is to include all the dependencies in our solution if they are not already present in the test environment; otherwise, the solution import will fail. Also, we cannot delete any solution component if that component has dependencies on another solution component.

While releasing any update to an existing solution, we can create a solution patch and can only include recently updated or new items. For example, if we added a new attribute to the Account entity, we could only include those attributes in our solution instead of including all the components from the Account entity, such as forms, views, and all fields.

 To view more details about solution patches, refer to `https://docs.` `microsoft.com/en-us/dynamics365/customerengagement/on-premises/` `customize/use-segmented-solutions-patches-simplify-updates`.

Now that we have an understanding of solutions, let's customize our Dynamics 365 CE environment.

Working with entities

Entities are used to store Dynamics 365 CE data and metadata. Every entity in Dynamics 365 CE represents a table in a Dynamics 365 CE database. When we set up a Dynamics 365 CE organization, we can acquire many out-of-the-box entities that can be used for different purposes. Entities can be divided into two broad categories:

- System entities
- Custom entities

Let's look at each of these categories in detail.

System entities

System entities are the entities that we get with a Dynamics 365 CE setup. Most of the system entities, such as lead, account, contact, opportunity, quotes, and orders can be customized easily. For example, we can change the form design of these entities; we can modify views available in these entities; we can add new fields for these entities. But some of the entities—such as Rule Item, Customer Relationship, and Wall View—are not available for customization.

In the default solution, we can check which of the out-of-the-box entities are customizable, and which of the entities are not customizable, using the Customizable column.

Custom entities

Custom entities are created by us. If our requirements can't be fulfilled with any out-of-the-box system entities, we can create custom entities. We can create two types of custom entities: standard entities and activity-type entities. Standard entities are similar to out-of-the-box standard system entities such as Account, Contact, and Lead. Activity-type entities are a special entity where we get different special PartyList fields, whereby we can select multiple types of entity records. For example, to a field in an email entity, we can send an email to an account, contact, or user.

When we create a solution, we can add existing entities to our solution using the **Add Existing** button, or we can create new entities. While adding existing entities to our solution, we should always only include components that we want to customize instead of adding the whole entity to our solution. This way, we can keep our solution light for distribution.

Now that we have an understanding of Dynamics 365 CE entities, let's discuss how we can create custom entities.

Creating a custom entity

Let's imagine that we want to create the entity that we discussed in the *Understanding Functional and technical design* section in `Chapter 4`, *Preparing Functional and Technical Design Documents*. We are going to create a vehicle entity to store our customer's vehicle information using the following steps:

1. First, we will create our custom solution. Let's imagine we want to name it **HIMBAP Auto Service**. Navigate to **Solutions** from `make.powerapps.com` and click on the **New solution** button. We can follow the numbering sequence shown in the screenshot here:

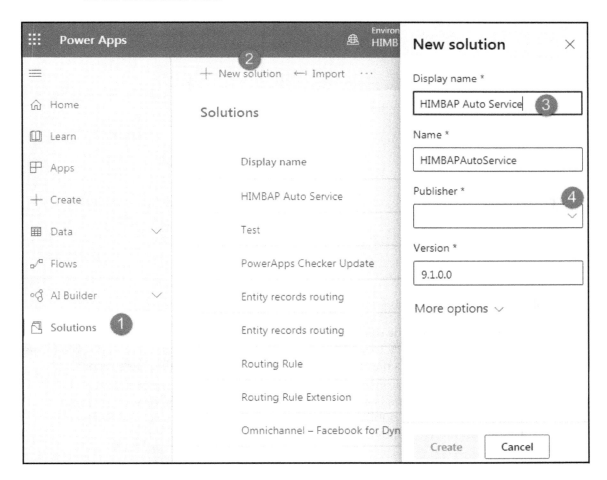

2. Let's say we want to create our new publisher. So, select the **Publisher** dropdown, and then select the **+ Publisher** option. This will open the **New Publisher** window, as shown in the following screenshot. While creating the publisher, we can fill in the information shown in the following numbered sequence:

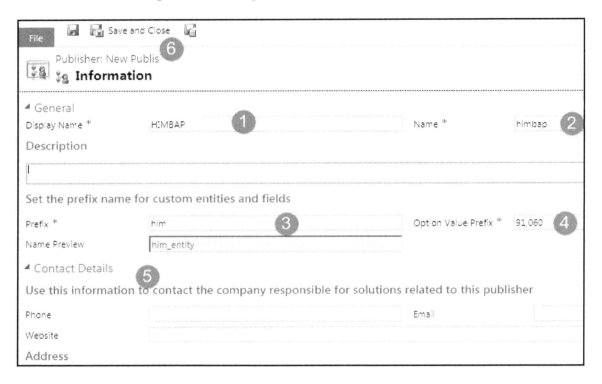

Let's look at the important fields in this section, as follows:

- **Display Name** will be displayed for the publisher under publisher lookup. For example, when we try to select a publisher for our solution, we will be able to see this name. Using this name means we can identify our publisher's record.
- The **Name** field is automatically filled by the system, but we can change it if required. This name is assigned by the system internally, or we can assign it while working with publisher records using the Dynamics 365 CE **Software Development Kit** (**SDK**).

- **Prefix** is a very important field in **Publisher** and can be used to identify who has customized or created this field. The default publisher for our organization uses the **new** prefix, but we can change it based on our requirements. When we change the prefix, we can see how it will be used for naming new entities in a preview.
- The **Option Value Prefix** value represents the number sequence that will be used for new option set values. By default, this is automatically filled by the system, but it can be changed if required.

In addition to the preceding information, we can also include our company details—such as contact information and address—while creating a publisher. Keep in mind that once we have created a new entity and its field using our new publisher, we can't modify the prefix of the entity. In case you want to change the prefix, you have to delete the entity and need to recreate this under another publisher.

Once our solution is created, navigate to the **Entities** option and click on **New** from the right-hand side solution component command bar. This will open an entity editor for us. While creating an entity, we can use the following information:

- The **Display Name** label will be used to display our entity in the Dynamics 365 CE application.
- The **Plural Name** label will be used in all the navigation area.
- The **Name** label will be used to set up an entity table in the Dynamics 365 CE database, and we will be using this name while working with SDK code.
- The **Virtual Entity** field is used to create virtual entities. We can use this type of entity to display data from different databases from outside of Dynamics 365 CE.
- The **Ownership** field is used to handle entity security requirements. We can set up entity ownership using the following two options:
  - **User or Team**: We use this option when we want to control the visibility of the entity using security roles. When this option is selected, we can set up an entity record owner as an individual user or team. This option allows us to control the security of this entity at various levels. We will discuss access levels when looking at security roles.
  - **Organization**: When we use this option to create an entity, the entity will be available to all Dynamics 365 CE users, or not available to any users at all.

While setting up ownership, we need to make sure we are setting it up correctly, based on requirements. If we want to make our entity available to all users without any restrictions, we can create an organization-level entity, or we can create a user- or team-level entity.

- The **Define as an Activity Entity** option is used to create an activity-type entity. This adds some additional `PartyList` fields and enables the default setting to automatically be applied to our entity.
- **Primary Image**: This field can be used to set up an entity image. We can create an image-type field for our entity and can select that field here after our entity is created.
- The **Color** field is used to set up the entity icon color.
- **Description** provides an entity description—for example, the reason why we are going to use this entity.
- The **Areas that display this entity** section displays all of the possible navigation areas available in our Dynamics 365 CE organization. We can select areas in which we want to display our entity.
- The **Business Process Flows** option is used if we want to set up business process flows for our entity, which can guide users visually.

When an entity is created as an activity type, it adds some other mandatory settings, such as **Enable Attachments**, **Allow Feedback**, **Enable Connections**, **Enable Queues**, and **Duplicate Detection**. On the other hand, some of the options—such as activity task, send email to entity, and support mail merge—are not available for this type of entity.

Communication and Collaboration

These settings can be used to relate our entity with other entities and services, for better communication and collaboration. We have the following options available under these settings:

- The **Feedback** option is used to capture feedback from the user for the entity record. For example, we can use this setting to capture customer service experiences with HIMBAP Auto Service Center in the **Auto Service** entity.
- The **Notes** option is used as a free text area in an entity record, where we can also upload documents to our entity record.

- The **Activities** option is used to allow activity support for our entity. If we want to create activity records related to our entity, we can select this option.
- The **Connections** option is used if we want to relate our entity record with another entity.
- The **Sending Email** option allows us to send emails to this entity. When this option is selected, an email field will be added to our entity.
- The **Mail Merge** option is enabled if we want to use mail merge functionality with our entity.
- The **Document Management** option is used to enable SharePoint integration for our entity.
- The **OneNote Integration** option can be used to access Office 365 OneNote integration if we have enabled SharePoint integration.
- The **Access Teams** option allows us to use lightweight access teams for our entity without using security roles. We can use **Access Teams** if we want to share our entity records with other users.
- The **Queues** option can be used if we want to utilize queue functionality for our entity. Queues can be used for sharing purposes as well.
- The **Knowledge Management** option is used to enable knowledge-base management for our entity. If this option is selected, we can associate knowledge-base articles with our entity.
- The **Enable for SLA** option can be used to enable **service-level agreement (SLA)** support for our entity.

Some of the preceding options can't be disabled once enabled, so proper planning should be done to avoid any unnecessary relationships being created for our entity. If we are not sure about enabling any particular option at the time of the entity being created, it is recommended that we enable that option later on, after proper planning.

Data services

These settings are used to manage entity data. We have the following settings available under this option:

- The **Allow quick create** option can be used to set up quick create forms for our entity, in which we can capture key information quickly to create an entity record.
- The **Duplicate detection** option is used to enable duplicate detection for our entity. Once this option is enabled, we can set up duplicate detection rules for our entity.

- If the **Auditing** option is enabled, we capture our entity data changes. Further to this, we can enable auditing for a particular field in which we want to monitor changes.
- The **Change Tracking** option is used to enable the monitoring of data changes for our entity. We can use this option while integrating our entity with external systems when we want to fetch data that has been changed during a specific interval.

Auditing

In addition to the enabled auditing features for the entity, there are new auditing settings available where we can enable read access for entity records. This setting has two options: to track auditing for a single record that corresponds to an SDK retrieve event (this event is fired when we fetch a single record); and to track auditing for multiple entity records that correspond to an SDK retrieve multiple records event (this event is fired when we retrieve multiple entity records). This is also known as activity logging.

Outlook and mobile

These settings are used to enable our entity for Outlook and mobile devices. We have the following options available under this setting:

- **Enable for phone express**: Using this option, we can enable our entity to be available under the Phone Express app from Microsoft.
- The **Enable for mobile** option can be used to enable our entity for mobile apps that are available for different mobile devices such as iOS and Android. We can enable our entity to be used in offline mode as well so that we can use our entity even if we are not connected to the Dynamics 365 CE server.
- The **Reading pane in Dynamics 365 for Outlook** option allows us to enable our entity for a read-only view in Outlook.
- The **Offline capability for Dynamics 365 for Outlook** option allows us to access our entity data in offline mode of the Outlook app. This option is useful if users want to use this entity from Outlook when they are not connected to the Dynamics 365 CE server.

If read-only in mobile is activated for an entity under **Enable for mobile** and this entity is used in a sub-grid in a new **user interface** (**UI**), it is not possible to create new records in the sub-grid in the new UI, even though it is still possible to create new records in the same sub-grid in the classic design.

Help

Dynamics 365 CE now allows us to set up custom help for our entity. We can use this setting to provide a custom help URL to users, which will be presented when the user tries to access help for this entity.

Setting up a primary field

While creating an entity, we can set up the primary field of the entity. This field holds the record name for our entity, and this field is used for lookup fields in another entity. For example, let's say we have an account lookup in our custom entity. When we click on this lookup field, we see the account name under the lookup and are able to select a particular account record. We can click on the **Primary Field** tab to set up a primary field. We have the following properties available under this tab:

- The **Display Name** option is used to provide a display name for our primary field. By default, this is set to **Name**, but we can change it. As an example, let's imagine we want to call it **Vehicle name**.
- **Name** is used to refer SDK.
- The **Field Requirement** option is used to set up field requirements for the **Name** field. We have three options here:
  - **Business Required**: If this option is set for the user for the field, the user has to fill in the **Name** field. This will add a red star to the field.
  - If the **Business Recommended** option is selected, it will add a blue plus (+) sign to the field, which means it is recommended to enter this value.
  - **Optional**: The user can skip entering a value for this field.

  We should set these options based on our requirements. It is recommended that we keep the primary field as **required** because this field is used for the lookup field. So, if the user left this field blank, we wouldn't be able to see any value under this entity lookup field.

- **Data Type** is fixed to **Single Line of Text**.
- **Format** is fixed to **Text**.
- **Maximum Length**: A **Single Line of Text** field can contain a maximum of 4,000 text characters.

Now that we have an understanding of entity properties and primary fields, let's create a vehicle entity in our solution. We can create a new entity using the numbered steps shown in the following screenshot:

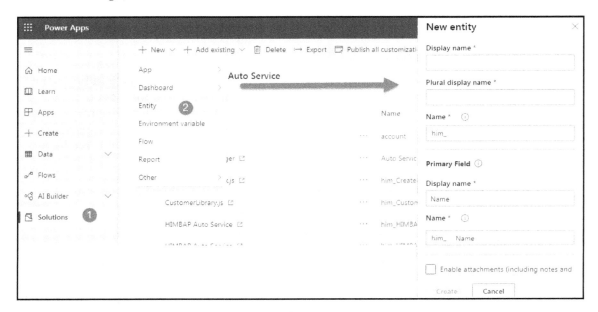

Keep all other settings as their defaults, as follows:

Display name	Vehicle
Plural display name	Vehicles
Primary Field	
Display name	Vehicle Name

After entering these details, click on **Create**. Once the entity is created, we need to add attributes to this entity, so let's discuss entity attributes and their data types.

 We can change the display name of the existing entities based on our requirements—for example, if we need to rename the opportunity entity to **Auto Service**.

Understanding entity attributes

We know that every entity represents a database table in Dynamics 365 CE, and similarly, every attribute represents a table column in a Dynamics 365 CE database. We can use an attribute to store different types of information based on their data type. Every attribute is created with a specific data type that defines the type of data we can store in that field. When we create an entity in Dynamics 365 CE, Dynamics 365 CE Power Platform creates many out-of-the-box attributes, as shown in the following screenshot:

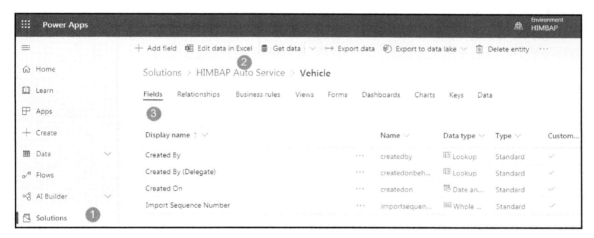

For the **Vehicle** entity, 19 fields were created automatically, with different data types. Let's discuss the data types available for Dynamics 365 CE entities.

Single Line of Text

If you want to store text within a single line, we can use this option. This data type allows us to store text, numbers, and alphanumeric characters in this field. When storing numbers in this field, they are treated as text values; so, if we need to use stored numbers in a calculation, we need to use a conversion function to convert these text values to numeric values. We can store a maximum of 4,000 text characters in this field.

Multiple Lines of Text

This is another text field that can be used to store multiple lines. We use this field when we need to store more lines of text data—for example, in a description. This field permits us to have 1,048,576 text characters within it.

Option Set

We can consider this field as a dropdown in traditional web applications, in which we have many options available. We can select one option, so this is a single selection field in which every option has a specific value and label. In earlier versions of Dynamics 365 CE, this field was known as a picklist. By using default values, the number sequence for the option set is dependent on the solution that we are using for our customization.

Multiple Option Set

As the name suggests, this option set allows us to select more than one option. This field was added with the Dynamics 365 CE version 9.0 release.

Two Options

If we have a requirement to store a Boolean field, we can use this data type that contains two options: **Yes** or **No**. In this field, **1** represents yes, and **0** represents no. If required, we can change the default label for the options.

Image

While creating the entity, we discussed primary image fields, and we can use this data to create an image field for the entity. For example, for our **Vehicle** entity, we could use the image field to display a vehicle image. We can only create one image field per entity.

Whole Number

This field is used to store whole integer numbers. We can store positive or negative numbers in this field, within the range -2,147,483,648 to 2,147,483,647. While creating this field, we can set a maximum and minimum value for this field, which will restrict users to only entering values within that range. We have the option to format this field with duration, time zone, and language, which allows us to set the value of this field according to these options. For example, the following is a screenshot of a whole number field with the time zone format configured:

We can see from the preceding screenshot how this field will provide all of the possible time zone options to select. When users select any time zone, the corresponding value of the selected time zone is stored in this field.

Floating Point Number

This field is used to store decimal values. It allows us to store decimal numbers up to five decimal places within the range -100,000,000,000 to 100,000,000,000. Based on this range, we can set minimum and maximum values, thereby restricting users to only entering decimal numbers within this range.

Decimal Number

This field is also used to store decimal values, and it enables us to store decimal numbers of up to 10 decimal places within the range -1,00,00,00,00,000.0000000000 to 1,00,00,00,00,000.0000000000. Similar to other fields, we can also set a minimum and maximum range for this field.

Currency

This field is used to store monetary values within the range -92,23,37,20,36,85,477.0000 to 92,23,37,20,36,85,477.0000. We can use four decimal places for this field, and we can also specify minimum and maximum values.

Date and Time

If we need to store date and time values, we can use this field. We can configure it to store only date values, or we can store both date and time values. Another important property we need to configure properly while creating the **Date** and **Time** field is its **Behavior**. We can use the following options:

- **User**: If this option is selected, date and time will be displayed in the user's local time and formatted as per their current portal language/locale.
- **Date only**: If this option is selected, it will only contain a date value without time zone conversion. The time will always be 12:00 A.M.
- **Time-Zone Independent**: If this option is selected, the date and time will be displayed with no time zone conversion. All users will be able to see the same date and time.

Lookup

This is a reference data type in which we can create a link between two entities. We can select our target entity and can configure the relationship name. Dynamics 365 CE set up an *N:1* relationship as a result of this field between the current entity and the target entity. We can set up a relationship with all entities that are available for customization.

Customer

This field is used to store customer details. A customer can be either an account or a contact, so this is used for a lookup field where we can set up a relationship between the current entity and an account or contact entity.

In addition to the preceding data types, there are some special data types that are not available for setting up custom fields—for example, **Unique Identifier**, **Status**, and **Status Reason**. These data types are used by Dynamics 365 CE only to set up fields during entity creation. Now that we know all of the possible data types, let's understand field editor options. While creating a new custom field, we can configure the following options:

- **Display Name**: This label is used for the field on the entity form and views.
- **Name**: Dynamics 365 CE uses this option to set up a column name for this field, and we can use this name to refer to the field while working with the SDK.
- **Field Requirement**: We can use this option to set up field requirements, such as making them optional fields, which means users can leave this field blank. We could also choose **Business Recommended**, which means filling in this field is recommended, but the user can leave this field blank if they want to. **Business Required** means that users have to enter a value for this field in order to save the entity record. It won't allow users to leave this field blank.
- **Searchable**: This option allows us to configure whether this field will show under **Advanced Find** or not. If it is set to **No**, we can't search the entity record using this field.
- **Field Security**: We can use this option to apply field-level security to this field. Field-level security allows us to restrict field values based on the field-level security profiles. We will discuss field-level security further in a later section.

- **Auditing**: Auditing allows us to capture changes in this field for later use. For example, if we want to monitor changes in this field value, we can enable auditing for this field. Keep in mind that enabling this option unnecessarily for the field can increase a Dynamics 365 CE database's size.

- **Description**: We can use this option to provide details about this field. We can also use this field to show tooltips for users. Any information provided here will be displayed to the user when the user hovers their mouse on the label of this field (after publishing changes).

- **Appears in global filter and Sortable in interactive experience**: These options enable this field to be used in interactive experience dashboards for customer service.

- **Data Type**: We can select available data types that we discussed in an earlier section.

- **Field Type**: We can select the field type based on the data type selected for this field. We will discuss possible field types in the next section.

- **Format**: Some data types have format options available. We can select these based on our requirements.

- **Range Options**: Some data types allow us to set up minimum and maximum range values that will restrict users to entering values within that range only.

- **IME Mode**: This option defines the editor mode for this field. This option is used to deal with the special characters used in the Chinese, Japanese, or Korean languages. When set to **Auto**, the editor mode is automatically selected by Dynamics 365 CE.

Now we have learned the various field editor options, let's create the following field for our **Vehicle** entity. Navigate to **Fields** and click on the **Add field** button command bar to create a new field. Let's add an image field for our **Vehicle** entity so that we can show a vehicle image of the record. Fill in the following options in the field editor:

- **Display name**: Vehicle Image
- **Data type**: Image

Keep all other options set as their defaults. You can see the preceding steps in the following screenshot:

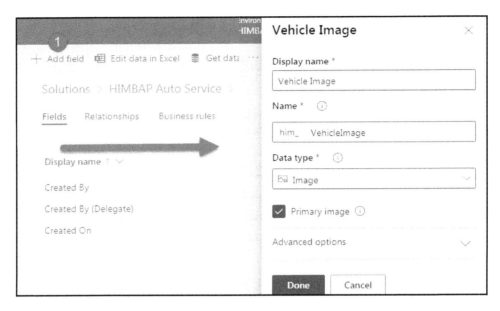

Click on the **Done** button to save the image field, and click on the **Save Entity** notification on the screen to save your changes for the entity. As soon as we create an image field, this field is automatically set under the **Primary image** field. We can click on the **Add field** button again to open the editor and create a new field option set to store the vehicle type. Fill in the following details for the **Vehicle Type** field:

- **Display name**: Vehicle Type
- **Requirement**: Yes
- **Searchable**: Yes
- **Data type**: Option Set
- **Option set**: +New Option set
- Add the following items:
- Coupe
- Crossover
- Hatchback
- MPV
- Sedan
- SUV

We can add options using an option set editor. Click on **Add new item** and enter labels one by one, as shown in the following screenshot:

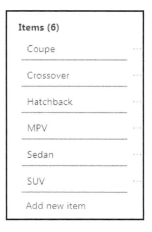

Click on **Done** to create the field.

In the **Vehicle** entity, we have a number of lookup fields, so let's see how we can set up a lookup field in the **Vehicle** entity. Before setting one up, we must make sure we have created a parent entity whose lookup we want to create in the **Vehicle** entity, like so:

- Click on **Add field** under field list
- Write **Customer** in **Display name**
- Select **Lookup** from **Data type**
- Select **Customer** under **Related entity** (the entity whose lookup we want to create)

Click on **Done**. Similarly, we can set up other lookup fields for the **Make**, **Model**, and **Year** entities.

Understanding field types

While creating custom fields, some data types allow us to configure the field type. This defines whether we can input values into this field or if values will be calculated for this field. We can set up the following field types:

Simple field type

This is used for a field that does not require any automatic calculation.

Calculated field type

This is used to autocalculate values based on the formula used. We can use calculated fields for the following data types:

- Single Line of Text
- Option Set
- Two Options
- Decimal Number
- Currency
- Date and Time

We can use a formula by using the **Edit** button available next to the field type option. Let's imagine we have an **Issue Date** field in the **Vehicle** entity that displays when the vehicle was issued, and we now want to add a **Vehicle Expiry Date** field. By default, the vehicle expires 15 years after the issue date. Take the following step to add **Issue Date** and **Registration Expiry** fields to the **Vehicle** entity:

Click on the **Add field** button and fill in the following options:

- **Display name: Issue Date**
- Set **Data type** as **Date and Time**

Keep all options as their defaults and then click on **Done**, and click on the **Add field** button to create an **Expiry Date** field. To set up **Registration Expiry** as a calculated field, click on the **New** button and fill in the following options:

- **Display name: Expiry Date**
- Set **Date type** as **Date** and **Time**
- Click on the **+ Add** button under **Calculated** or **Rollup** and select **+ Calculation**.
- Click on the **Save** button on the entity save notification.
- Reopen the field and click on the **Open Calculation** link under the field property window. Fill in the formula, as shown in the following screenshot:

Here, the **him_issuedate** field is the date field that we created in the earlier step. Now, the **Registration Expiry** field value is autocalculated based on the issue date field value.

Rollup field

This is also a calculated field; however, this field is used to calculate the aggregated value using aggregate functions such as **SUM, COUNT, MAX, MIN**, and **AVG** from a related entity. Similar to the calculated field, we can also set up our rollup formula for the rollup field calculation. Values for rollup fields are calculated using an asynchronous system job in the background. We can see all of the rollup system jobs by navigating to **Settings** | **System Jobs** | **View** | **Recurring System Jobs**.

 More details on rollup fields can be obtained from `https://docs.`
`microsoft.com/en-us/dynamics365/customer-engagement/customize/`
`define-rollup-fields.`

Now that we know how to create fields and set up field properties, we can refer to Appendix A for complete field details for the Vehicle entity and add them in the same way that we added the preceding fields. Once we have set up all the fields, we can design our vehicle form. Let's first understand form types in Dynamics 365 CE.

Understanding form types

Dynamics 365 CE forms are like web pages that are used to display Dynamics 365 CE records for users. Users can create and update records using forms. Dynamics 365 CE contains the following forms.

Main forms

This is the main form that is displayed to a user irrespective of the device they are using to access a Dynamics 365 CE application. This form is automatically created with the primary fields as soon as an entity is created. Later, we can modify this form and other controls as required. We can also create multiple forms and apply form security, so as to display this main form to users based on their security roles. For example, we may create one type of main form that is displayed to salespersons, and create another main form for administrators.

Quick view forms

Quick view forms are used with lookup control to display additional details of the entity record selected in the lookup field. In this form, data is presented in a read-only format, so we can't modify any field values. This form type allows us to add **Section, Sub-Grid, Space**, and **Timer** control only.

Quick create forms

These forms are used to create entity records quickly with key fields. We can set up multiple quick create forms and can set their order. The quick form that is first in the order will be displayed to the user. For example, in the following screenshot, we can see that we have two quick create forms:

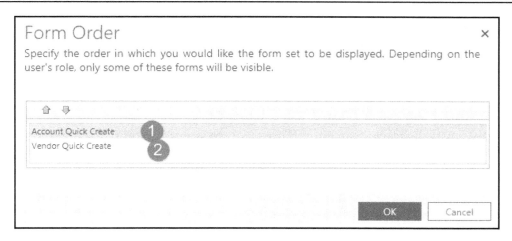

However, as the **Account Quick Create** form is the first in order, only this quick create form will be visible to the user for the Account entity.

Quick forms for any entity are only available to users if the **Allow quick create** option is selected under the entity definition. We can use the quick create option using the **Quick create** button on the top navigation bar, as shown in the following screenshot:

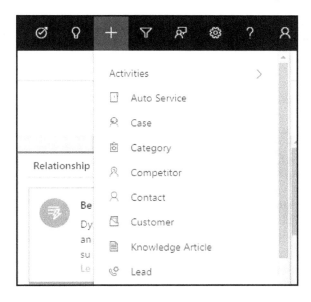

A quick create form can also be opened from a sub-grid if the quick create form is available for the entity for which we have configured a sub-grid; otherwise, the main form is opened.

Card forms

These forms are used in Unified Interface apps for lookup control and views.

Now that we have learned about entity forms, we are going to modify the main form of the vehicle entity. So, let's navigate to **Forms** and double-click on the **Information** main form. The three areas of main forms that can be used to display fields are as follows:

- **Header** is the top section of the main form where we can place a key field. We can select **Header** and can drag which fields we want to see on the form. Make sure to enable **Display options.** The form head will show a maximum of only four fields that will be read-only. Any additional fields will be moved to the drop-down flyout. We can also edit fields from the flyout, but the field on the header will be read-only. We can see an example of a **Header** form in the following screenshot:

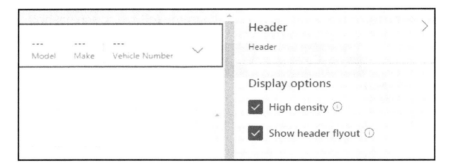

Let's add three fields to the **Header** section shown in the preceding screenshot by dragging fields from the Field Explorer.

- **Body** is the main form area where we mainly design our entity form for users by adding multiple sections, tabs, and other controls from the **Insert** tab under the Entity form editor command bar. We can add new tabs and sections and change their properties by double-clicking on the section or tab, or we can select any control and click on the **Change Property** button. Let's modify the existing section to add a field based on the following design:

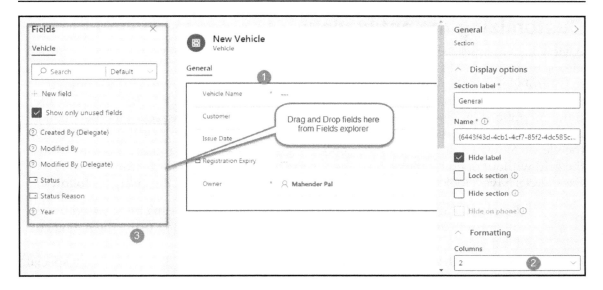

Select the **General** section on the **General** tab and select **2** under
the **Columns** dropdown, under the **Formatting** option. Once the **General** section
has two columns, drag fields from the Field Explorer and drop under this section,
as in the preceding screenshot.

- **Footer** is the third section of the form in which we can place controls. However,
  fields in this section are not editable, as they are in the Header and Body sections.
  As can be seen in the following screenshot, all of the fields are read-only, which
  means these fields can't be modified from the **Footer** section:

Let's add the preceding fields to the **Footer** section.

Further details pertaining to the form editor can be found here: `https://`
`docs.microsoft.com/en-us/dynamics365/customer-engagement/`
`customize/form-editor-user-interface-legacy`

Now that we have designed our vehicle form, let's work on the view customization for our
vehicle form.

Customizing the entity view

A view in Dynamics 365 CE is a list of records for a specific entity. We can create multiple views, or we can modify existing views based on the requirements. Dynamics 365 allows us to control views for both our custom views and our system views. We can add/remove columns to the view in order to display different information from the entity. We can alter different options on views; for example, we can double-click on the record to open it and make a change in the record, and we can also edit multiple records by selecting them from the views. Now, we can also set up an editable grid so that we can modify a record using the grid without opening the record, and we can export a list of records from the view to Excel. Let's have a look at the different types of views available for the entity, as follows:

- **Personal Views** are created and owned by the user and can't be accessed by other users unless they are shared. These views are created using the **Advanced Find** view.

- **Quick Find View** is created automatically by Dynamics 365 CE. This is a special view that is available in every view screen, and we can use it to search for specific data based on the **Find Columns** added to this view. We can add **Find Columns** while customizing a quick find view.

- **Advanced Find View** is used to display the results of the Advanced Find view. This view is also created automatically by Dynamics 365 CE when an entity is created. If required, we can modify this view and can add/remove columns accordingly.

- **Associated View** is used to display the result of the association between entities. For example, let's imagine we have a *1:N* relationship between an A and B entity. We can see all of the related entity B records in the associated view of entity A. This view is also a system view created by Dynamics 365 CE when the entity is created.

- **Lookup View** is displayed to users when searching records for lookup. This is also a system view and is created by Dynamics 365 CE automatically when the entity is created.

- **Custom View** also allows us to create our own custom view if required, in which we can add entity fields and set up filter criteria to show specific records under this view. To create a custom view, open our entity from our solution and navigate to the **view** section. Click on the **+ Add view** button, as shown in the following screenshot:

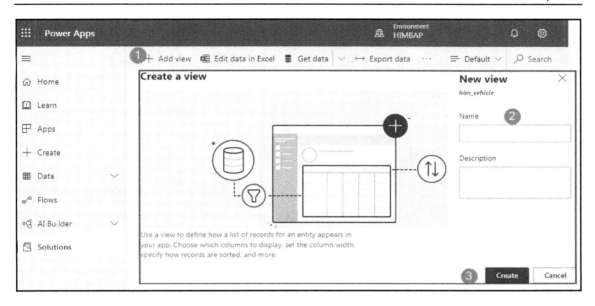

Once you have clicked on the **Create** button, that will open a new view designer for us, as shown in the following screenshot:

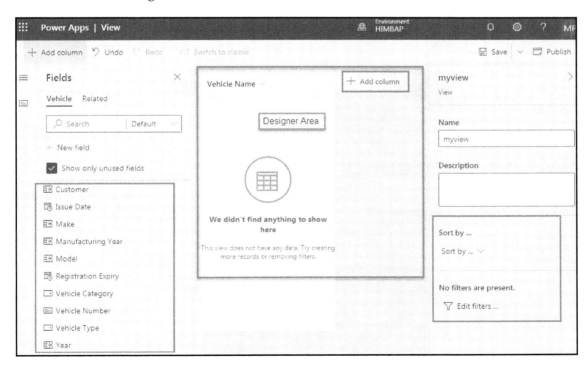

We can view the display name under the **Name** field and can design our view by means of drag and drop columns from the left-hand side of the **Designer Area**, or we can click on the **+ Add column** button to add columns. We can resize the column width by simply using the mouse. We can use the **Edit filters** option to add our filter criteria for the view that controls the list of records to display in the view. We can use the **Sort by** option to configure sorting for the record displayed under the view. We can configure sorting for two columns.

Now that we have an understanding of view customization options, let's modify the view for the vehicle entity. We will add the following fields to the vehicle view. Navigate to **Views** and double-click on the **Active Vehicles** view, and perform the following steps:

- Select **Created On** and click on the **Remove** button under the **Common property** dropdown.
- Click on **+ Add Column** and select the following fields from the list, one by one:
  - **Vehicle Name**
  - **Vehicle Number**
  - **Customer**
  - **Make**
  - **Model**
  - **Year**
- Click on **Save.**
- Click on **Publish.**

We can follow the same steps to modify all views in a similar manner to add the preceding fields.

Setting up security options

We can set up Dynamics 365 CE security options by navigating to `make.powerapps.com` and selecting **Settings** | **Advanced settings**, as shown in the following screenshot:

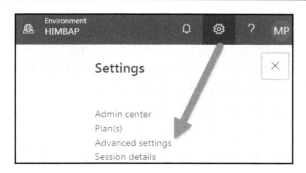

After that, we can navigate to **Settings** | **Security**, and we will get the following options to set up **Security**:

In the preceding screenshot, you can see all the security-related options are available here. Let's discuss how we can use these options, one by one.

Users

User options can be used to work with users for our organization. New users for our organization can be added from the Office 365 admin portal. After that, we can make changes in user profiles within Dynamics 365 CE—for example, assigning security roles to users, approving their email ID, and changing their business unit or manager.

Teams

Dynamics 365 CE teams are groups of users that can be related to the same business or a different business unit. We can use Teams to perform a set of actions on a group of users instead of an individual user. For example, let's imagine that a case is created, and we want to assign or share it with a number of users so that all of the technicians can access that case. Instead of doing it for individual users, we can set up a team of technicians, and assign or share records with that team. All of the team members will have access to the records. We can see all the owner teams of our organization by navigating to **Settings** | **Security** | **Teams**. When we set up a Dynamics 365 CE organization, a default team is created that has the same name as the organization and that contains all the users from the current organization. For example, the following screenshot shows the default team for our organization:

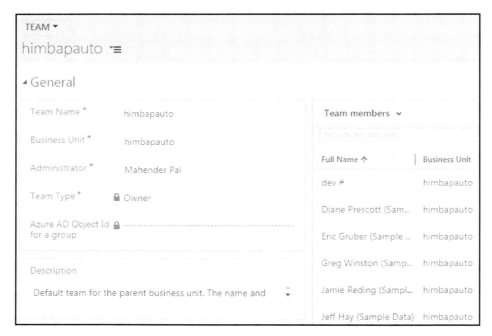

In Dynamics 365 CE, we have the following two types of teams:

- An **owner team** was first introduced during Dynamics CRM 2011, and they require security roles. These teams can own entity records. We can assign security roles to an owner team, and those security roles are inherited by all the team members.
- An **Azure Active Directory (Azure AD) group team** can also own entity records. We can assign them a security role, just as with an owner team. We can create these teams based on two groups: Security and Office 365.
- **Access teams** are lightweight teams that do not require a security role assignment. These teams can't own entity records. In the case of access teams, we define access team templates that are used to define access rights for all team members. We can easily add or remove users from access teams.

 You can obtain more details about teams from `https://docs.microsoft.com/en-us/power-platform/admin/manage-teams`.

Security role

The security of our customer data is controlled by security roles in Dynamics 365 CE. Security roles are nothing but a combination of different privileges and access levels. Dynamics 365 CE contains many out-of-the-box security roles. Roles can be customized based on our specific requirements, or we can create a new security role if required. It is recommended that you copy an existing security role that matches most with your requirement, and then modify it. Security roles are mainly configured to match different job profiles in any organization—such as a salesperson, sales manager, customer executive, application administrator, and customizer— for roles that make metadata changes in an application.

Dynamics 365 CE allows us to configure different security roles based on user profiles. We can assign these security roles to users so that they can only access data that is required by them. We can assign single or multiple security roles to any user, but every Dynamics 365 CE user should be associated with at least one security role.

We can assign a security role to a single user, or we can add a user to a team and assign a security role to teams. Security roles are managed based on business units. All child business units inherit security roles that are available in the root business unit automatically. So, when creating security roles, keep in mind that it is best to create security roles in the root business unit because we can only include security roles in the solution that is created in the root business unit. Any security role created in the child business unit can't be added to the solution. So, if you want to move your security roles to another environment, create them under the root business unit. In the following screenshot, we can see different privileges and access levels that we can configure for an entity list:

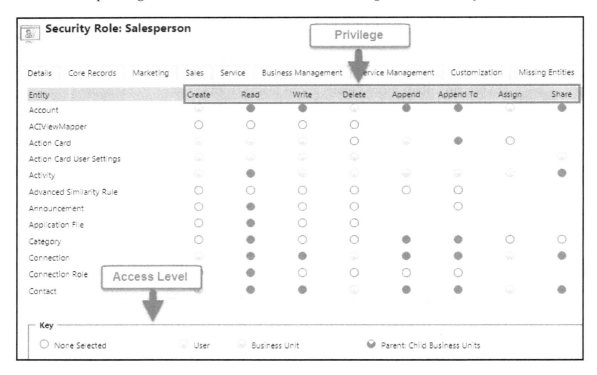

We need to configure both privileges and access levels for entities. We can see different entities that are divided into multiple tabs such as **Core Records, Marketing, Sales,** and **Service** based on their functionality.

Now that we have an idea about how security roles work, let's discuss privileges and access levels.

Privileges

A privilege can be defined as the permission to perform specific actions on a Dynamics 365 CE record. By using privileges, we can control what action the current user can perform on an entity record. We can configure the following entity privileges in security roles:

- **Create** permissions define whether the current user can create entity records.
- **Read** permissions define whether an entity will be visible to the user. If the user has a **Read** permission on the entity only, then this entity will be visible to the user.
- **Write** permissions are used to control update actions that can be performed on the entity.
- **Delete** permissions help us configure whether the user can delete this record.
- **Append** permissions can be used to allow us to associate the current entity record with other entity records.
- **Append To** permissions are used to allow us to associate other entity records with the current entity record.
- **Assign** permissions are used to allow the user to assign an entity record to another user or team. This action changes the ownership of the record.
- **Share** permissions are used to share a record with other users.

As we have now learned about the different privileges, let's discuss different access levels.

Access levels

Access levels define the level to which a user can perform read, create, update, delete, and other actions on an entity. We can understand the access-level hierarchy with the following diagram:

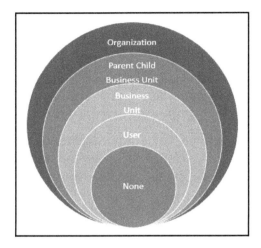

Let's discuss these access levels in detail, as follows.

- **None:** If the access level is set to **None**, the user can't perform any access on any level of the entity record.
- The **User** access level allows the user to access entity records owned by them, shared with them, and assigned to them. All these operations can be associated with the user directly or can be done by their team. For example, a user can access records owned by themself or by their team.
- A **Business Unit** access level allows users to access records within their business unit. They can access records for all the other users available under their business unit. Let's imagine that a manager of a business wants to access records from all the users under their business unit. We can thus configure business unit-level access to the manager. Business unit-level access means the user will have user-level access automatically.
- A **Parent Child Business Unit** access level allows a user to access data from their business unit as well as all the child business under their business unit.

Now that we know about security roles, let's look at how we can customize them.

It is recommended to keep a copy of the security role before modifying it.

Navigate to **Settings** | **Security** and click on **Security Roles**. Let's open the **Salesperson** security role and customize it. Take the following steps to customize it:

1. Open the solution that we are using to store our customization.
2. Navigate to the **Security Roles** link and click on **Add Existing**.
3. Select the **Salesperson** role from the available security roles.
4. Change the role name to **HIMBAP Auto Service**.
5. Navigate to the **Custom Entities** tab and, in the **Make** entity row, select all the privileges, as shown in the following screenshot:

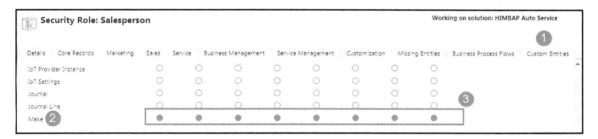

In the preceding screenshot, we have set the **Make** access level for the organization, which means any user who has the **HIMBAP Auto Service** security role will be able to access the **Make** record created by all the organization's users. Similarly, we can do the same thing for the **Model**, **Year**, and **Vehicle** entities as well. Click on the **Save and Close** button to save our changes. Similarly, we can customize other security roles based on our requirements, or we can create a new security role. We can assign a security role to an individual user, or we can use owner teams, whereby security roles are assigned to a team and security roles are inherited by team members.

Business units

This option is used to set up additional business units for our organization. By default, a business unit is set up by Dynamics 365 CE during our organization setup. This business is created with the same name as our organization. This business unit is known as the root business unit. We can't rename or delete this business unit. We can use this business unit to create a further child business unit.

Security roles in Dynamics 365 CE are maintained based on the business unit. When we change the business unit of the user, all of its security roles are removed automatically. To create a new business unit, we can navigate to **Business Units** | **New** and add our child business, as shown in the following screenshot:

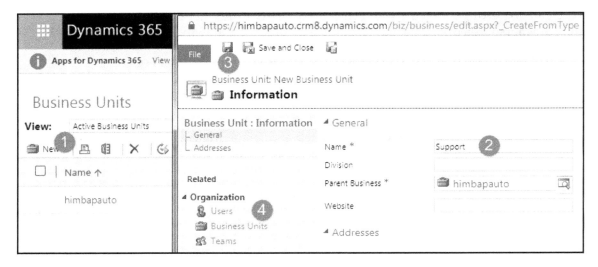

As can be seen in the preceding screenshot, the **Parent Business** unit field is automatically filled with the root business unit. Once the business unit is created, we can add users to our business unit.

Field security profiles

Security roles are used to control access for entities, but if we want to control the security of the field, we use field-level security. Using field-level security, we can control whether a user can read, create, or update a particular field. By default, field-level security is disabled. We can change the field-level security properties from the **Field Property** window. We can see all the security profiles created for the organization by navigating to **Settings** | **Security** | **Field Security Profiles.**

Let's say we want only the service manager to be able to apply manual discounts to total service amounts. To implement this, we need to create a field-level security profile. Let's see how we can create it using the following steps:

- Navigate to our solution and click on **Field Level Security Profiles.**
- Click on **New** and use the name **Auto Service Manager**.

- Click on **Field Permission**. Here, we can see all the fields where field-level security is enabled.
- Double-click on the **Discount amount** field, and set **Yes** for all operations, as shown in the following screenshot:

- Click on **Users** and add all CSR managers.
- Similarly, we can configure field-level security for discount percentages.

We need to set up another field-level security profile for the non-CSR user, and in there, we need to set field-level security for both the fields, as shown in the following screenshot:

In the preceding configuration, we are allowing the user to see the discount amount and percentage, but they won't be able to update or create a value for this field. In this profile, we need to use other members who will be working with auto-service records.

Hierarchy Security

We can use **Hierarchy Security** to implement complex security requirements. It lets us access data of the immediate reportee, the person who works under us. By default, **Hierarchy Security** is disabled. We can enable it and select which type of hierarchy security we are going to use. We can also set the depth of the hierarchy security, which defines the level at which we will be able to access data in the reportee hierarchy. We can exclude an entity if we don't want to access its data, as shown in the following screenshot:

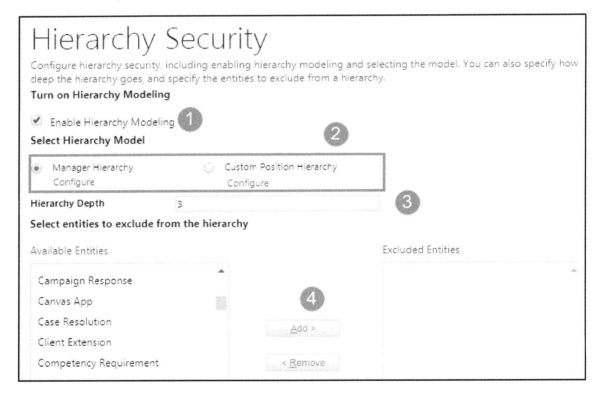

There are two types of hierarchy security:

- **Manager**: This type of hierarchy security is implemented within the same business unit. Let's say we have three users A, B, and C, where user A is the manager of user B, and user B is the manager of user C. All of the users have user-level access in their security role, which means they can only access records owned by them, shared with them, and assigned to them. After implementing **Manager** security, user A can access and modify data of user B, as well as being able to access data of user C who is under their direct reportee (in our case, user B is the manager of user C).

- **Position**: This type of hierarchy is used to implement security based on the position of the user, and it is implemented in cross-business units. This security works similar to **Manager** security but is based on the position of the user instead of the manager.

Positions

A position lets us define the hierarchy of a position based on organizational requirements. For example, we can see in the following screenshot that we have a sales position hierarchy where the **Salesperson** position comes under **Sales Manager**, and the **Sales Manager** position comes under the **Sales VP** position:

If we want to use the position hierarchy, we need to first define the position, and then we can provide access to data based on the position using the position hierarchy.

Access team templates

Access team templates let us define access rights for the access teams. By creating this template, we can select multiple permissions that we want to share with the users, as shown in the following screenshot:

The preceding screenshot shows an out-of-the-box opportunity sales team template. Any user added to this access team will be able to read, edit, and associate opportunity records with other entity records. Access to the team template can be created only for those entities that have the **Access Teams** option enabled under the **Communication and Collaboration** setting in the entity definition.

This is how we can set up security in Dynamics 365 CE. Let's now see how we can customize sitemap in Dynamics 365 CE.

Changing navigation

Navigation in Dynamics 365 CE is controlled by sitemap, which is an XML file that defines different sections for navigation. We can understand sitemap with the help of the following screenshot:

Depending on the Dynamics 365 model-driven app we are using, certain areas will be visible to us. In the preceding screenshot, we are using the Sales app, so we are able to see a **Sales** area. This area contains multiple groups. These groups share Dynamics 365 CE entities. Under the groups, we have different sub-areas. These areas can represent different components, such as entities, views, and dashboards. Earlier, we used to have a single sitemap, but in Dynamics 365 CE, we have a sitemap for every app. We can open the **Default Solution** and can see all the sitemaps under **Client Extensions**. To customize sitemap, we can double-click on any app's sitemap, and it will open the sitemap designer, where we can execute changes to the sitemap.

Let's quickly create a model-driven app and configure a sitemap for our app using the following steps:

1. Open our solution and click on the **New** button to create a model-driven app. We can follow the numbering sequence listed in the screenshot here:

2. Fill in the new app dialog as in the following screenshot, and click on the **Next** button:

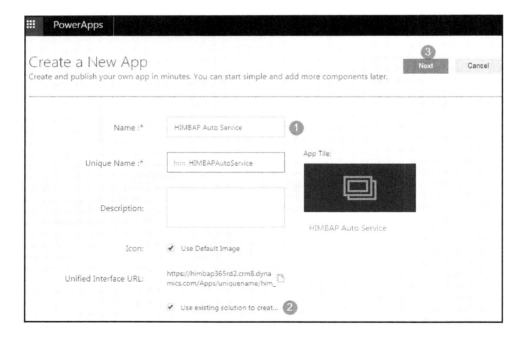

3. In the next screen, set up options shown in the following numbering sequence, and click on **Done**:

This will create a new app for us, and we will be taken to the following screen:

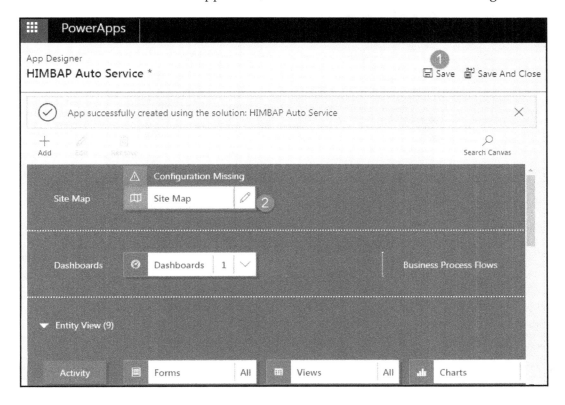

4. Click on the **Save** button, and then click on the **Site Map** edit button to change the sitemap for our app.
5. Next, observe the following steps:

- Drag **Area** from components and drop it before **Sales.**
- Write **Auto Service** under the **Title** field of **Area.**
- Next, drag **Group** and drop it under **Auto Service**, and name it **Service Extension**.
- Next, drag **SUB AREA** and leave it under the **Service Extension** group.
- Configure **SUB AREA** to show the **Vehicle** entity, as follows:

Similarly, we can configure other entities and groups, and **Save** our changes. We can also add other components such as Dashboard, Web Resource, or URL to the sub-area from the **Type** dropdown. Once all changes are done, we can **Publish** our sitemap.

Customizing dashboards and charts

Dynamics 365 CE provides us with an out-of-the-box business intelligence feature that includes Dynamics 365 CE reports, Power BI reports, Dashboards, and Charts. All of these options can be used by the customer based on their requirements. We can use Dynamics 365 CE's inbuilt editor to customize most of the components. For example, we can use the report wizard to write reports; we can design dashboards and charts using inbuilt editors. In this section, we are going to discuss dashboards and charts, so let's proceed.

Dashboards

In Dashboards, we can use multiple controls to represent a 360-degree view of customer data such as views, web resources, charts, and iframes. There are many out-of-the-box dashboards available for every app of Dynamics 365 CE by default. For example, if you navigate to the Sales app, you can see that Microsoft has provided many dashboards for this, and we can simply use them without any changes. If required, we can enable Security on the dashboard; therefore, we can configure the dashboard for particular users. For example, we can configure the dashboard for **Salesperson**, meaning that if a user has a salesperson role, they will be able to access the dashboard. We do have the option available to set up a default dashboard to access daily while accessing our Dynamics 365 CE app. In Dynamics 365 CE, we can create two types of dashboards: system dashboards and personal dashboards.

System dashboards

These dashboards are created from solutions and can be deployed to another environment using solutions. These dashboards are organization-owned. As these are system dashboards, they are available to all of the users in the organization. System dashboards can be created by users who have System Administrator or System Customizer security roles.

Personal dashboards

These dashboards are created by individual users and are owned by the user or team. We can create these dashboards directly from the Dashboard section, which means they are created outside the solution. We can't add these dashboards to a solution. These dashboards are not available to other users unless they are shared with other users.

We can navigate to the dashboard area to create a new personal dashboard. We can click on **New** and select dashboard layouts from the following available options:

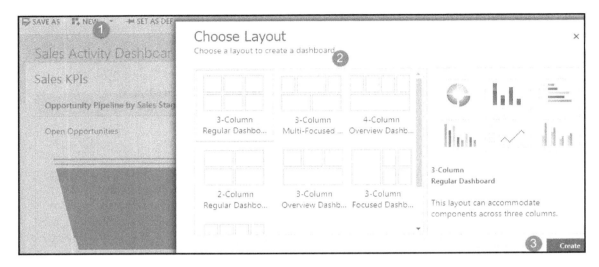

Once we have our layout available, we can add the following controls to our dashboard:

- Chart
- List
- Web resource
- Iframe
- Relationship assistant

Once the dashboard design is completed, we can save our changes and close.

Chart customization

This is another way to present a 360-degree view of the data using charts. We can create different charts against customer data and can use them in a dashboard or in a view. Similar to a dashboard, we have different charts available out of the box. In Dynamics 365 CE, we can create two types of charts: a system chart or a personal chart.

System charts

System charts are available to all the users of an organization. These charts are created from solutions and can only be created by the users who have System Administrator or System Customizer security roles. We have many out-of-the-box system charts available that can be customized if required.

Personal charts

Personal charts are created by individual users, so these can only be seen by the user who created them, or they can be seen by users with whom they have been shared. To share personal charts, the user should have proper share permissions.

To create a system chart, we can open a solution and navigate to **Charts** under the entity for which we want to create a chart. In the following screenshot, we can see the high-level steps for creating a chart:

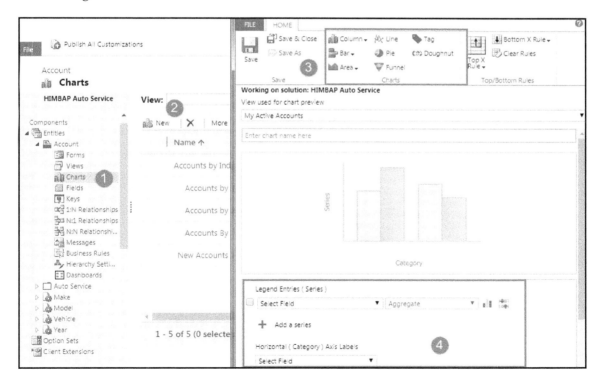

We can select different chart categories from the toolbar section, and then configure vertical and horizontal fields for our chart. Once the chart is created, it can be referenced in our dashboard or views.

Summary

In this chapter, we learned Dynamics 365 customization features. We discussed how we can create a new entity and create views for that entity. We discussed different data types available in Dynamics 365 CE. We also learned about different types of views available in Dynamics 365 CE and how we can customize views. Further to this, we discussed how we can set up security in Dynamics 365 CE, and learned about customizing security roles. Finally, we discussed how to customize dashboards and charts.

In the next chapter, we are going to discuss how to implement custom business logic for Dynamics 365 CE.

Extending Dynamics 365 CE 7

This chapter will help you understand how to extend the behavior of Dynamics 365 CE using custom code. We will learn about the extendibility architecture of Dynamics 365 CE and the layers where we can extend Dynamics 365 CE. We will discuss how we can write client-side code for entity forms and fields. We will also discuss options for retrieving entity data using Web API code. Later, we will discuss details about plugin development, such as writing plugin assembly, registering plugin assembly, and debugging plugin code to implement our custom logic using server-side code. Debugging plugins will help you troubleshoot any issues with plugin development.

The main topics that we are going to discuss in this chapter are as follows:

- Extendibility architecture
- Implementing client-side logic
- Implementing server-side logic
- Implementing custom logic using plugins
- Debugging plugin code

Technical requirements

The following are the technical requirements for this chapter:

- Access to Dynamics 365 CE or an on-premise environment.
- .NET Framework 4.6.2 or later should be installed.
- Visual Studio 2012 or later version should be installed.
- Windows Identity Foundation 3.5 should be installed on your development machine.
- The Dynamics 365 CE Plugin Registration Tool should be downloaded.

You can find the code bundle for this chapter at `https://github.com/PacktPublishing/Implementing-Microsoft-Dynamics-365-Customer-Engagement/tree/master/Chapter%207%20Code`.

Extendibility architecture

The Dynamics 365 CE application is known as a highly extendable business application. Its extendibility platform gives us many options to extend the capability of Dynamics 365 CE, such as customizing business entities or creating new entities, writing client-side extensions, developing custom plugins, and so on. In `Chapter 6`, *Customizing Dynamics 365 CE*, we discussed customizing entities and views and creating new business entities, fields, forms, and site maps without the need for any coding. We also discussed the solution concept, which makes it easy to move our changes from one environment to another.

Another great feature of Dynamics 365 CE is its support for writing code in commonly used languages such as JavaScript, jQuery, HTML, and .NET. We can also write custom components outside of Dynamics 365 CE while utilizing Dynamics 365 CE APIs for integration purposes. We have different methods and functions available in Dynamics 365 CE APIs that we can integrate with other third-party applications.

We can understand the extendibility architecture of Dynamics 365 CE using the following diagram:

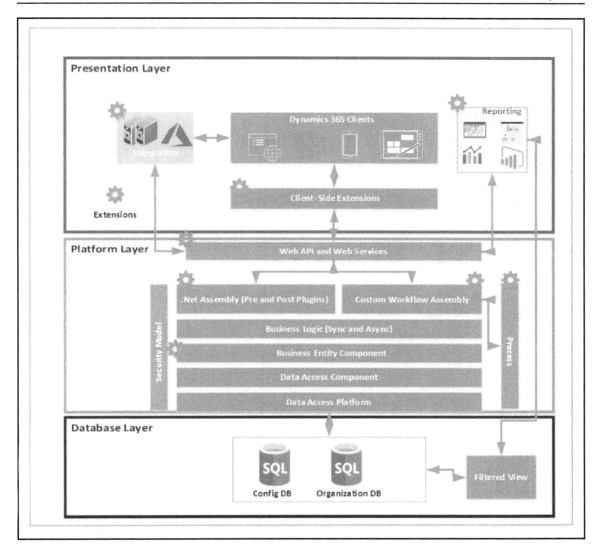

As you can see, we can divide the Dynamics 365 CE architecture diagram into the following three layers:

- The **Presentation Layer**
- The **Platform Layer**
- The **Database Layer**

Let's discuss these layers in detail.

The presentation layer

The first layer we can see in the preceding diagram is the presentation layer, which is responsible for providing the interface for the user for accessing Dynamics 365 CE. This layer provides many points that we can extend. Let's look at all of the items included in this layer.

Client-side extensions

In Chapter 6, *Customizing Dynamics 365 CE*, while discussing customization, we learned how we can customize the site map. By changing the site map, we can provide a personalized experience for end users. We can remove site map areas that are not required by the customer. For example, if the sales department only uses the sales area, other areas can be hidden from that department. Dynamics 365 CE now allows us to create custom apps that can also be used to define tailored apps for users.

Business entity component

We learned about entities and their components in Chapter 6, *Customizing Dynamics 365 CE*. We can create custom entities if required. As soon as a custom entity is created, out-of-the-box components such as main forms, views, and fields are added to the entity by the Dynamics 365 CE platform. These components can be customized based on our requirements and we can add new forms, views, and fields.

Command and ribbon buttons

There are different command buttons on entity forms and views. We can use these command buttons to initiate different actions. All the new forms, which are also known as updated forms, contain command buttons, while all the old forms still contain ribbon buttons. In the following screenshot, we can see the command buttons of an entity form and a subgrid:

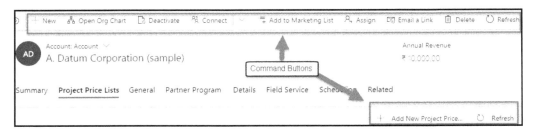

We can add new command buttons or modify the existing command buttons by modifying `RibbonDiffXml`:

```
<RibbonDiffXml>
  <CustomActions />
  <Templates>
    <RibbonTemplates Id="Msorm.Templates"></RibbonTemplates>
  </Templates>
  <CommandDefinitions />
  <RuleDefinitions>
    <TabDisplayRules />
    <DisplayRules />
    <EnableRules />
  </RuleDefinitions>
  <LocLabels />
</RibbonDiffXml>
```

We can customize `RibbonDiffXML` manually by exporting our solution, which should include our entity, to where we want to add a new custom command button. However, adding a command button manually can be error-prone, so it is recommended to use a tool to add command buttons quickly. One of the popular tools in the Dynamics 365 CE community is Ribbon Workbench. This tool refers to our solution and modifies the ribbon definition by simply using drag and drop controls on the command button editor. Make sure that you keep your solution components to a minimum; otherwise, customizing and publishing changes can be time-consuming.

You can download Ribbon Workbench from `https://www.develop1.NET/public/rwb/ribbonworkbench.aspx`.

You can find out more about working with the Ribbon Workbench editor at `https://ribbonworkbench.uservoice.com/knowledgebase/articles/71374-1-getting-started-with-the-ribbon-workbench`.

We can also use the Ribbon Workbench from XrmToolBox. You can find out more at `https://www.xrmtoolbox.com/plugins/RibbonWorkbench2016/`.

Web resources

Another way to extend the capabilities of Dynamics 365 CE is to use web resources. Web resources are different types of files such as XML, HTML, JavaScript, CSS, and images. We can use these web resources for different purposes: we can use HTML web resources to create custom screens; JavaScript web resources are used for storing client-side code; CSS files can be used to store style sheets; and image web resources can be used to store different formats of image files.

Dynamics 365 CE supports the following web resources types:

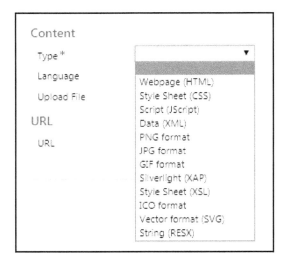

Web resources are stored in Dynamics 365 CE and can be referred to by their unique URLs. We will work with web resources in the *Creating web resources* section of this chapter.

Business intelligence extensions

Although Dynamics 365 CE provides many out-of-the-box reports, dashboards, and charts, if required, we can develop our own business intelligence extensions in Visual Studio or develop them in the Dynamics 365 CE application itself. We can develop two types of reports for Dynamics 365 CE, which are as follows:

- **FetchXML**: FetchXML reports are developed for Dynamics 365 CE online, where we write our query in XML-like syntax, which is known as FetchXML.
- **SQL Server Reporting Services** (**SSRS**): These reports are developed for Dynamics 365 CE on-premise, where we can write our query using SQL.

We will discuss reporting in detail in `Chapter 9`, *Business Intelligence and Reporting*.

Custom applications

Dynamics 365 CE provides rich API support that can be leveraged to integrate custom applications with Dynamics 365 CE. We can develop custom web or Windows applications using Microsoft or non-Microsoft language tools.

The platform layer

The platform layer in the extendibility architecture diagram represents many components, such as Dynamics 365 CE web services and custom business logic using plugins. Let's discuss these components one by one.

Dynamics 365 CE web services

Dynamics 365 CE provides many APIs that we can use in our custom application to connect with Dynamics 365 CE data. We have the following APIs available for Dynamics 365 CE, which we will look at in the following subsections:

- The Web API
- The Organization service
- The Discovery service

The Web API

This is a new set of APIs that was introduced in Dynamics CRM version 8.0. In earlier versions of Dynamics CRM, such as 2016 and earlier, developers used to work with the SOAP endpoint to connect to Dynamics CRM data. Using SOAP, it was easy to connect through a .NET application, but for a non-.NET application, it was difficult to connect. Later, the REST API was introduced to make non-.NET applications easy to connect with Dynamics CRM data. This REST API is also known as OData endpoints.

Although it is easy to connect to Dynamics CRM data using the REST API, it only provides a limited set of methods for us to work with Dynamics CRM data. To overcome this limitation, a new Web API was introduced in Dynamics CRM version 8.0, which made it easy for .NET and non-.NET applications to connect with data and also provided a full set of methods. Sometime in the near future, the Web API is going to replace the Dynamics 365 CE Organization service as well. We will discuss more details about the Web API in the *Working with the Web API* section of this chapter.

The Organization service

This is another service that we can to work with Dynamics 365 CE data and metadata. We can use the Organization service in applications outside of Dynamics 365 CE and can perform different operations. It contains different requests, such as create, update, retrieve, retrieve multiple, and delete. In the future, this service will be replaced by the Web API. We will discuss the methods that are available in the Organization service in later sections.

The Discovery service

Dynamics 365 CE is a multi-tenant business application, which means that, in a single-tenant, we can have a multiple-organization setup. In the case of an online environment, we can create different organizations such as Dev, QA, and Prod to use as our development, testing, and production environments. If multiple organizations are created, using the Discovery service, we can get the correct endpoint URL for the user.

Plugin assemblies

Dynamics 365 CE allows us to register our custom server-side business logic using .NET assemblies. We can write plugins on different triggers, which can run before or after the main database operations. Plugins are one of the most commonly used ways to extend Dynamics 365 CE behavior. We are going to discuss plugins in a more detailed manner in the *Implementing custom logic using plugins* section.

Custom workflow assemblies

Dynamics 365 CE provides rich support for workflows, which is mainly available to business users. Workflows provide the most commonly used triggers and operations, which we can use to perform different tasks such as creating and updating records, sending emails, and assigning records. But on top of that, we can also write custom workflow assemblies to extend the capability of workflows.

Business entities

We know Dynamics 365 CE has many out-of-the-box domain-specific entities available, but we can create custom entities if required, which allows us to extend the business entity collection of Dynamics 365 CE. We discussed the creation of entities in `Chapter 6`, *Customizing Dynamics 365 CE*.

The database layer

This layer is hidden from Dynamics 365 CE users and is responsible for storing customer data and organization data for other layers. We can't make direct changes to Dynamics 365 CE databases (although it is technically possible, it is not supported, or documented in the Dynamics 365 CE SDK). Dynamics 365 CE has two main databases:

- The configuration database
- The organization database

Let's look at them in detail.

Configuration database

This database stores the metadata of Dynamics 365 CE. This database is created at the time of setting up a Dynamics 365 CE environment. For example, if you are installing Dynamics 365 CE on-premise, this database will be created with the Dynamics 365 CE organization database. However, if a new organization is created using the Deployment Manager, it won't create a configuration database again; instead, it will reuse an existing configuration database. This database will be created with the name `MSCRM_Config`.

Organization database

This database stores customer data and is created for every organization. For example, if we have created three organizations—namely, Dev, QA, and Prod—we will have three databases for every organization. Every database is created based on the name of the organization; for example, if our Dev organization name is `HIMBAPDev`, then the name of the organization database will be `HIMBAPDev_MSCRM`. This database contains a table for every entity in Dynamics 365 CE. The organization database also contains a special view for every entity, called a filtered view. This view presents data according to the user's security role. All of the reports that are created for Dynamics 365 CE use these views.

With that, we have discussed all the layers of Dynamics 365 CE and also discussed all the extension points that allow us to enhance the capability of Dynamics 365 CE. Now, let's discuss all these extension points in detail. First, we are going to discuss implementing client-side logic in Dynamics 365 CE.

Implementing client-side logic

Client-side logic executes on the client machine; for example, data validation that's been implemented using client-side code runs in the browser. Dynamics 365 CE allows us to use client-side language tools such as JavaScript's jQuery to implement client-side logic. We can use client-side code on entity forms to implement data validation or to display data from other entities. To implement client-side logic for entities, first, we need to understand the client-side API object model. We can do so using the following diagram:

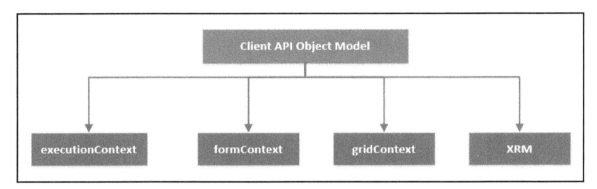

As shown in the preceding diagram, we have four main contexts that come under the client API object model root.

executionContext

The execution context is used to get context regarding where our code is executing. While writing client-side code for entity forms and controls for forms, we can pass this parameter to get context. We can pass `executionContext` to our code using the options explained in the following two subsections.

Using an event handler

To add an event handler to entity form fields, we can double-click on the particular entity field and click on the **Add** button under **Event List**. While associating possible events with controls, we can enable the **Pass execution context as first parameter** option, as follows:

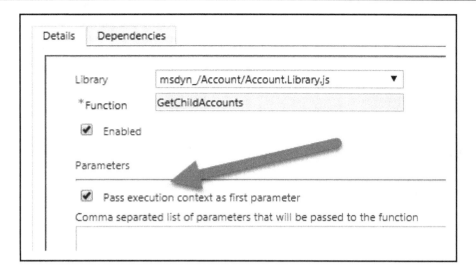

Furthermore, in our code, we can use this execution context. We can only use a context such as `formContext` if this option is selected under the **Event** tab, but if this option is not enabled and we try to use `formContext`, we will get an error.

Using an event handler in code

Sometimes, we need to associate an event with entity fields using JavaScript code. In those cases, the execution context is automatically passed as the first parameter to the function. For example, let's say we have one field named "amount" and we want to execute a function when the user changes the value of that field. To implement this requirement, we can use the following code:

```
formContext.getAttribute("him_amount").addOnChange(amountOnChange);
```

We can use the preceding code to associate the `OnChange` event with this field. By doing this, the execution context will be automatically passed to our `amountOnChange` function.

formContext

This is the most commonly used context and allows us to access entity forms and entity form controls. In earlier versions, we used to use `Xrm.Page` to get an entity form and its controls. With the release of Dynamics 365 CE version 9, `Xrm.Page` is deprecated and we now use `formContext`. `formContext` contains many objects that we can use to access different controls.

We can understand all of those objects using the following diagram:

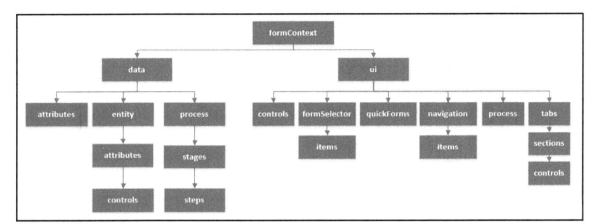

As you can see, under `formContext`, we mainly have two objects: `data` and `ui`. Let's discuss these objects in detail, one by one.

data

This object allows us to work mainly with entity data. Under `data`, we have three objects.

attributes

This object is used to work with collections and is only supported in the new Unified Interface client.

entity

This object helps us work with the current entity record; for example, accessing entity properties. The following methods are available under this object:

`addOnSave`	We can use this method to call our specific function on saving the entity form. We can use this method as follows: `formContext.data.entity.addOnSave(accountOnSave)`
`getDataXml`	We can use this method to find out which field is updated on an entity form. This method provides us with an XML string where we can see the field that will be saved to the Dynamics 365 CE database: `formContext.data.entity.getDataXml();`

`getEntityName`	If we want to know the logical name of the current entity using client-side code, we can use this method. For example, if we use the following code in our vehicle entity, it will return `him_vehicle`: `formContext.data.entity.getEntityName()`
`getEntityReference`	We can use this method to get a lookup reference. We can use it in the following code: `formContext.data.entity.getEntityReference();` This method returns an object that contains the following three properties: • `entityType`: The logical name of the entity • `id`: The GUID of the entity record • `name`: The primary field value of the entity
`getId`	This method can be used to get the GUID of the current record: `formContext.data.entity.getId();`
`getIsDirty`	If we want to know whether any field values have changed in the form or not, we can use this method. We can use the following code: `formContext.data.entity.getIsDirty();`
`getPrimaryAttributeValue`	As we know, every entity has one primary field of text type. If we want to get the value of the primary field, we can use the following code: `formContext.data.entity.getPrimaryAttributeValue();`
`isValid`	This method can be used to find out whether all the entity field data is valid: `formContext.data.entity.isValid();`
`removeOnSave`	If we want to remove a function on saving the entity form, we can use the following code: `formContext.data.entity.removeOnSave(accountOnSave);`

`save`	This method is used to save an entity record. We have a different parameter for the `save` method, where we can define whether we want to close the entity form or want to open a new entity form after saving:
	`formContext.data.entity.save(saveOption);`
	For example, if we want to open a new entity form after saving, we can use the following code:
	`formContext.data.entity.save("saveandnew");`

We can use the preceding methods to interact with Dynamics 365 CE entities.

process

This object provides methods so that we can work with business process flows. Business process flows are used to guide users on how to complete a predefined process by following different steps and stages in a business process flow. The following common methods are available under this object:

`getActiveProcess`	If we want to get an active process, we can use this method: `formContext.data.process.getActiveProcess();`

`setActiveProcess`	If we want to set any process as active based on the process ID, we can use the following code:
	`formContext.data.process.setActiveProcess`
	`(processId, callbackFunction);`

`getProcessInstances`	We can use the following method to get all the process instances of the entity record:
	`formContext.data.process.getProcessInstances`
	`(callbackFunction(object));`

`setActiveProcess Instance`	This method is used to set a process instance as an active instance:
	`formContext.data.process.setActiveProcessInstance`
	`(processInstanceId, callbackFunction);`

`getInstanceId`	The following method is used to get the GUID of the process instance: `formContext.data.process.getInstanceId();`
`getInstanceName`	We can use the following method to get a process instance's name: `formContext.data.process.getInstanceName();`
`getStatus`	We can use the following method to get the status of a process instance: `formContext.data.process.getStatus();`

`setStatus`	We can use this method to set the status of a process instance:
	`formContext.data.process.setStatus`
	`(status, callbackFunction);`

`moveNext`	We can use the following method to move to the next stage:
	`formContext.data.process.moveNext`
	`(callbackFunction);`

`movePrevious`	We can use the following method to move to the previous stage:
	`formContext.data.process.movePrevious`
	`(callbackFunction);`

`getActivePath`	This method is used to get the current stages collection in an active path: `formContext.data.process.getActivePath();`

`getEnabledProcesses`	This method is used to get all of the processes that have been enabled for an entity:
	`formContext.data.process.getEnabledProcesses`
	`(callbackFunction(enabledProcesses));`

`getSelectedStage`	If we want to get the currently selected stage, we can use this option: `formContext.data.process.getSelectedStage();`

We can use the preceding methods to interact with business process flows based on our requirements.

ui

This object internally contains other objects that provide methods that are mainly for working with the Dynamics 365 CE user interface. Let's go over the methods that are available under this object.

Control

This object allows us to work with the different controls that are available in Dynamics 365 CE. The following are the commonly used standard control type methods that are available under this object:

addNotification	We can use this method to display a notification for the field or to display an error message to the user based on the value. We can also suggest an action under the notification: `formContext.getControl(arg).addNotification(notification);`
clearNotification	This method clears notifications that have been displayed using the addNotification method: `formContext.getControl(arg).clearNotification(uniqueId);`
getAttribute	We can use this method to get an attribute associated with a control: `formContext.getControl("controlname").getAttribute();`
getControlType	If we want to know the type of a control, we can use this method: `getControl("controlname").getControlType();` It will return a control type such as `lookup`, `iframe`, or `optionset`.
getDisabled	We can use this method to find out whether a control is disabled: `formContext.getControl("controlname").getDisabled();`
setDisabled	We can use this method to disable a control: `formContext.getControl("controlname").setDisabled(bool);`
getVisible	We can use this method to find out whether a particular control is visible or not: `formContext.getControl("controlname").getVisible();`
setVisible	This method can be used to set the visibility of a control: `formContext.getControl("controlname").setVisible(bool);`
setFocus	We can use this method to set the focus of a control: `formContext.getControl("controlname").setFocus();`

All of the preceding methods are useful for working with controls such as hiding and showing controls based on the different conditions and to show notifications to users.

formSelector

This object allows us to work with form items. The following are the methods that are available under this object:

get	We can use the following code to get all the controls of a form. We need to pass the GUID of the form to get the controls: `formContext.ui.formSelector.items.get("Form GUID");`
getCurrentItem	We can use this method to get the current entity form reference: `formContext.ui.formSelector.getCurrentItem();`

The preceding methods are useful if we are using multiple forms for entity; we can use the preceding methods to get form details.

navigation

This object provides methods that are used to work with the navigation items in the navigation bar. The following are some of the methods that are available under this object:

getId	We can use this method to get the navigation item ID: `navigationItem.getId();`
getLabel	We can use this method to get the label of the navigation item: `navigationItem.getLabel();`
getVisible	We can use this method to check the visibility of the navigation item: `navigationItem.getVisible();`

We can use the preceding methods to interact with navigation items.

process

This object provides methods that we can use to work with business process flows on a form. The following are some of the methods that are available under this object:

getDisplayState and setDisplayStage	We can use these methods to find out and set the display state of a business process flow:
	`formContext.ui.process.getDisplayState();`
	`formContext.ui.process.setDisplayState();`

getVisible and setVisible	We can use these methods to get and set the visibility of a business process flow:
	`formContext.ui.process.getVisible();`
	`formContext.ui.process.setVisible();`

We can use the preceding methods to show and hide the business process flow bar on the entity form.

quickForms

This object provides methods that we can use to work with the quick view form controls that are available on a form. We can use the following method to get our quick view form control:

```
quickViewControl=formContext.ui.quickForms.get("name of quick view");
```

Once we have quick view form control, we can use its methods to interact with a quick view form control. The following are some of the methods that are available for a quick view form:

getControlType	This method provides the control type. We can use it as follows: `quickViewControl.getControlType();`
getLabel	We can use this method to get a quick view form label, as follows: `quickViewControl.getLabel();`
isLoaded	We can use this method to find out whether a quick view control has been loaded fully or not: `quickViewControl.isLoaded();`
refresh	We can use this method to refresh data in a quick view form, as follows: `quickViewControl.refresh();`

setVisible	We can use this method to hide or display a quick view control by passing `true` or `false`:
	`quickViewControl.setVisible(true); //to show`
	`quickViewControl.setVisible(false); //to hide`

In the preceding table, we have just mentioned common methods. You can find more `quickForms` methods at https://docs.microsoft.com/en-us/powerapps/developer/model-driven-apps/clientapi/reference/formcontext-ui-quickforms.

tabs

This object provides methods that are used to interact with tab controls on entity forms. It's a common requirement to hide and show tabs on an entity form based on some logic. We can use the following code to hide and show tab controls on an entity form:

```
formContext.ui.tabs.get("TAB1").setVisible(true); //to
showformContext.ui.tabs.get("TAB1").setVisible(false); //to hide
```

You can find more tab functions at `https://docs.microsoft.com/en-us/` `dynamics365/customer-engagement/developer/clientapi/reference/` `formcontext-ui-tabs`.

In the preceding code, `TAB1` is the name of the tab control. We can check the tab's control name from the control property. We can open it by double-clicking on the tab. Now that we are familiar with `ui` methods, let's discuss how to work with grid controls.

gridContext

We can use `gridContext` to work with grids or subgrids. A subgrid represents data in a list format. We can use a subgrid to display data on an entity form from a related or non-related entity. Grid controls are available on the entity home page. We get `gridContext` by using `formContext` on the form. The following are some common methods that are available for `gridContext`:

addOnLoad	If we want to call a method when our subgrid loads, we can use this method. We can use the following code to do so: `gridContext.addOnLoad(FunctionName);`
getEntityName	We can use this method to find out the entity name, which is displayed under the grid: `gridContext.getEntityName();`
getFetchXml	We can use this method to find out about a FetchXml query, which displays data in the subgrid: `gridContext.getFetchXml();`
getGrid	We can use this method to get a subgrid object: `gridContext.getGrid();`
getGridType	We can use this method to find out whether the grid control is a grid or a subgrid: `gridContext.getGridType();`
refresh	If we want to refresh a grid control, we can use this method, as follows: `gridContext.refresh();`

The preceding methods are commonly used for grid control. You can find out more about grid methods at `https://docs.microsoft.com/en-us/dynamics365/customer-engagement/developer/clientapi/reference/grids/gridcontrol`.

Xrm

This object has multiple internal objects for working with different components. The following are the high-level objects that come under this object:

- Xrm.Device: This object has a method that is used to work with mobile devices.
- Xrm.Encoding: This object provides a method for encoding and decoding string text.
- Xrm.Navigation: This object includes a method for working with navigation; for example, opening URLs, files, and prompts.
- Xrm.Panel: This object includes a method that's used to display a web page in the side pane of Dynamics 365 CE.
- Xrm.Utility: This object contains many utility methods. For example, one of the methods that's available under this object is used for displaying a progress indicator. In the past, we used to write unsupported code for this, but now, we have supported methods available. We can show a progress indicator as follows:

```
Xrm.Utility.showProgressIndicator("Fetching entity records....");
```

This will be displayed to the user as follows:

```
                    Fetching entity records....
```

When we want to close the progress indicator, we can use the following method:

```
Xrm.Utility.closeProgressIndicator()
```

- Xrm.WebApi: This object contains a method for working with the Web API. We can use methods to work with entity records. These methods support both the online and offline modes of Dynamics 365 CE. We will discuss the methods that are available in Xrm.WebApi in a later section.

Now that we understand the client-side API object model, let's look at the events that are exposed to entity forms and the fields in which we can associate our client-side script.

Understanding client-side events

Dynamics 365 CE allows us to write client-side scripts that are associated with different events that are exposed to entity forms and form controls. Let's discuss these events.

Entity form events

Dynamics 365 CE entity events let us implement our custom logic on entity changes; for example, when an entity form loads data or when an entity form saves data to a Dynamics 365 CE database. An entity form has the following two events exposed:

- `OnLoad`
- `OnSave`

Let's discuss these two events in detail.

OnLoad

This event triggers when an entity form loads. If we want to run our script as soon as an entity form is loaded—for example, auto-populating entity field values and showing and hiding fields—we can associate our script with this event. We can bind our functions to this event using form properties like the following:

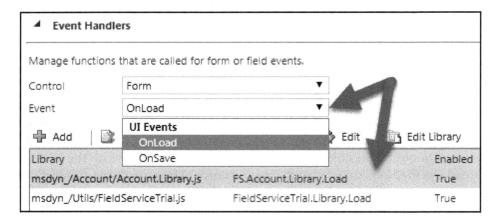

We can also bind a function to an `OnLoad` event using the `addOnLoad` method, as follows:

```
formContext.ui.addOnLoad(accountOnLoadFunction)
```

OnSave

This event triggers when an entity form is saved. We can save an entity form manually or a form can be saved automatically if the autosave feature is enabled. We can also bind our function to this event using form properties or can use the following code to associate our function with an `OnSave` event:

```
formContext.data.entity.addOnSave(accountOnSaveFunction)
```

Entity field events

Similar to an entity form, an entity field also has events exposed where we can associate our custom code for validation or for other entity operations such as retrieving data from other entities. The following are the events that are available for entity fields.

OnChange

This event triggers when a field focus is lost after changing the value of a particular field. Similar to the `OnLoad` and `OnSave` events, we can associate our function with this event using a field property or we can use the following method to associate our function to the field's `OnChange` event:

```
formContext.getAttribute("name").fireOnChange();
```

PreSearch

This event is available for lookup controls and can be used to filter them. We can only associate a JavaScript function with this event using code; it is not available under field events. We can get our `Filter` condition, add a customer filter using the `addCustomFilter` method, and then call `addPreSearch`, as follows:

```
formContext.getControl("lookupfieldname").addPreSearch(FilterLookupFilter);
function FilterLookupFilter()
{
var filter= "<filter type='and'><condition attribute='emailaddress1'
operator='like' value='mpal@himbap.com'/></filter>";

 formContext.getControl("lookupfieldname").addCustomFilter(filter);

}
```

Grid events

Grid events are associated with grid controls and are where we can use our custom logic to perform different validation or changes. The following events are available for grid controls:

- OnChange: This event occurs when the value of a cell in a grid is changed.
- OnLoad: This event occurs when a grid is loaded or refreshed.
- OnRecordSelect: This event occurs when a single record is selected in a grid.
- OnSave: This event occurs when data is saved through a grid.

 You can refer to my post at http://himbap.com/blog/?p=2529 to learn more about how we can work with grid events.

Tab events

A tab control has one event exposed, TabStateChange, which triggers when the display state of the tab is changed. If required, we can add our JavaScript function to this event using the **Tab Properties** dialog or we can use the addTabStateChange method to associate our JavaScript function with this event.

IFrame events

An IFrame control has the OnReadyStateComplete event exposed, which occurs when the content of an IFrame is completely loaded.

Knowledge base search control events

A knowledge base search control is used to search for knowledge base articles. The following are the events that are available for a knowledge base search control:

- OnResultOpened: This event occurs when we open a knowledge base article from a knowledge base search control.
- OnSelection: This event occurs when a knowledge base article is selected.
- PostSearch: This event occurs when a knowledge base article search is completed.

Process flow events

The following events are available for business process flows:

- OnProcessStatusChange: We can use this event to call our JavaScript function when the status of the process instance changes.
- OnStageChange: If we want to call our JavaScript method on stage change of business process flow, we can use this event.
- OnStageSelected: We can use this event to call our JavaScript function on business process flow stage selection.

Now that we know about forms and form events, let's learn how to use these events to write our JavaScript function using web resources.

Creating web resources

We can use script web resources to store our JavaScript libraries. Once created, they can be reused in multiple entities. Let's say we want to hide the manager lookup on a customer form based on the customer type. We only want to show the manager lookup if the customer type is a customer. Let's follow these steps to create web resources for our script:

1. Navigate to **Settings** | **Solutions** and open the **HIMBAPAutoService** solution.
2. Click on **Web Resources** | **New** and fill in the following details:

   - **Name**: CustomerLibrary.js
   - **Display Name**: CustomerLibrary.js
   - **Type**: Script (Jscript)

3. Click on **Text Editor** and use the following script:

```
var HIMBAP = window.Sdk || {};
(function() {
 this.customertypeOnChange = function(executionContext) {
 //get formContext
 var formContext = executionContext.getFormContext();
 //validate if field is available and it's value is nont null
 if (formContext.getAttribute("customertypecode") != null &&
 formContext.getAttribute("customertypecode").getValue() !== null)
 {
 //get customer type value
 var customertype
 formContext.getAttribute("customertypecode").getValue();
 if (customertype == 3) {
```

```
//show manager field
formContext.getControl("him_manager").setVisible(true);
} else {
//hide manager field
formContext.getControl("him_manager").setVisible(false);
}
}
}}).call(HIMBAP);
```

In the preceding code, we have to define our namespace, HIMBAP, using the following line of code:

```
var HIMBAP = window.Sdk || {};
```

Here, we have created our customertypeOnChange function, which takes executionContext as a parameter. When associating our function with an entity form or field, we need to pass executionContext. Furthermore, we have retrieved formContext from executionContext. We can get an entity attribute reference using formContext and then we can get the value of the field using the getValue method. For the customer option, the value is 3, so we are checking whether the customer type is equal to 3. We want to make sure the manager field is visible; otherwise, we will be hiding it. Now that we have our script ready, click on **Save** to save our script changes.

 When a web resource is saved for the first time, we don't need to publish it, but for web resources that have been re-edited after creation, we need to save and publish our changes.

Now, we will call our method on the customer entity form load and customer type field. We have changed the display name of the account entity to customer and the account form display name to customer. Follow these steps to associate our script function with these events:

1. Navigate to the customer entity and double-click on the customer form to open it. We will associate our method with the OnChange event, as well as on the OnLoad form event.

2. Double-click on the **Relation Type** field and click on the **Event** tab. First, we need to add our customer library. Later, we will call our method when the field changes. While adding the event, we can call our function using the following syntax:

```
<Namespace>.functionname
```

3. We need to make sure that we enable **Pass execution context as first parameter** so that we can pass the context, like so:

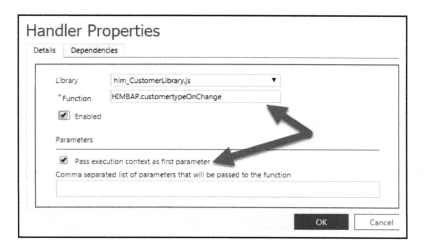

4. Similarly, we need to call this function when the account entity form loads. Adding our JavaScript library and event association should be completed by following the steps labeled with numbers in the following screenshot:

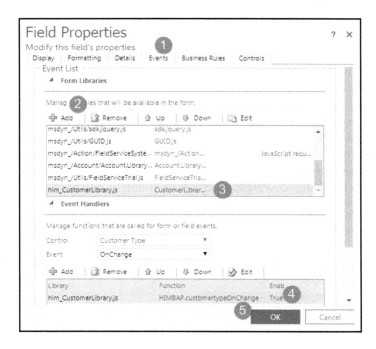

5. After this, we will see that if we select any option other than **Customer**, it will hide the manager lookup:

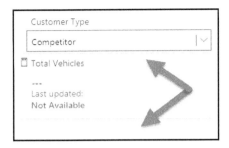

6. However, if we select **Customer**, it will show the manager lookup, as follows:

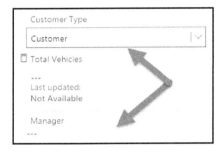

Now we know how to create a library and associate our function with an entity or field event. While planning to implement form validation, for example, setting a default value for the entity form field, hide/show entity form field, we can also consider using business rules. Business rules can be created using a visual designer, where we can apply different actions based on the condition. The business rule fires on load of the entity form and on change of the field where the business rule is associated. This is a very useful feature for business users or functional consultants as it does not require using any code. By using business rules, we can work with current entity fields, so if we need to apply form validation based on the value of a field from another entity, we need to use JavaScript.

You can find out more about business rules at `https://docs.microsoft.com/en-us/dynamics365/customerengagement/on-premises/customize/create-business-rules-recommendations-apply-logic-form`, which should help you understand more about business rules as well as how to create and use them.

In the next section, we are going to discuss using the Web API.

Working with the Web API

Another common use for JavaScript is to work with Dynamics 365 CE entity data. We can use the Web API, OData V4, which was introduced in Dynamics CRM 2016, or we can use `Xrm.WebApi`, which was introduced in Dynamics 365 V9. Let's say we have a requirement to copy an email from the primary contact in the customer form when the primary contact lookup is selected. Let's learn how to write JavaScript using both of these options. We can write these requests manually or we can use a community tool such as CRM REST Builder to write a Web API request. To use CRM REST Builder, follow these steps:

1. Download the latest release of CRM REST Builder from `https://github.com/jlattimer/CRMRESTBuilder/releases` and import the solution into our organization.

2. Once the solution has been imported, we can refresh our browser session and we will see a **CRM Rest Builder** button, which we can use to open CRM REST Builder.

3. Once **CRM REST Builder** is open, we can simply generate our script using the following sequence:

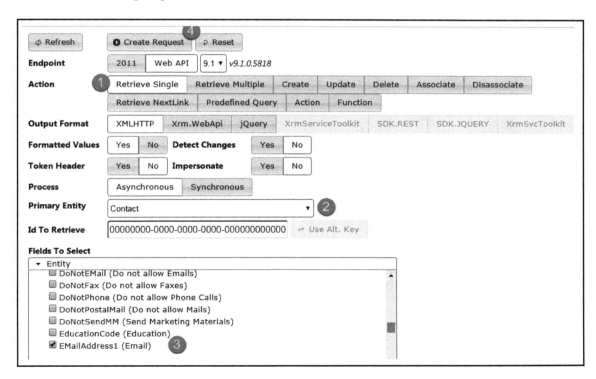

Different methods are listed under **Action**, which we can use to write our Web API request.

4. We can select our source entity from the **Primary Entity** drop-down list and we can select which entity field we want to retrieve in our request. We want to retrieve a contact record based on the contact's primary field (key), so we are using the **Retrieve Single** request.

5. Once we have designed our request, we can click on the **Create Request** button to generate the request. It will open the **Code** tab with the request generated, which we can use in our JavaScript web resource.

We are going to use our existing account library file and add a method that will trigger when the primary contact changes. The following script is used to populate the email field of the account entity form once the primary contact field has been selected:

```
this.primarContactOnChange = function(executionContext) {
var formContext = executionContext.getFormContext();
//get global context
var globalContext = Xrm.Utility.getGlobalContext();
//get primary contact id
if (formContext.getAttribute("primarycontactid") != null &&
formContext.getAttribute("primarycontactid").getValue() != null) {
var contactid =
formContext.getAttribute("primarycontactid").getValue()[0].id.substring(1,
37);
//prepare request
var req = new XMLHttpRequest();
req.open("GET", globalContext.getClientUrl()+ "/api/data/v9.1/contacts(" +
 contactid + ")?$select=emailaddress1", true);
req.setRequestHeader("OData-MaxVersion", "4.0");
req.setRequestHeader("OData-Version", "4.0");
req.setRequestHeader("Accept", "application/json");
req.setRequestHeader("Content-Type", "application/json; charset=utf-8");
req.onreadystatechange = function() {
if (this.readyState === 4) {
req.onreadystatechange = null;
if (this.status === 200) {
var result = JSON.parse(this.response);
var emailaddress1 = result["emailaddress1"];
if (emailaddress1 != null)
formContext.getAttribute("emailaddress1").setValue(emailaddress1);
} else {
 console.log(this.statusText);
}
}
};
```

```
req.send();
 }
}
```

In the preceding code, first, we get the GUID from the primary contact field. Once we have the primary contact ID, we can simply retrieve the contact's email ID using the following syntax:

```
req.open("GET", Xrm.Page.context.getClientUrl() +
"/api/data/v9.1/contacts(" + contactid + ")?$select=emailaddress1", true);
```

After that, we prepare the request head, which is almost the same for every request, and then we check whether the execution is completed and that an OK status has been returned. We do this using the following syntax:

```
if (this.readyState === 4) {
 req.onreadystatechange = null;
 if (this.status === 200) {
//code to process result
}}
```

We can call our HIMBAP .primarContactOnChange method on OnChange of the primary contact lookup, just like we added an OnChange event for the Relationship type field. Similarly, we can generate an Xrm.WebAPI request by clicking on the Xrm.WebApi button under the Output folder. The following code is the Xrm.WebApi request to get the email ID:

```
this.primarContactOnChange = function(executionContext) {
var formContext = executionContext.getFormContext();
 //get entity id
 if (formContext.getAttribute("primarycontactid") != null &&
formContext.getAttribute("primarycontactid").getValue() != null) {
 var contactid =
formContext.getAttribute("primarycontactid").getValue()[0].id.substring(1,
37);
Xrm.WebApi.online.retrieveRecord("contact", contactid,
"?$select=emailaddress1").then(
 function success(result) {
 var emailaddress1 = result["emailaddress1"];
 formContext.getAttribute("emailaddress1").setValue(emailaddress1);
 },
 function(error) {
 console.log(error.message);
 }
 );
 }
}
```

Now we know how we can use client-side requests to work with entity data. So far, we've discussed how to query data in traditional ways using Web API requests and how to use `Xrm.Webapi` to get data from an entity. Now, let's discuss what options are available for working with an entity and its data from the server-side.

Implementing server-side logic

Now that you know how to use client-side code for Dynamics 365 CE, it is very important to learn about writing server-side code for Dynamics 365 CE since we want to run some of the business logic over a server instead of a client. At the time of writing, we have the following options for writing server-side code:

- Organization service endpoints
- Web API endpoints

The first option is to use Organization service endpoints. Organization service endpoints have been used since Dynamics CRM 2011 and will be deprecated in some Dynamics 365 CE future releases. We can use Organization service SOAP endpoints in applications outside of Dynamics 365 CE to connect to customer data. As shown in the following screenshot, we have two endpoints available when navigating to **Settings | Customizations | Developer Resources**:

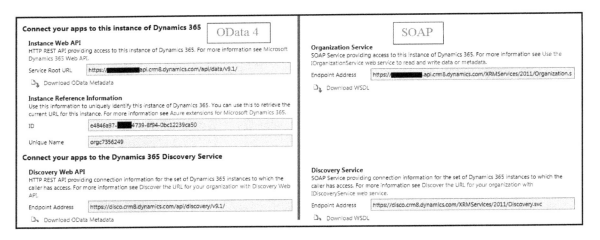

The Web API uses OData V4 and provides better compatibility with different languages. At the time of writing, we can use both endpoints to work with entity data and metadata. We are going to discuss the Organization service methods here. If you want to work with the Web API, you can refer to `https://docs.microsoft.com/en-us/dynamics365/customer-engagement/developer/webapi/get-started-web-api`.

Using the Organization service

The Organization service provides us with different methods that can be used to work with entity data and metadata. Let's discuss the most commonly used Organization service methods.

Retrieve

This method is used to get data based on the primary key. In a request, we can specify the entity name, the entity primary key, and the columns that we want to fetch. We can use the following code to get data from the `vehicle` entity:

```
Entity vehicle = OrgService.Retrieve("him_vehicle", new Guid("F8D74085-
C38D-E911-A969-000D3A29FEA4"), new ColumnSet(new string[] {
  "him_name",
  "him_make",
  "him_model"
}));
```

In the preceding code, we are passing a specific entity record. Keep in mind that the preceding code is for demo purposes. It is not recommended to hardcode a GUID; instead, we should retrieve multiple requests to get a record's GUID based on the required condition.

RetrieveMultiple

This method is used to retrieve data based on a parameter other than the primary key. We can create our query and specify the parameter that we want to retrieve data from. We can use the two classes to create our query, both of which we will cover in the following subsections.

QueryByAttribute

This class is used to retrieve data from an entity based on a simple query where we can check attributes for equality. It only supports the logical AND operator, and we can only combine two conditions using the AND operator:

```
// Create query using querybyattribute
QueryByAttribute querybyattribute = new QueryByAttribute("him_vehicle");
querybyattribute.ColumnSet = new ColumnSet("him_name", "him_make");
querybyattribute.Attributes.AddRange("him_name");
querybyattribute.Values.AddRange("Tata");
EntityCollection retrieved =
_serviceProxy.RetrieveMultiple(querybyattribute);
```

In the preceding code, you can see that we are fetching the `vehicle` entity's data based on its name.

 You can find out more about the `QueryByAttribute` class at `https://docs.microsoft.com/en-us/powerapps/developer/common-data-service/org-service/use-querybyattribute-class`.

QueryExpression

This class can be used to create a query for a complex scenario where we have multiple conditions. It supports both the AND and OR logical operators. We can retrieve data from the related entity using the `QueryExpression` class. For example, if we want to write the preceding `QueryByAttribute` query, where we used `QueryExpression`, we could use the following code:

```
QueryExpression query = new QueryExpression() {
EntityName = "him_make",
```

In the following code, we have defined conditions using `Criteria`:

```
ColumnSet = new ColumnSet(new string[] {
"him_name"
}),
Criteria = {
Filters = {
new FilterExpression {
FilterOperator = LogicalOperator.And,
Conditions = {
new ConditionExpression("him_name", ConditionOperator.Equal, "Tata")
},
}
```

```
    }
  }
};
```

In `Criteria`, we can define filter conditions.

 You can find out more about the `QueryExpression` class at https://docs.microsoft.com/en-us/powerapps/developer/common-data-service/org-service/use-queryexpression-class.

Now that we know how to query Dynamics 365 CE entities using `QueryExpression`, let's discuss how to create an entity record using the `Create` method.

Create

This method is used to create an entity record. This method takes an entity object as a parameter and returns an entity ID after a record has been created. The following code sample creates a `vehicle` entity record:

```
Entity vehicle = new Entity("him_vehicle");
vehicle["him_vehiclename"] = "Tata Nexon";
vehicle["him_make"] = new EntityReference("him_make",
makes.Entities[0].Id);
vehicle["him_model"] = new EntityReference("him_model",
models.Entities[0].Id);
vehicle["him_vehicletype"] = new OptionSetValue(910600005);
vehicle["him_vehiclecategory"] = new OptionSetValue(910600001);
Guid vehicleId = OrgService.Create(vehicle);
```

In the preceding code, we set the different attributes of the `vehicle` entity, where we are setting the lookup, option set, and text fields. Once the record has been created, it will return the GUID of the record.

Update

This method is used to update an existing entity data based on the primary key or an alternate key. The following is some sample code that can be used to update data based on the primary key:

```
Entity vehicle = new Entity("him_vehicle");
vehicle.Id = new Guid("E8D74065-C38D-E911-A969-000D3A29FEA9");
vehicle["him_vehicletype"] = new OptionSetValue(910600005);
OrgService.Update(vehicle);
```

In the preceding code, we are updating the `vehicle` entity record based on the GUID. You can refer to `http://himbap.com/blog/?p=1522` to learn how to update data based on an alternate key.

Delete

This method is used to delete an entity record. We need to specify the entity's name and the record the GUID that we want to delete, like so:

```
OrgService.Delete("him_vehicle", new Guid("F8D74085-C38D-E911-
A969-000D3A29FEA4"));
```

The preceding code will delete the `vehicle` entity record that matches the GUID that was passed.

Execute

This method is used to create a request where we can specify an entity operation for which there is no direct method available. We should only use this method to perform entity operations that we do not have a direct method for.

 You can refer to `https://docs.microsoft.com/en-us/dotnet/api/microsoft.xrm.sdk.iorganizationservice?view=dynamics-general-ce-9` to find out more about the Organization service.

All the preceding code can be used on the console application for demo purposes. Alternatively, you can download a quick-start sample application for Dynamics 365 CE at `https://code.msdn.microsoft.com/Sample-Quick-start-for-650dbcaa`.

Implementing custom logic using plugins

Plugins are basically .NET assemblies where we can write custom logic that we want to register in Dynamics 365 CE for specific events. Every plugin is associated with an event. You can view all the predefined plugin events for Dynamics 365 CE at `https://docs.microsoft.com/en-us/dynamics365/customer-engagement/developer/supported-messages-entities-plugin` or you can create your own custom events using actions in Dynamics 365 CE.

You can find out more about actions at `https://docs.microsoft.com/en-us/dynamics365/customer-engagement/customize/actions`.

Once the development of our assembly is complete, we need to register it in Dynamics 365 CE. When registering our plugin for Dynamics 365 CE, we need to specify the execution stage. These execution stages identify whether our custom logic will run before or after Dynamics 365 CE's main database operation:

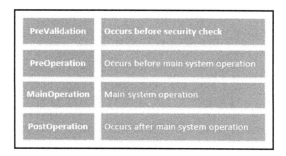

Registering a plugin consists of the following stages:

1. **PreValidation** is the first stage, which occurs before the main database operation. At this stage, the security role of the user is checked to verify whether they have the required permissions to perform entity operations.

2. **PreOperation** is the second stage, which also runs before the main database operation. At this stage, all the security checks are performed for the user to make sure they have the correct permissions to perform entity operations. We can use this stage to prepopulate entity fields; for example, by generating an entity number for an entity. We can also use this stage to run logic that we want to run before data is saved in the primary entity that our plugin is registered in. For example, let's say we want to create the record for entity A before entity B is created; here, we can write a pre-operation plugin on entity B, and there, we can write logic to create entity A.

3. **MainOperation** is the stage in which the system performs the main database operation. We can't associate any logic at this stage.

4. The **PostOperation** stage runs after all the main database operations. We can use this stage to run logic that should run after the database operations are complete. Let's say we want to create a customer record in a legacy system once it has been created in Dynamics 365 CE; here, we can write a PostOperation plugin on the customer entity and write our logic there to create a legacy system record.

Apart from the plugin stages, we can also decide whether we want to run our plugin logic synchronously or asynchronously. A synchronous plugin runs immediately after the trigger and waits until the logic is executed completely. The system won't respond until the execution is complete, which means we can't use the system until the plugin is executed. An asynchronous plugin is run in the background by an asynchronous service. These plugins don't immediately run our logic as there may be other processes in the asynchronous process queue. While this plugin is executing, we can use the system and perform other operations since this plugin doesn't keep the system busy and runs in the background.

All synchronous plugins run under a transaction, which means that if we are running our logic in a synchronous plugin and an error occurs, all the changes that were made by our logic will be rolled back. To understand this clearly, let's say that, in our plugin, we are creating three entity records. During the execution of our plugin, while creating the third entity record, if we get an error, it will roll back the first and second entity records we created as well. Asynchronous plugins do not support transactions.

We can write our plugin and register it manually using the plugin registration tool or we can use the developer toolkit. We will demonstrate writing and deploying plugin code manually in the next section.

 The developer toolkit can be downloaded from `https://marketplace.visualstudio.com/items?itemName=DynamicsCRMPG.MicrosoftDynamicsCRMDeveloperToolkit`.

Now that we have learned about plugins, we'll learn how to write one. Before writing a plugin, make sure you have downloaded the Dynamics 365 CE plugin registration tool from `https://www.nuget.org/packages/Microsoft.CrmSdk.XrmTooling.PluginRegistrationTool/`.

Writing a sample plugin

Let's say we want to write a plugin for the logic that we previously implemented using JavaScript, where we auto-populated the **Email** field in an account entity record from a selected contact. Let's use the following steps to write our plugin:

1. Navigate to **Visual Studio** | **New** and select **Class Library** (.NET Framework).

While creating the solution, keep in mind that we can use .NET Framework version 4.6.2 or later for Dynamics 365 CE.

2. Once the project has been created, we can rename the class based on our requirements; for example, we have renamed it `SetEmailFrmContactOnAccountPreCreate`.

3. Let's add Dynamics 365 CE assemblies to our project. Right-click on our project and select the **Manage NuGet Packages** option.

4. Add some Dynamics 365 CE assemblies, as shown in the following screenshot. You need to follow the numbered steps indicated in the following screenshot to do this:

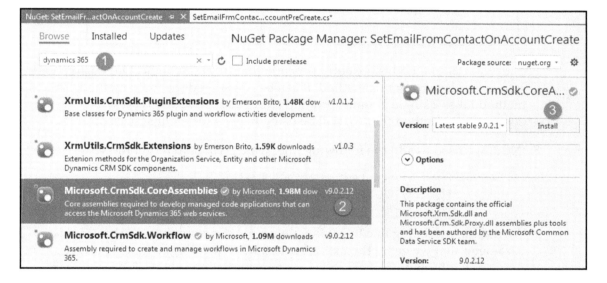

5. Accept the license prompt. This will add all the required assemblies to our project.

6. We need to add the following two namespace references to our class:

```
using Microsoft.Xrm.Sdk;
using Microsoft.Xrm.Sdk.Query;
```

The `Microsoft.Xrm.Sdk` namespace is the core namespace for working with Dynamics 365 CE entities. This namespace also has an **IPlugin** interface, which we need to implement to write a plugin. The `Microsoft.Xrm.Sdk.Query` namespace contains classes that we will be using to query Dynamics 365 CE data.

7. After that, we need to inherit the IPlugin interface and implement its **Execute** method. We can do this by following the numbered steps shown in the following screenshot:

```
public class SetEmailFrmContactOnAccountPreCreate : IPlugin  ①
{
    public void Execute(IServiceProvider serviceProvider)  ②
    {
        //write code here
    }
}
```

The `Execute` method is the entry function for our plugin logic. Our custom logic starts executing from this method. It can be considered the main method. This method takes a single parameter of the `IServiceProvider` type, which has a `GetService` method that we will be using to get a different service object.

8. Next, we need to add the following line, which will help us get the service object:

```
IPluginExecutionContext pluginContext =
(IPluginExecutionContext)serviceProvider.GetService(typeof(IPluginE
xecutionContext));
```

We use the preceding line to get the plugin context from the `serviceProvider` parameter that we get in the `Execute` method of the plugin. It helps us get contextual information about the environment that our plugin is executing in. Using `pluginContext`, we can get different properties, such as business units and parameter collection.

You can see a full list of properties at `https://docs.microsoft.com/en-us/dotnet/api/microsoft.xrm.sdk.ipluginexecutioncontext?view=dynamics-general-ce-9`.

While working with the plugin, we can handle exceptions and create tracing logs. All the tracing-related methods are available in the `ITracingService` class:

```
ITracingService tracingService =
(ITracingService) serviceProvider.GetService(typeof(ITracingService)
);
```

9. Next, we need to use the following two lines to get the `IOrganization` service object. The `IOrganization` service provides us with different methods that we can use to work with entity data and metadata:

```
IOrganizationServiceFactory serviceFactory =
(IOrganizationServiceFactory) serviceProvider.GetService(typeof(IOrg
anizationServiceFactory));
IOrganizationService orgService =
serviceFactory.CreateOrganizationService(pluginContext.UserId);
```

In the preceding code, we are creating an Organization service object using `pluginContext.UserId`, which means it will use the user that's been configured in the plugin registration tool in the **Run in User's Context** field. By default, calling the user is configured in this field, which means it will create an Organization service object based on the initiating user.

10. Next, we need to get an entity from the input parameters. The input parameters are a collection of parameters that we can get from the plugin context that we collected earlier. What parameter we get in the input parameter collection depends on the plugin event that we used to register our plugin. For example, in the case of the Create message, we will always get a `Target` parameter. We can get it and validate whether it is an entity class type as follows:

```
if (pluginContext.InputParameters.Contains("Target") &&
pluginContext.InputParameters["Target"] is Entity)
```

11. Once we have checked the `Target` parameter, we can get the entity and look for the fields that we want to validate. In our case, we want to check whether the user filled in **Primary Contact** in the account form or not. If **Primary Contact** is available, we can fetch it and query the contact entity based on the primary contact, as follows:

```
try {
  Entity account = (Entity) pluginContext.InputParameters["Target"];
  if (account.LogicalName != "account") {
    return;
  }
  if (account.Contains("primarycontactid")) {
```

```
Entity contact = orgService.Retrieve("contact",
account.GetAttributeValue < EntityReference >
("primarycontactid").Id, new ColumnSet(new string[] {
"emailaddress1"
}));
if (contact.Contains("emailaddress1"))
account.Attributes.Add("emailaddress1", contact.GetAttributeValue
< string > ("emailaddress1"));
}}
catch (FaultException < OrganizationServiceFault > ex) {
tracingService.Trace(ex.Message + " : " + ex.StackTrace);
throw ex;
} catch (Exception e) {
tracingService.Trace(e.Message + " : " + e.StackTrace);
throw e;
}
}
```

In the preceding code, after fetching the primary contact entity, we added the `emailaddress1` field under the account entity attributes collection. We are going to register our plugin on `PreCreate` so that it will pass the `emailaddress1` field in the account object with input parameter collection and be saved with the main database operation:

```
account.Attributes.Add("emailaddress1",
contact.GetAttributeValue<string>("emailaddress1"));
```

12. If we want to change an entity after it has been created, we need to use the `Update` method specifically. We also need to handle the exception in our code. As you can see, we have written our code under a try-catch block. After catching the exception, we can add an exception under the trace log for better troubleshooting.

13. Now, we need to sign our assembly to provide a strong name. Right-click on the project and select **Properties**. This will open some property windows where we can select the signing option to give our assembly a strong key name, as follows:

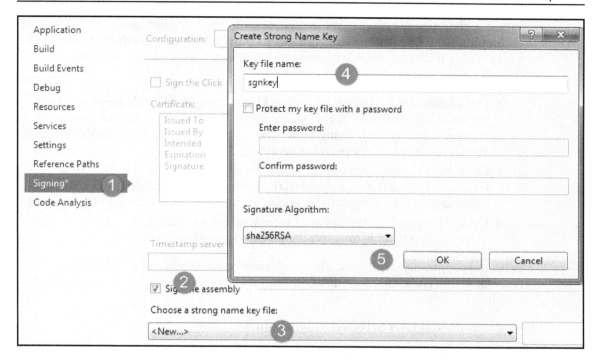

Once you've built your project to generate an assembly file, you can register the plugin.

Deploying plugin code

Navigate to the plugin registration tool folder and open `PluginRegistration.exe`. We need to take the following steps to register a plugin:

1. Click on the **CREATE NEW CONNECTION** button to open a connection window. Fill in your Dynamics 365 CE credentials after selecting your data region; for example, for me, this is India.
2. Click on **Login** to be connected to your Dynamics 365 CE default organization. If you have multiple organizations, you can also check the **Display list of available organizations** checkbox while entering credentials. This will show you a list of organizations that are accessible to you.
3. Click on the **Register** dropdown and select **Register New Assembly**.
4. Browse your assembly file and keep all the options in the dialog as their defaults.

When registering the plugin, we need to specify the isolation mode. In the case of Dynamics 365 CE Online, we need to select **Sandbox**. **None** is selected when we are working with on-premise organizations. We can register our assembly in three locations:

- **DataBase**: This is the best option as you can register your assembly where the assembly is stored in the organization database. If required, we can also retrieve our assembly using code. This option is available for both Dynamics 365 CE Online and on-premise versions.
- **Disk**: When using this option, our assembly is stored in our hard disk location. This option was used in the early versions of Dynamics CRM for better debugging support and is only available for on-premise deployments.
- **GAC**: When using this option, our assembly is stored in the global assembly cache. This option is only available for on-premise deployment.

With these options, we should always deploy our assembly to the database because it is secure and assembly code can be retrieved from the database if we lose it.

5. Click on the **Register Selected Plugins** button.

 Keep in mind that your plugin class should be public; otherwise, you won't be able to see any plugin details after browsing your project assembly while registering the plugin.

6. Look for your assembly in the assembly list and expand it to see all the available plugins. Right-click on the plugin and select **Register New Step**.

When registering the plugin, we need to specify the following details:

- **Message**: Here, we specify the event that we want to register our plugin on; for example, **Create, Update, or Delete**.
- **Primary Entity**: Here, we provide the logical name of the entity that we want to register our plugin on.
- **Secondary Entity**: Some events require two entities; for example, the `SetRelated` event. So, here, we specify the second entity.
- **Filtering Attributes**: This option is used for update events where we can specify the entity attribute. If we do this, our plugin will only execute when these attributes are updated.
- **Event Handler**: This provides details about the plugin assembly. We don't need to change anything here.

- **Step Name**: This provides details about the plugin step. This is automatically filled.
- **Run in User's Context**: By default, **Calling User** is selected here. If we want to run our plugin using a specific user, we can specify that user here.
- **Execution Order**: If multiple plugins are registered on the same event, we can specify the execution order of our plugins here.
- **Description**: Description of the plugin.
- **Event Pipeline Stage of Execution**: We can select options such as **PreValidation**, **PreOperation**, and **PostOperation** from here, which we discussed in detail in the *Implementing custom logic using plugins* section.
- **Execution Mode**: Here, we specify whether we want to run our plugin in synchronous or asynchronous mode.
- **Deployment**: Here, we specify that our plugin should be available to the server only or whether we want to run our logic in offline mode as well; for example, when Outlook is running in offline mode.
- **Delete AsyncOperation if StatusCode=Successful**: We can use this option to save disk space. It will delete all completed async operation records.
- **Unsecure Configuration**: Here, we specify unsecured configuration data for our plugin, which can be read by any user. These settings are transferred to another organization within the solution.
- **Secure Configuration**: These configurations can only be read by the system administrator and are not transferred to another environment within the solution.

We need to use the following details for our plugin:

- **Message**: Create
- **Primary Entity**: Account
- **Event Pipeline Stage of Execution**: PreOperation

Keep all the details as their default.

Make sure that you disable the OnChange event for the primary contact field where we associated our JavaScript function on the account entity form. Now, when we create an account and fill in the primary contact ID, it will auto-populate with the email from the contact entity when we hit **Save**. Our logic will run before the save operation.

Similarly, we can write plugins for other events. Now that we know how we can register our custom logic in Dynamics 365 CE using plugins, let's learn how to debug our Dynamics 365 CE Online plugins.

Debugging plugin code

Let's say that, in our plugin, we have misspelled some of the field names or we are getting some other exception and we want to debug our plugin. We can take the following steps to debug our plugin:

1. Install the profiler in our organization by clicking on the **Install Profiler** button in the plugin registration tool.

2. Once the profiler has been installed, select the number 1 shown in the following screenshot and click on **Start Profiling**, as shown in the following screenshot under number 2:

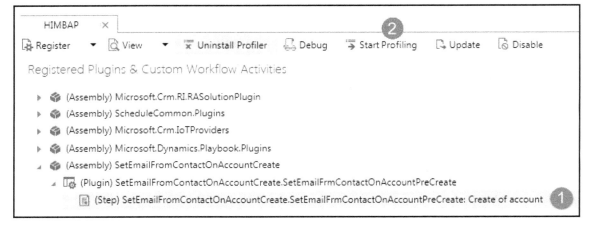

3. Keep the default settings on the profiling dialog and click on **Ok**.

4. Now, try to execute your logic; for example, we registered our plugin upon account creation. When we try to create an account, it will generate a log file with the error details and will store it under the **Plugin Profile** entity.

5. You can verify log recording in Dynamics 365 CE from **Advanced Find** by getting a record from the **Plugin Profile** entity.

6. Navigate to **Visual Studio| Debug** and click on the **Attach to Process** option. We need to search for the PluginRegistration.exe process and then click on **Attach**.

7. Set the breakpoint in our code.

8. Now, select our plugin step again and click on the **Debug** button from the toolbar. This will open a dialog where we need to select a log file, as shown in the following screenshot:

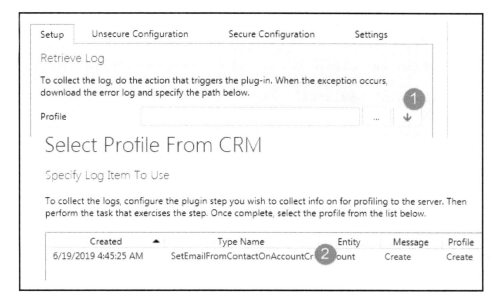

9. Next, we need to select our assembly and click on **Start Execution**. This will bring focus onto our source code in Visual Studio so that we can start debugging:

```
20    IOrganizationService orgService = serviceFactory.CreateOrganizationService
21    if (pluginContext.InputParameters.Contains("Target") && pluginContext.Input
22    {
23        try
24        {
25            Entity account = (Entity)pluginContext.InputParameters["Target"];
26            if (account.LogicalName != "account")
27            {
28                return;
29            }
30            if (account.Contains("primarycontactid")) 62ms elapsed
31            {
32                Entity contact = orgService.Retrieve("contact", account.GetAttrib
33                if (contact.Contains("emailaddress1"))
34                    account.Attributes.Add("emailaddress1", contact.GetAttribute
35            }
```

With that, we've learned how to debug our plugin code and fix any development issues.

Here, we learned about writing a sample plugin and how to deploy it. More details on plugin development can be found in the Dynamics 365 CE SDK. Similar to plugin development, we can also develop custom assemblies to extend the capabilities of Dynamics 365 CE workflows, which can be registered to Dynamics 365 CE just like plugins.

These workflow assemblies are not associated with any events; instead, they are used when designing workflows from Workflow Designer.

 You can find out more about developing custom workflow assemblies at `https://docs.microsoft.com/en-us/dynamics365/customer-engagement/developer/custom-workflow-activities-workflow-assemblies`.

Summary

In this chapter, we learned about extending Dynamics 365 CE. We learned about the different layers of the Dynamics 365 CE platform and how to extend them. We learned about implementing client-side code using the Web API and writing form and field event scripts using web resources. Later, we discussed the options for writing server-side code. We also discussed plugin development details and how to deploy a plugin assembly. Finally, we discussed how to debug plugin code if there are any issues in it. This chapter should help you develop solutions for Dynamics 365 CE if some customer requirements can't be mapped with out-of-the-box features.

In the next chapter, we will discuss the integration options for Dynamics 365 CE. We will also discuss how we can integrate Dynamics 365 CE with other applications, such as Microsoft Flow and PowerApps using connectors.

8
Integrating Dynamics 365 CE with Other Applications

This chapter will help you understand how to integrate Dynamics 365 CE with other applications, such as Power Automate and PowerApps. We will create a sample workflow to send an SMS notification to customers when an automobile service is complete, so you will learn how to send an SMS using Power Automate. We will also create a sample application using PowerApps Studio to create an automobile service request. You will also learn how to use PowerApps Studio, the controls available in PowerApps Studio, and how to create Dynamics 365 CE entity records using PowerApps. Later, we will discuss the **Dynamics 365 CE Software Development Kit** (**SDK**), which will help you to understand how to create console application utilities, using the Dynamics 365 CE SDK to interact with customer data.

The main topics that we are going to cover in this chapter are as follows:

- Dynamics 365 CE integration options
- Using the Dynamics 365 CE SDK
- Integrating Dynamics 365 CE with Power Automate
- Integrating Dynamics 365 CE with PowerApps

Technical requirements

The following are the technical requirements for this chapter:

- Access to a trial of Dynamics 365 CE Online
- .NET Framework 4.6.2 or later should be installed on your machine
- Visual Studio 2017 should be installed on your machine
- Windows Identity Foundation 3.5 should be installed on your development machine
- A Power Automate trial setup
- A Twilio trial setup

You can find the code files of this chapter on GitHub at `https://github.com/ PacktPublishing/Implementing-Microsoft-Dynamics-365-Customer-Engagement/tree/ master/Chapter%208%20Code/SampleConsole`.

Dynamics 365 CE integration options

Dynamics 365 CE provides very rich out-of-the-box features that we can leverage to automate our day-to-day business activities. It is nonetheless common to integrate Dynamics 365 CE with other applications that customers use for their business purposes. These applications may be part of Microsoft Office 365 applications; for example, the SharePoint, Power Automate, PowerApps, Microsoft Teams, and **enterprise resource planning** (**ERP**) apps included in Microsoft Dynamics 365. We can use Microsoft SharePoint as a document management system. We discussed how to configure SharePoint integration in `Chapter 5`, *Configuring Your Dynamics 365 CE Organization*. Power Automate and PowerApps have different purposes, and we will be discussing these applications in later sections. Microsoft Teams is a collaboration application that can be used to chat with people, have video meetings, and share content. We can use Microsoft Teams and Dynamics 365 CE integration in collaboration with our colleagues and customers, to share information and content. You can find more details about integrating Dynamics 365 CE with Teams at `https://docs.microsoft.com/en-us/dynamics365/teams-integration/ teams-integration`.

Apart from these applications, it is common to integrate Microsoft applications with non-Microsoft applications as well. It may be a non-Microsoft ERP system, or it may be some other application where a customer needs to send Dynamics 365 CE data. Such integration requires the passing of customer data back and forth. The main objective of these types of integration is to synchronize data between Dynamics 365 CE and other systems. Data synchronization between Dynamics 365 CE and other applications is done using the following two common approaches:

- On-demand data integration
- Batch processing

Let's look at each of these approaches in detail.

On-demand data integration

On-demand data integration is associated with some logic that initiates data integration between two applications. This integration happens as soon as the logic runs, without any waiting period. The following diagram represents the high-level idea of on-demand data integration:

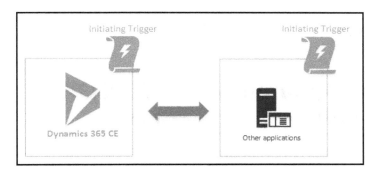

Here, we can see that we are initiating a trigger on each side, which is responsible for starting the movement of data between Dynamics 365 CE and the other applications.

On the Dynamics 365 CE side, we can utilize plugins to use as a trigger to initiate data integration. For example, let's say the other applications need customer sales order details from Dynamics 365 CE. We can write a post plugin on the sales order entity to send sales order details data to the other applications. On-demand data integration normally processes a single record at a time.

Batch processing

With this type of data integration, more than one record is normally processed. These types of processes don't execute when records are modified; instead, they wait for a specific time period to initiate data integration. The following diagram represents the high-level idea of batch processing:

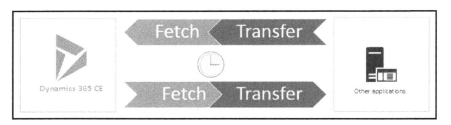

As you can see, this process is associated with a timer logic that waits for a specific period. Normally, it runs after office hours, when no one is using the system. There is a logic associated with this process, which fetches data from the source system based on some criteria; for example, it may want to send records that were modified today.

Both integration options utilize the Dynamics 365 CE API to work with Dynamics 365 CE data. We can use utilities developed in-house for this data integration, or we can use different connectors that are available on the market for these integrations.

Using the Dynamics 365 CE SDK

In Chapter 7, *Extending Dynamics 365 CE,* we discussed how we can use the Dynamics 365 SDK in plugins to implement server-side logic and IOrganizationService methods. We can also use the CRM SDK to develop applications that run outside of Dynamics 365 CE. Furthermore, we can use the Dynamics 365 CE SDK to perform different tasks, such as creating, updating, and deleting bulk entity records. We are going to create a sample console application that connects to the Dynamics 365 CE application. When developing a plugin or a custom workflow assembly, it is easy to test our logic using the console application first; after that, we can move our logic to a plugin or a custom workflow assembly. Let's create our console application, which will import **Make** and **Models** data from CSV files. We will be using the IOrganizationService method in our console application to import data.

Creating a console application to import data

We will use Visual Studio 2017 to create our data import utility for importing Make and Models data. Follow these steps to create this utility:

1. Start Visual Studio, go to **New Project**, and select **Console App**, as shown in the following screenshot:

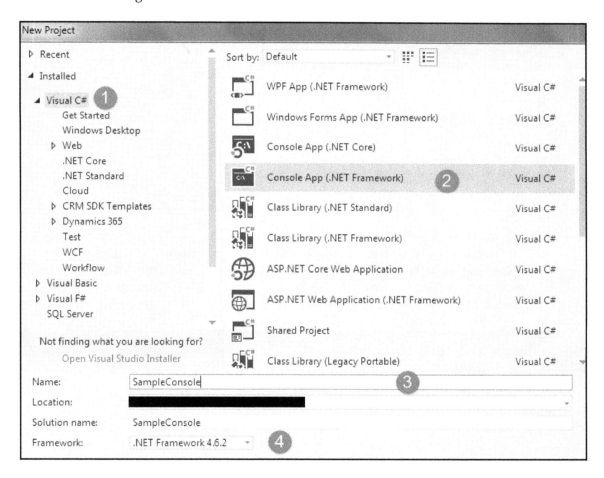

2. Next, let's add a Dynamics 365 Core SDK reference to our sample console application. Right-click on the project, select **Manage NuGet Packages**, and follow the steps shown here:

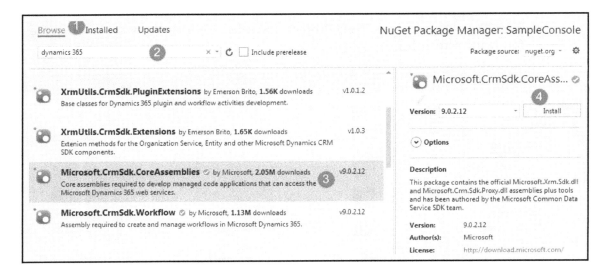

3. Let's add our configuration data in `App.config` so that we can make changes if and when required. First, we need to get the **Organization Service** using the following steps. Navigate to **Settings | Customizations | Developer Resources** as shown in the following screenshot, and copy the **Endpoint Address** from the **Organization Service**, as follows:

We also need to get the path of our CSV files, so we can store all these details in our `App.config` file, as follows:

```xml
<?xml version="1.0" encoding="utf-8" ?>
<configuration>
  <appSettings>
    <add key="Makers" value="███████████████████Maker.csv"/>  ①
    <add key="Model" value="██████████████████Models.csv"/>  ②                    ③
    <add key="OrgURL" value="https://himbapauto.api.crm8.dynamics.com/XRMServices/2011/Organization.svc"/>
    <add key="UserName" value=██@himbapauto.onmicrosoft.com"/>  ④
    <add key="Password" value=████████ />  ⑤
  </appSettings>
  <startup>
      <supportedRuntime version="v4.0" sku=".NETFramework,Version=v4.6.2" />
  </startup>
</configuration>
```

We will be using all the preceding keys to get configuration data in our utility code.

4. Next, right-click on the project name from the Solution Explorer and select **Add | Class**, and let's name it `Dynamics365Utility`.

5. Next, we need to add a reference for the Dynamics 365 CE assemblies and other assemblies that we will be using, like so:

```
using System.Configuration;
using Microsoft.Xrm.Sdk;
using Microsoft.Xrm.Sdk.Client;
using Microsoft.Xrm.Sdk.Query;
using System.IO;
using System.Data;
```

The Dynamics 365 CE SDK helps us to work with entities and classes. `System.IO` is used to work with `StreamReader`, which will help us to process data available in CSV files. `System.Data` is used to work with data tables and rows.

6. Let's first add a constructor to our class, as follows, to create a connection with the Dynamics 365 CE organization:

```
public Dynamics365Utility()
{
ClientCredentials credentials = new ClientCredentials();
        credentials.UserName.UserName = ConfigurationManager
        .AppSettings["UserName"];
        credentials.UserName.Password = ConfigurationManager
        .AppSettings["Password"];
        Uri serviceUri = new
```

```
Uri(ConfigurationManager.AppSettings["OrgURL"]);
OrganizationServiceProxy proxy = new
OrganizationServiceProxy(serviceUri, null, credentials, null);
proxy.EnableProxyTypes();
service = (IOrganizationService)proxy;
}
```

In the preceding code, you can see that we are getting our configuration data from the App.config file by passing a key. Once we have an Organization Service URL and credentials, we can pass them to the OrganizationServiceProxy class. We can get an Organization service object from the OrganizationServiceProxy.

7. Next, let's add a method to read our CSV files, as follows:

```
private DataTable GetCSVFile(string keyname) {
  string path = ConfigurationManager.AppSettings[keyname];
  string fileText = string.Empty;
  DataTable source = new DataTable();
  try {
  using(StreamReader sr = new StreamReader(path)) {
  while (!sr.EndOfStream) {
  fileText = sr.ReadToEnd().ToString();
  string[] rows = fileText.Split('\n');
  for (int i = 0; i < rows.Count() - 1; i++) {
  string[] rowValues = rows[i].Split(','); {
  if (i == 0) {
  for (int j = 0; j < rowValues.Count(); j++) {
  source.Columns.Add(rowValues[j]);
  }
  } else {
  DataRow dr = source.NewRow();
  for (int k = 0; k < rowValues.Count(); k++) {
  dr[k] = rowValues[k].ToString();
  }
  source.Rows.Add(dr);
  }
  }
  }
  }
  } catch (Exception e) {
  throw e;
  }
  return source;
}
```

The preceding method takes a key name as a parameter that is used to get the value from the `App.config` file, based on this key. Once we have a file path, we get the `StreamReader` class to read all the data available in the CSV file. In our code, we first get row data to store the data table's column name, and all the other data is stored in rows. Sometimes, when working with CSV, we may get the `\r` or `\n` character next to a column name or a data name, so let's add a method to remove these characters, as follows:

```
public static string GetRowValue(string value)
  //check for \r\n
    if (value.Contains('\r') || value.Contains('\n')) {
     //remove \r or \n
value = value.Substring(0, value.Length - 1);
    }
    return value; }
```

In our next method, let's use the `GetCSVFile` method and process it to import `make` entity data, as follows:

```
public void AddMakers() {
//get csv file data into data table
 DataTable makers = GetCSVFile("Makers");
 //loop all rows and get their data
 foreach(DataRow row in makers.Rows) {
  if (row["Name\r"].ToString() != "") {
   //Create Make record
   Entity make = new Entity("him_make");
   make["him_name"] = GetRowValue(row["Name\r"].ToString());
   service.Create(make);
  } }}
```

In the preceding code, we are using the `Create` method of the Organization service to create `make` entity record data. In the `make` entity, we have just one field, which is the primary field of the `make` entity, so we are only setting the `name` field of `make` while creating its record.

To import the `model` record, we need to import a `make` record first because a `model` entity has a lookup for the `make` entity. While importing `model` data, we need to get the **globally unique identifier (GUID)** of the `make` record to set the lookup field value. Let's add the following method to query the `make` record ID based on its name:

```
private Guid GetMake(string make) {
  EntityCollection results = null;
  Guid Id = Guid.Empty;
```

```
QueryExpression query = new QueryExpression() {
EntityName = "him_make",
 ColumnSet = new ColumnSet(new string[] {
 "him_name"
 }),
Criteria = {
 Filters = {
 new FilterExpression {
 FilterOperator = LogicalOperator.And,
 Conditions = {
 new ConditionExpression("him_name", ConditionOperator.Equal, make)
 },
 }
 }
 }
 };
 results = service.RetrieveMultiple(query);
 if (results.Entities.Count > 0)
 Id = results.Entities.FirstOrDefault().Id;
 return Id;
}
```

In the preceding code, we are using the QueryExpression class, where we have
added a filter expression that has one condition to compare the Make record name
based on the string parameter. Here, we are using the RetrieveMultiple
method, as we are querying data based on the non-primary key field. This
method will check whether we have a Make record available in Dynamics 365 CE.
If we have, it will return the record's GUID; otherwise, it will return an empty
GUID.

8. Next, we can use the following method to add model data, where we will also
   incorporate the GetMake method:

```
public void AddModel() {
 //get model file path
 DataTable models = GetCSVFile("Model");
 //process medle file records
 foreach(DataRow row in models.Rows) {
 if (row["Make"].ToString() != "" && row["Model\r"].ToString() !=
  "") {
 //create model
 Entity model = new Entity("him_model");
 model["him_name"] = row["Model\r"].ToString();
 //get make record id
 Guid makeId = GetMake(row["Make"].ToString());
 if (makeId != Guid.Empty) {
```

```
model["him_make"] = new EntityReference("him_make",
GetMake(row["Make"].ToString())));
}
service.Create(model);
}
}
}
```

The preceding method first calls the `GetCSVFile` method by passing the `model` key name and then processes `model` data row by row. This method also uses the `GetMake` method to get a `Make` record ID based on its name.

9. Finally, we can call our public methods from the main method of our sample console application. We will use the following code:

```
static void Main(string[] args) {
Dynamics365Utility utility = new Dynamics365Utility();
Console.WriteLine("Importing HIMBAP Auto Service Make and Models
  Data.....");
utility.AddMakers();
Console.WriteLine("Maker data imported correctly");
utility.AddModel();
Console.WriteLine("Models data imported correctly");
Console.ReadLine();
}
```

In the preceding code, first, we are creating an object of our `Dynamics365Utility` class, and then importing its **Make** and **Models** data into Dynamics 365 CE. When we run this application, we should see details on the screen like the following:

```
Importing HIMBAP Auto Service Make and Models Data.....
Maker data imported correctly
Models data imported correctly
```

We should see our data in Dynamics 365 CE. This is how we can create our own utility to interact with Dynamics 365 CE data. In the next section, we are going to discuss how we can use Power Automate to integrate Dynamics 365 CE with other applications.

Integrating Dynamics 365 CE with Power Automate

Another integration option we are going to talk about is Power Automate. If you are new to Power Automate, the simplest explanation would be to call it a cloud tool to automate your business processes. It is a workflow creation tool, whereby our workflow can be associated with a trigger and perform some predefined actions. We can consider it somewhat like our Dynamics 365 CE workflows, which are very useful, especially for business users. Before talking more about Power Automate, let's discuss the built-in workflow capabilities of Dynamics 365 CE a little bit, which are now known as classical workflows. For our integration purposes, we will be using a combination of Dynamics 365 CE workflows and Power Automate. Workflows perform different tasks based on our requirements. We can design a workflow using the workflow designer, where we can configure a workflow trigger that is responsible for starting the workflow and corresponding workflow actions. If you are an admin user or you have access to processes, you can see all the workflows created for your organization by navigating to **Settings** | **Processes**. When creating a workflow, we have the following options to configure it:

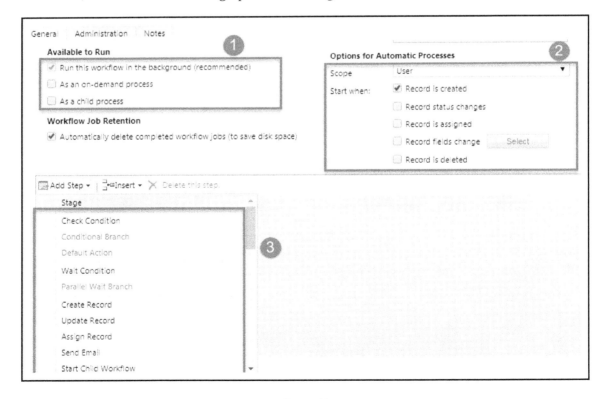

In the preceding screenshot, you can see three main areas. Let's discuss some details about these areas, as follows:

1. **Available to Run**: This area provides different ways to run our workflow. We can run our workflow as a background process, which means it will run as an asynchronous process in the background. It won't respond to actions immediately because of its asynchronous nature. We can also create a synchronous workflow, which is known as a real-time workflow. Real-time workflows will respond to our actions immediately, and they don't run in the background. Under this setting, we can configure our workflow to run on demand. These on-demand workflows are available to run for selected records from Dynamics 365 CE views, using the **RUN WORKFLOW** button. We can also configure our workflow to run as a child process, which means we can call our workflow from other workflows.

2. **Options for Automatic Processes**: In this area, we can set a scope for our workflow, where we have different options, similar to the access levels of security roles. The scope of the workflow defines the records on which you can run a workflow. For example, if the scope is set to the **User** level, you can run a workflow only on the record that you created; and if the workflow scope is **Organization**, then the workflow can be executed for all of the records of the Dynamics 365 CE organization. It is recommended to have your workflow scope set as **Organization**, to avoid any runtime errors. **Start when** options allow us to configure a trigger for our workflow; for example, if we want to run our workflow when a record is created or when any field is updated. We can select the field that we want to use to run our workflow by using the **Select** button. We can also run our workflow when a record status changes, when a field is assigned to another user, and when a record is deleted.

3. **Add Step**: This option allows us to configure actions such as create records, update records, assign records and send email records. We can also perform conditional checks before performing these actions. We also have options to use such as the wait option, which can be used to run the workflow after waiting for a specific time period.

We can extend the capability of a workflow by writing custom workflow assemblies, just like plugin assemblies. Although the out-of-the-box workflow tool is great for automating tasks inside Dynamics 365 CE, it does not provide any options for integrating Dynamics 365 CE with other applications. To overcome this limitation, we can utilize Power Automate's capabilities. If there are any requirements that can be fulfilled with a workflow tool, then we should always opt to do so. However, if we are looking to automate our business processes using multiple applications, then we should consider using Power Automate. We want to use Power Automate to send an SMS notification when a vehicle service is completed, but there is no direct option available to run Power Automate when any field is updated in Dynamics 365 CE. So, let's add a custom two-option field on an auto service (opportunity) entity and call it `Send SMS`. We will update this field to **Yes** when the status reason for the auto service is changed to **Completed**. We have added a new option to the Auto Service Status option set field. We need to place this on the form so that we can set this field from the workflow. Let's create our workflow to set this field, as follows:

1. Navigate to the **HIMBAP Auto Service** solution and select **Processes**.
2. Click on the **New** button, and fill in the following information:

   - **Process Name**: `Trigger SMS Notification`
   - **Category**: `Workflow`
   - **Entity**: `Auto Service`

3. Click on **OK**. It will open the workflow designer for us.
4. Set **Workflow Scope** as **Organization** and select **Record** field changes. We need to select the **Status Reason** field from the available options.
5. Click on **Add Step** and add a condition check from the dropdown. We need to check whether the **Status Reason** value is shown as complete, as shown in the following screenshot:

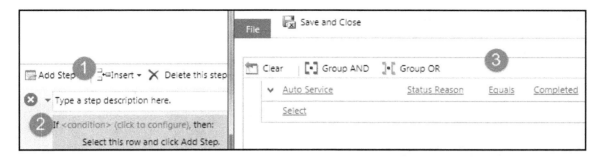

6. Select the row immediately after the check condition and add an update step from the **Add Step** option. We need to click on the **Set Properties** button and set our **Send SMS** field to **Yes**, as shown in the following screenshot:

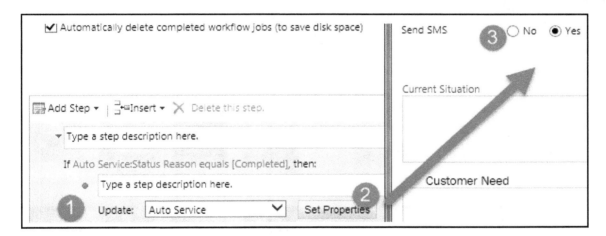

7. We have our workflow ready. When the vehicle service is complete, it will set this field to **Yes**, and in Power Automate, we will check this field. If it is true, we will send an SMS to the customer.

Now, let's talk about Power Automate. Power Automate provides the option to integrate it with different online services; for example, in the following screenshot, we can see some of the services that we can use in Power Automate:

Currently, Power Automate supports more than 300 connectors to connect with different applications. Similar to our Dynamics 365 CE classical workflows, Power Automate can be associated with a trigger to run automatically, or we can create a push-button flow. This type of flow can be initiated from mobile devices by simply tapping a button.

Power Automate has the following plans, which can be selected based on our requirements:

- Per User Plan: $15 per user/month
- Per Flow Plan: $500 per month

The Per User Plan will be able to create an unlimited number of flows to implement automation, whereas the second plan is for an organization and includes five flows per month. Additional flows can be purchased for $100 per month. Power Automate is included with the Dynamics 365 license, so there is no need to buy a separate license for Power Automate if you are a Dynamics 365 user. However, there is an API limit, depending on your Dynamics 365 license. For example, if you are using the Dynamics 365 Enterprise app, the number of API requests is limited to 20,000 per day; and if you are using the Dynamics 365 Professional app, API requests are limited to 10,000 per day.

You can refer to https://docs.microsoft.com/en-us/power-platform/admin/api-request-limits-allocations for more details on limits to API requests. And for more information about the plans, you can refer to https://flow.microsoft.com/en-us/pricing/

While working with Power Automate, we can design our own flow, or we can use an existing generic template to create a flow. These templates are divided into different categories based on their functionality. In the following screenshot, different template categories are shown, such as **Approval**, **Email**, **Events and calendar**, **Notifications**, and so on, which can be used to automate approval processes and other activities:

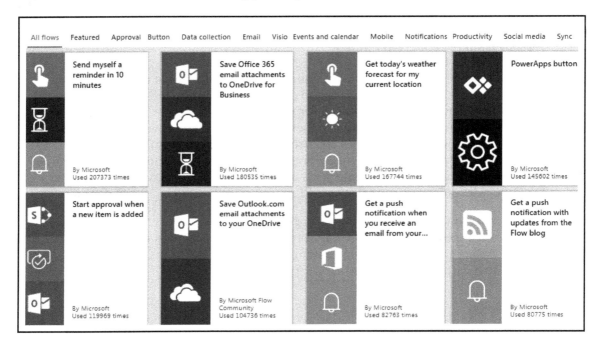

Dynamics 365 CE now contains a **FLOW** button, which we can use to create a flow or see a flow that we created for the current entity; for example, the following button is available on the account entity's home screen:

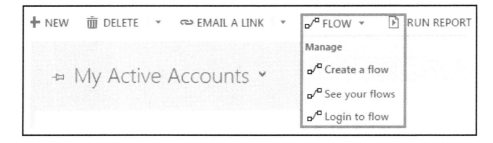

Now that we know some details about Power Automate, let's create a flow that will send a notification to the customer based on the **Send Notification** field, which is set by the workflow that we created in the previous step. To send an SMS, we first need to connect with a service that will help us to do this. We are going to use a trial account of Twilio. You can set up a trial account at `https://www.twilio.com`. Once you have your trial account set up, you can head to the console dashboard and get your **ACCOUNT SID** and **AUTH TOKEN** from there, like so:

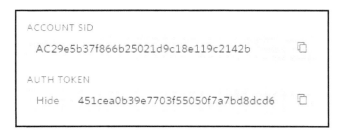

Let's use the following steps to create a flow:

1. Click on the Home button and select **Flow**, as shown in the following screenshot:

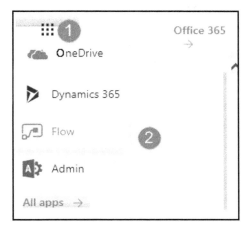

It may ask you to configure your country if you are starting Flow for the first time.

2. Navigate to **My flows** and create an **Automated—from blank** flow, as shown in the following screenshot:

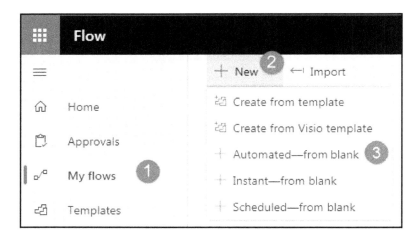

3. Let's use a flow name of `Send SMS Notification` and choose for the flow to be triggered when a Dynamics 365 record is updated.
4. Select the organization name and the entity name as `Auto Services`.
5. Click on **New Step** and add a condition control. We need to add a condition to check whether our **Send SMS** field is set to **true**. When you click on the text field, it will display the **Dynamic content** editor. From there, we can select our **Send SMS** field, as follows:

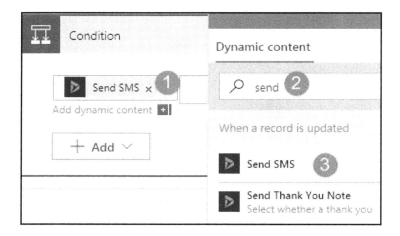

We need to compare it, as follows:

6. Click on **Add Action** under the **If yes** block after the preceding condition, search for Send SMS, and select **Send Text Message (SMS)** using Twilio, as follows:

7. Enter your Twilio account ID and the authentication token that you copied from the console dashboard.

8. We need to provide three things—our Twilio phone number, which we will use to send an SMS; the verified phone number of our customer (we need to set up a verified number in the Twilio app); and the SMS text that we want to send to our customers.

9. Finally, we need to add an **Update Step** to update the auto service record, and we need to set the **Send Notification** field back to **No**.

10. After all these steps, our flow should look as follows:

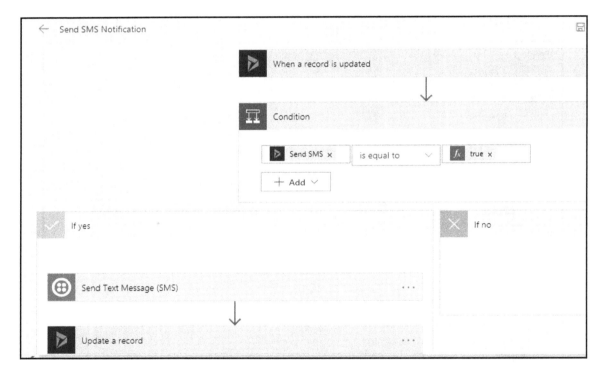

Now, when the **Auto Service** record status reason is set to **Completed**, our Dynamics 365 workflow will run, and it will set the **Send Notification** field to **true**. And finally, Power Automate will trigger and send a notification to the customer, as follows:

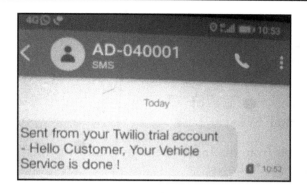

This is how we can use Power Automate to integrate Dynamics 365 CE with other cloud services.

Now that we know how to integrate Dynamics 365 CE with Power Automate, let's now see how we can use PowerApps canvas apps with Dynamics 365 CE.

Integrating Dynamics 365 CE with PowerApps

Let's say we want to create a quick mobile app for the HIMBAP Auto Service Center to create an auto service request for a customer. Let's see how quickly we can build our app using PowerApps Studio, by following these steps:

1. Click on the Dynamics 365 Home button (from where we selected **Flow** earlier) and select **PowerApps**.
2. Click on **Create** and select **Canvas app from blank**, and let's name our app `Auto Service Request`.
3. After clicking on **OK**, PowerApps Studio will open a new app that will have one screen by default.
4. Click on the right-hand side of **Screen1** and select the **Rename** option from the drop-down menu. Let's rename it `Service Request`.
5. Let's add the following controls to our screen, and name them as follows:

   - **Label**: `topiclbl`
   - **Text**: `topictxt`
   - **Label**: `customerlbl`
   - **Dropdown**: `customerdll`

- **Label**: vehiclelbl
- **Dropdown**: vehicledll
- **Label**: issueifanylbl
- **Text**: issuetxt
- **Label**: bookingdatelbl
- **Date Picker**: bookingdate

We can add these controls from the **Insert** menu by following the numbering sequence shown in the screenshot that follows:

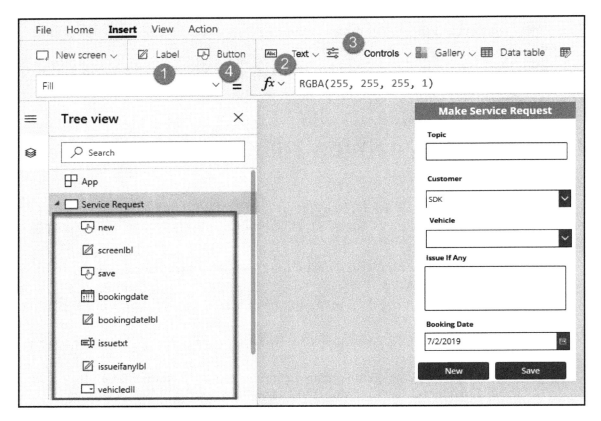

Let's place these controls on the screen as per the preceding screenshot. Now, let's add a Dynamics 365 CE data source to get data from Dynamics 365 CE entities, as follows:

1. Click on the **View** menu and select **Data Sources**.
2. Click on the **+ Add data source** button and select our current Dynamics 365 CE connection. Once it is connected, we need to select the following three entities, like so:

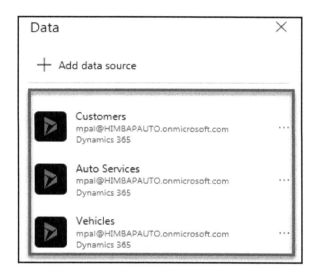

3. Now, let's bind our **Customer** dropdown to the Dynamics 365 CE customer entity, as follows:

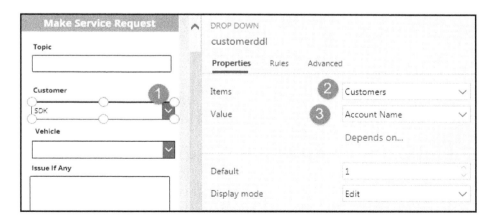

4. Next, we want to show the customer vehicle in the **Vehicle** dropdown, so we need to configure it by following the numbered steps shown in the following screenshot, after selecting the drop-down control from the screen. First, we need to select the **Vehicles** entity, and after that, we need to select the **Vehicle Name** field. Later, we can configure the **Depends on** options for this dropdown:

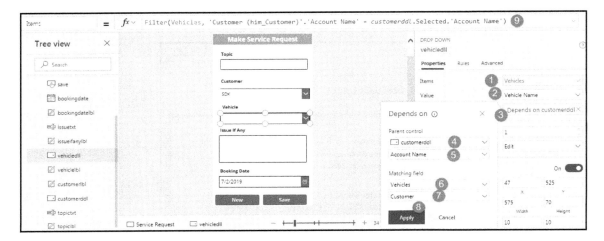

5. Next, let's use the `Reset` method to clear all the fields with a click of the **New** button. We can select the **New** button and use the `Reset` method on the formula bar, using the following number sequence:

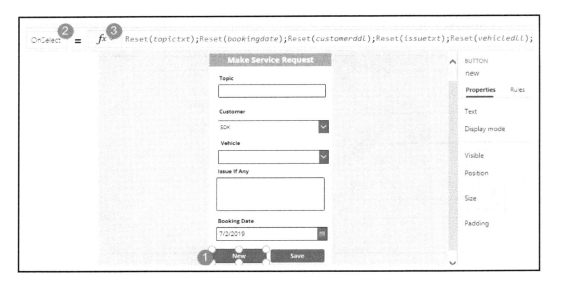

6. We need to write code for the **Save** button to store the current screen data to the Auto Service. We can select the **Save** button and write the following code for the `OnSelect` event of the button:

```
Patch('Auto Services',Defaults('Auto
Services'),{name:topictxt.Text},{currentsituation:issuetxt.Text},{h
im_servicebookingdate:bookingdate.SelectedDate},{_parentaccountid_v
alue:customerddl.Selected.Account},{_him_vehicle_value:vehicledll.S
elected.Vehicle});
```

In the preceding code, we are using the `Patch` method, which is used to create or update a record. When we want to use `Patch` to create a record, we need to use it with `Defaults`, which takes the table name as a parameter. In the preceding code, we have passed in the Auto Service entity name. Further, we can pass all the field names that we want to set.

7. Now, press *F5* to run our application. As soon as we select a customer name, we will be able to see their vehicle under the **Vehicle** dropdown, as in the following screenshot:

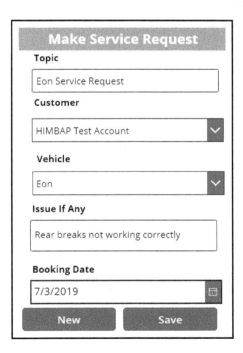

8. When we click the **Save** button, we will be able to see a record created in Dynamics 365 CE, like so:

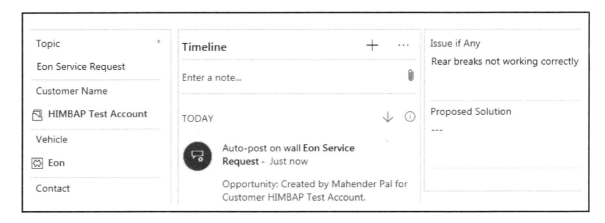

Finally, we can publish our app, and it can be used from a mobile device. To access our application, we first need to download PowerApps, and from there, we can access our PowerApps applications. This is a simple sample application, but we can create complex canvas apps in a similar way.

Summary

In this chapter, you learned about the integration options for Dynamics 365 CE. We discussed two Microsoft applications: Power Automate and PowerApps. You learned about Power Automate, its plans and templates, and how to use the flow designer. You now understand how to create a sample application to send SMS notifications using Flow. Later, you learned how to create a sample application using PowerApps, where you grasped how to use PowerApps Studio and its controls. Finally, you learned how to create Dynamics 365 CE entity records using PowerApps.

In the next chapter, we will discuss how to write reports for Dynamics 365 using the Dynamics 365 CE Report Wizard and Visual Studio.

Business Intelligence and Reporting

9

This chapter will help you to understand more about the business intelligence capabilities of Dynamics 365 CE. You will learn how to create reports using the Dynamics 365 Report Wizard. You will also learn how to create custom reports using Visual Studio. We will discuss how to add parameter and filtering capabilities in an **SQL Server Reporting Services** (**SSRS**) report. Later on in this chapter, we will discuss how to deploy an SSRS report to Dynamics 365 CE. Lastly, you will learn about connecting to Dynamics 365 CE from Power BI. You will also learn about using Power BI Desktop and Power BI online to create reports and dashboards, which will later be deployed to Dynamics 365 CE.

The main topics that we are going to cover in this chapter are as follows:

- Dynamics 365 CE BI capabilities
- Dynamics 365 CE reporting options
- Using the Report Wizard
- Writing a custom report in Visual Studio
- Report deployment
- Writing Power BI reports

Technical requirements

The following are the technical requirements for this chapter:

- Access to a Dynamics 365 CE Online subscription.
- .NET Framework 4.6.2, or later, should be installed.
- SQL Server Data Tools for Visual Studio 2012 or later.
- Windows Identity Foundation 3.5 should be installed on your development machine.
- Dynamics 365 CE Report Authoring Extension should be installed on your machine.

Dynamics 365 CE BI capabilities

We discussed Dynamics 365 CE's business intelligence capabilities in `Chapter 6`, *Customizing Dynamics 365 CE,* where we discussed dashboards and charts. Here, we are going to discuss another option for utilizing the business intelligence capabilities of Dynamics 365 CE, using reports. There are different methods of reporting in Dynamics 365 CE. Let's discuss these options one by one.

Excel reporting

Since the early days of Dynamics CRM, this has been the easiest way – and the traditional way—of analyzing customer data. We can download Dynamics 365 CE data using the **Export to Excel** option and can use formulas, charts, and pivot tables to analyze our data. Additionally, in Dynamics 365 CE, we can now utilize Excel templates; that is, we can use the formulas of Excel in an Excel template and import those templates into Dynamics 365 CE to use them. These templates can be shared with other users as well. Once a template is created for an entity, we can use that template for different views of the entity.

More details on how to use Excel templates in Dynamics 365 CE can be found at `https://docs.microsoft.com/en-us/dynamics365/customer-engagement/admin/analyze-your-data-with-excel-templates`.

FetchXML reporting

Dynamics 365 CE Online only supports FetchXML reports that use the FetchXML query to get data from Dynamics 365 CE. We can write a FetchXML query manually, or we can use Advanced Find and XrmToolBox to design queries. All reports generated using the Dynamics 365 CE Report Wizard are FetchXML reports. We can also develop a FetchXML report using Visual Studio's SQL Server Data Tools after installing the Microsoft Dynamics CRM 2016 Report Authoring Extension.

SQL reports

These reports are supported by the Dynamics 365 CE on-premises deployment, where we can use SQL queries for our reports. We use filtered views to get data from business entities instead of a SQL table directly. Filtered views are special views that restrict data based on security roles. We can only see the data that relates to the entity permissions we have.

Power BI reports

Power BI is another option to develop dynamic reports for Dynamics 365 CE. Power BI is a cloud service from Microsoft that provides integration options for Dynamics 365 CE. It also provides the option to apply complex formulas to Dynamics 365 CE columns, using chart visualization, and always provides real-time data. Power BI reports can automatically refresh data based on a schedule. We can build Power BI reports using different data sources. For example, you can develop a report where you can combine data from Dynamics 365 CE and your inventory system.

Dynamics 365 CE has around 25 general-purpose reports available out of the box. The following screenshot is of the default reports available in Dynamics 365 CE. We can use these reports as they are, or we can modify them:

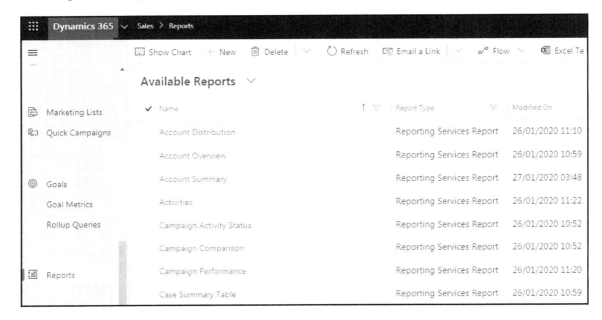

We can create reports for existing business entities or for new custom entities we create for our organization. Now we know about reporting options, let's discuss how to use Dynamics 365 CE's out-of-the-box Report Wizard to create a report.

Using Report Wizard

Report Wizard is an easy way to develop reports in Dynamics 365 CE. It provides an option to create a report by following multi-screen steps.

To create a report we can navigate, we can take the following steps:

1. Navigate to **Reports** and click on the **New** button.
2. Enter `Make And Model Report` under **Report name** and click on the **Report Wizard** button.

3. Keep the **New report** option as the default and click on the **Next** button.
4. Set up the entity information as follows and click on **Next**:

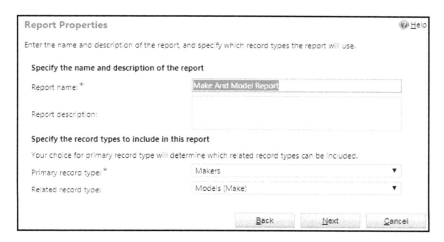

5. Keep the report filtering option as it is and click on the **Next** button.
6. Set up reporting by following the numbered steps shown in this screenshot:

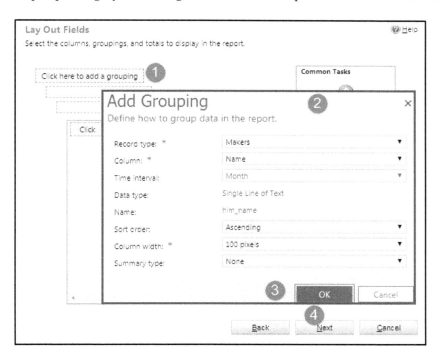

7. Click on **Click here to add the column** and set this column as the **Models** entity, as shown in the following image:

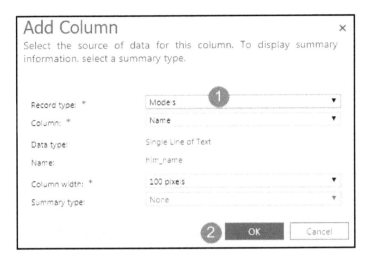

Once we have added the required column, we can perform other tasks from the **Common Tasks** section, such as sorting based on the primary entity field. Click on the **Next** button:

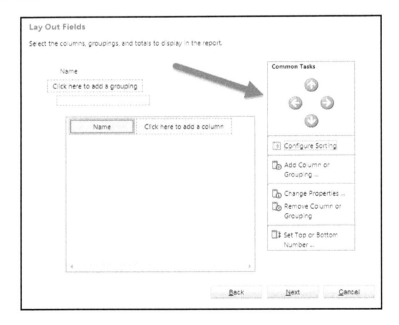

8. Set the **Format Report** option to **Table**. We can also select both the table and chart options as well.
9. Click on the **Next** button and review the report summary. Finally, click on the **Finish** button.
10. Click on the **Run Report** button from the report toolbar and you should get a report like the following:

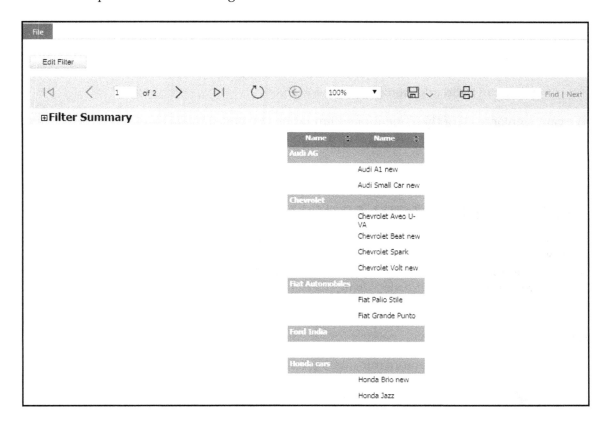

Once the report is finished, we can select it and can click on the **Edit** button to change the report if required. This is how we can use the Report Wizard to develop reporting using the Dynamics 365 CE application. Although the Report Wizard is a good option for generating a report for business users, customers, and admins, the Report Wizard has the following limitations:

- We can only use a first-level related entity when designing our report.
- We don't have many options for customizing our report's layout; for example, we can't use headers or footers in reports generated using the Report Wizard.
- We can't use any custom controls such as shapes or images.
- We can't use expressions to perform calculations.
- We can't add additional rows or columns.

We can overcome all of these mentioned limitations by developing custom reports in Visual Studio. So, let's discuss how we can create a report in Visual Studio for our Dynamics 365 CE online organization.

Writing a custom report in Visual Studio

Sometimes, we need to develop complex reports, for example, reports that involve more than one related entity or where we need to use expressions (we can use expressions in reports to define the content of SSRS controls) to validate the value of a field. These types of reports are not possible to develop using the Report Wizard, so we use Visual Studio to develop them. In order to write custom reports in Visual Studio, we need to make sure SQL Data Tools is installed with the Report Authoring Extension for Dynamics 365 CE. The Report Authoring Extension is needed for writing FetchXML reports.

You can find more information on expressions here: https://docs. microsoft.com/en-us/sql/reporting-services/report-design/ expression-examples-report-builder-and-ssrs?view=sql-server-2017.

We can use the following steps to write a report using Visual Studio; here, we are using Visual Studio 2012 SQL Data Tools:

1. Start SQL Server Data Tools for Visual Studio 2012 and follow the steps shown in the following screenshot to create the project:

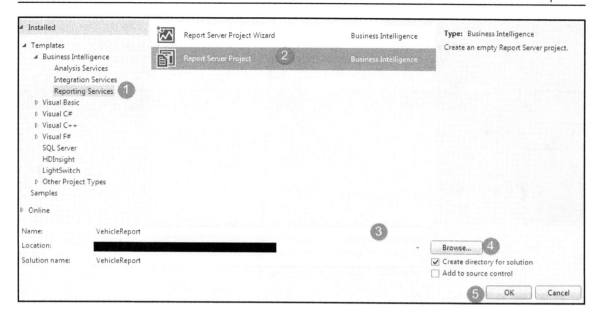

2. Once the project is created, we can right-click on the **Reports** folder under **Solution Explorer** to **Add** a new report, as follows:

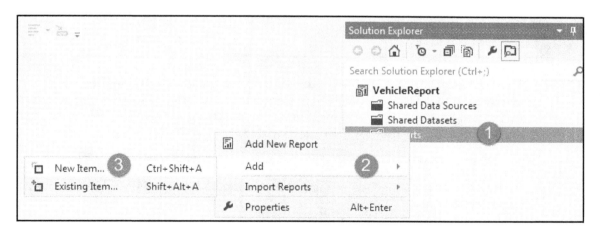

3. Right-click on **Data Sources** from **Report Data** and select **Add Data Source**.

4. If we want to connect to Dynamics 365 CE Online, we can use the following connection details:

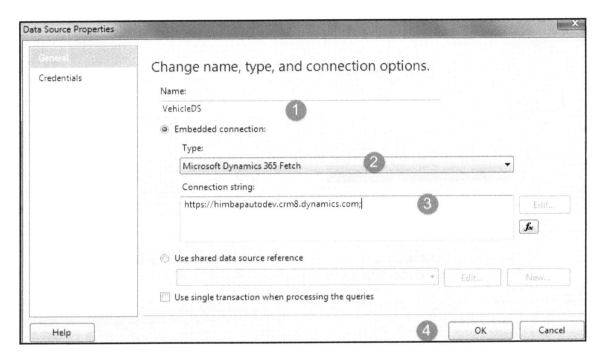

Here, you can see that, under **Connection string**, we have provided the organization URL only. Currently, we only have one organization in our tenant but, if you have multiple organizations, then you need to mention the organization name after the URL, as follows:

```
https://himbapauto.crm8.dynamics.com;HIMBAPAutoDev;
```

In the preceding connection string, we are connecting to our HIMBAP Auto Dev organization only.

5. Next, click on **Credentials** and enter your Dynamics 365 CE credentials, which you use to connect with your Dynamics 365 CE organization:

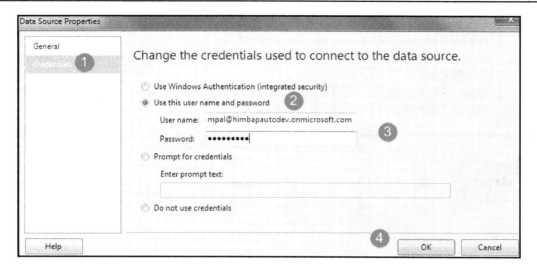

6. If you are working in a Dynamics 365 CE on-premises environment, you can set up a connection with your Dynamics 365 CE on-premises by clicking on the **Edit...** button to set up a connection string:

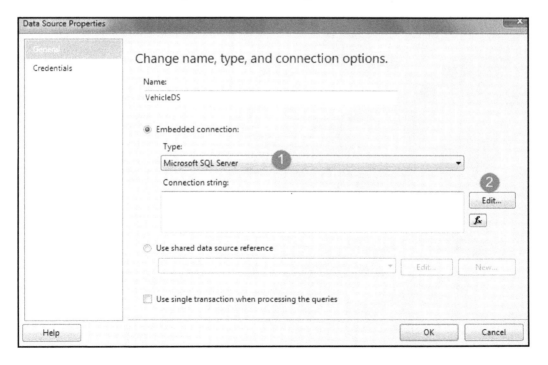

7. Once we have our data source created, we need to set up a dataset where we will connect to our entity. To create a dataset, we need to add a FetchXML query. As mentioned earlier, we can get FetchXML from **ADVANCED FIND** or we can create it using XrmToolBox.

8. Open **ADVANCED FIND**, select an entity, add the required field, and then click on the **Download Fetch XML** button:

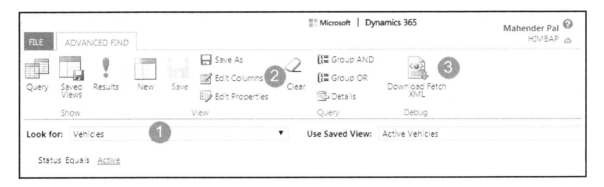

This will download the FetchXML query for this view. We can open the downloaded file and copy the query for use in the dataset.

9. Go to our report project, right-click on **Datasets** and select **Add Data Set**. After that, we configure it by following the steps shown in the screenshot:

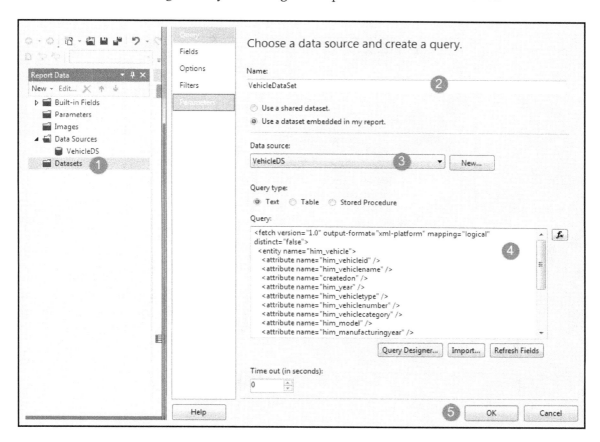

10. After clicking on the **OK** button, it will connect to Dynamics 365 CE and will show all the fields of this entity, which we can use in the Report Designer area, as follows:

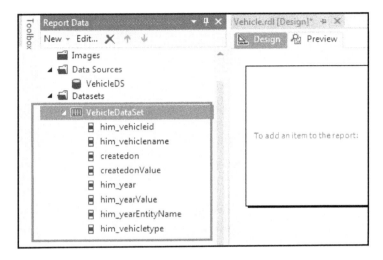

11. Let's first add a table to display the entity information. Click on the **Toolbox** view form on the left-hand side and drag a table control over the Report Designer. Click on the first column in the data row and then let's select **him_vehiclename** to display under it:

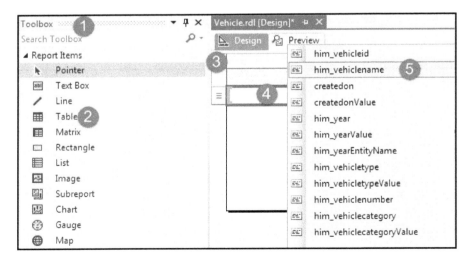

12. We can add more columns to the table by taking the following steps:

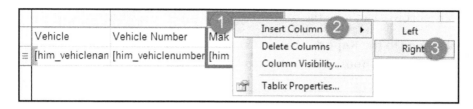

We can remove or hide columns using the **Delete Columns** and **Column Visibility...** options. We can also increase the column width by simply expanding the column width up to the required width.

13. Let's add the following fields and change their labels as follows:

Display name	Logical name
Vehicle	[him_vehiclename]
Vehicle Number	[him_vehiclenumber]
Make	[him_make]
Model	[him_model]
Category	[him_vehiclecategory]
Type	[him_vehicletype]

We can select the field and use formatting toolbars to format columns based on our requirements.

14. Click on the **Preview** button. You should be able to see all the vehicle data in your report.

15. Build a report project so that you can upload it to Dynamics 365 CE.

Now our simple report is ready. Let's take a look at how to deploy our report to Dynamics 365 CE.

Deploying a report

To upload a report, we can take the following steps:

1. Navigate to the **Reports** area and click on the **New** button.
2. Click on the **Choose File** button to look for RDL:

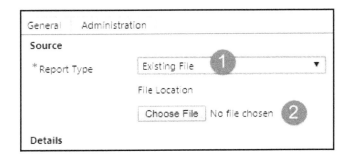

Once the file is uploaded, click on **Save** to save our file. Now we can click on the **Run report** button to run our report and it will show the data for the vehicle entity. Now, let's modify our report and add more options, such as adding grouping and a parameter to filter the report.

Adding grouping to a report

Let's say we want to add grouping to our report and we want to see the vehicle list according to the customer. We can take the following steps to add grouping to our report:

1. Click on **Details** under the **Row Groups** section and follow the steps shown here:

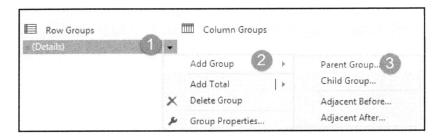

2. Under the **Parent Group** dialog, use the configuration shown in the following screenshot:

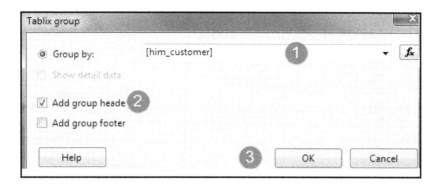

3. We can format the header and add some background color. After that, we can upload our new RDL file in the same report row (Dynamics 365 CE will ask you to verify overwriting the original file). Now, when we preview the report, we should be able to see it based on the customer, as follows:

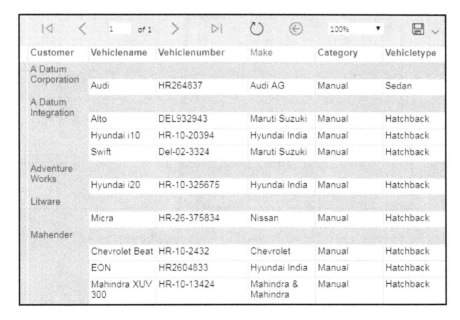

Next, we'll see how we can add a filter to our report.

Adding a filter to a report

Currently, our report doesn't provide an option to filter data, so when we open our report in Dynamics 365 CE, it won't show an option to add conditions to our report. However, if we want to add a filter to our report, we can do so using the following two options.

Adding pre-filtering support

We can add pre-filtering support to our report, which will allow us to filter it like **ADVANCED FIND**. We can apply a pre-filter to both the primary entity and related entities, if a related entity is used on our query, by following the steps that follow:

1. To add pre-filtering, we can simply enable the pre-filtering option on our `entity` node, as follows:

   ```
   <entity name="him_vehicle" enableprefiltering="true">
   ```

2. After adding pre-filtering to our report, when we upload the report and try to run it, you will see the **Edit Filter** button, as shown in the following screenshot:

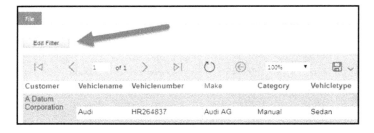

3. We can click on the **Edit Filter** button to edit the filter criteria and then click on the **Return to Report** button:

Our report will be filed based on our conditions. Now, let's demonstrate how to add a parameter to our report.

Adding a parameter to a report

Let's say we want to give the user a parameter option where the user can select the vehicle category from the drop-down menu. To create this parameter, first, we need to create a new dataset and we need to refer it to the parameter. Let's see how we can do that:

1. Create a new dataset, as we did earlier, and use the following query:

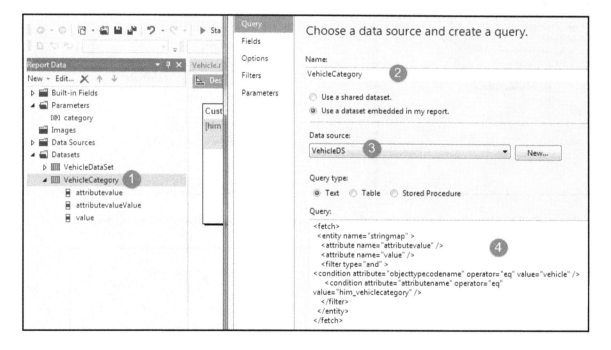

In the preceding query, we are querying the `stringmap` entity, which stores all the Option Set labels and values. Now, we need to configure the parameter to use this dataset.

2. Right-click on the parameter, select **Add Parameter**, and fill in the general details, as shown here:

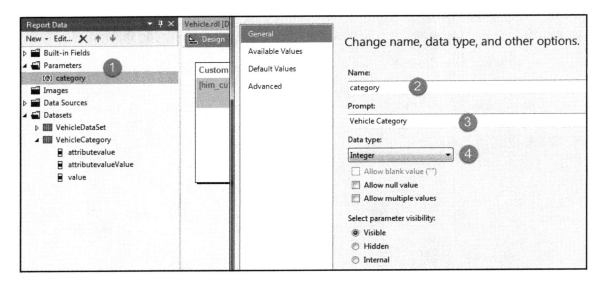

3. Click on the **Available Values** option and set the properties as follows:

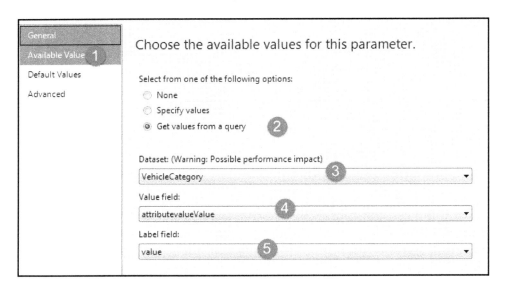

We are using the dataset that we created to get the Option Set details from the `stringmap` entity, and selecting which field is used for the display label and which field will be used to track its index value.

After making these changes, when we preview our report, we should see the drop-down parameter, as follows:

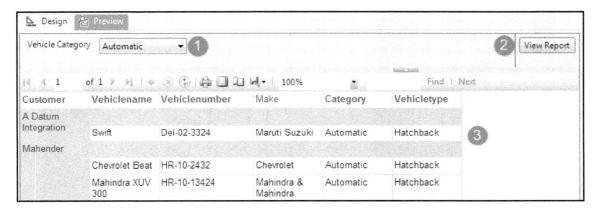

So, this is how we can develop reports using the Report Wizard or using Visual Studio. In the next section, we will discuss how to create a Power BI report for Dynamics 365 CE.

Writing Power BI reports

Power BI is a cloud service from Microsoft that provides integration options for Dynamics 365 CE. Using Power BI, we can develop rich reports and share them with users. Here, we are going to develop a sample report using Power BI; so, first, we need to set up a Power BI trial at `https://powerbi.microsoft.com`. You can use your same Office 365 credentials to set up this trial. We will develop our report using Power BI Desktop, which you can download at `https://powerbi.microsoft.com`.

Let's perform the following steps to develop our sample report:

1. Download Power BI Desktop and complete the installation steps.
2. Open Power BI Desktop and click on **Get data**:

3. Connect to Dynamics 365 CE by taking the following steps:

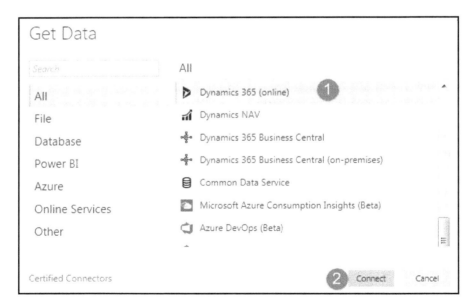

4. As soon as we click on **Connect**, a new dialog will appear, in which we can provide a **Web API URL**. We can copy it from the **Settings** | **Customization** | **Developer Resources** section:

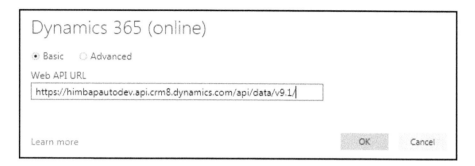

It may ask you to connect to your Dynamics 365 CE organization if you are using it for the first time. Use your Dynamics 365 CE credentials.

5. Now we are connected to our Dynamics 365 CE organization, we need to select which entities we want to use in our report. Let's select the **accounts**, **him_makes**, **him_models**, and **him_vehicles** entities. Power BI Desktop will connect to Dynamics 365 CE and we should be able to see all the selected entities in the Report Designer, as follows:

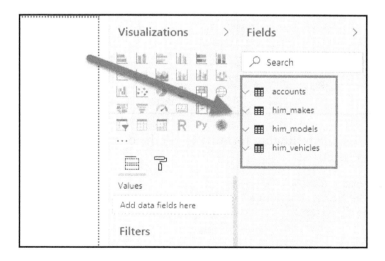

6. Let's expand the **him_vehicles** entity and select **him_vehiclename**, **him_vehiclenumber**, and **_him_customer_value** from the list. We can change the label of the fields by taking the following steps:

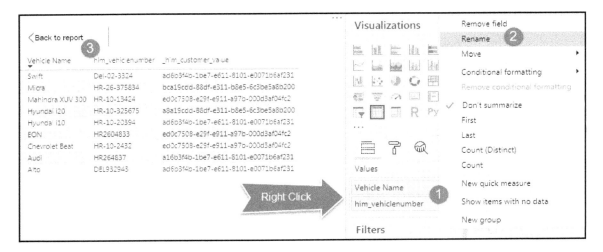

7. You will notice that the customer name is not displayed; instead, it will display the GUID of the customer record. To get the customer name, we need to add a new column and use the `LookupValue` method, so let's do that.

8. Click on the **New Column** button and change the label to `Customer Name`:

9. We will use the following formula to get the display name of the customer based on their GUID:

```
Customer Name=
LOOKUPVALUE(accounts[name],accounts[accountid],him_vehicles[_him_cu
stomer_value])
```

Here, the first parameter represents which column we want to get from the related entity, the second parameter is based on which column we want to get data, and the last parameter represents the GUID field of the current entity, which holds the customer ID. Now, we can uncheck the **him_customer_value** field and check our new **Customer Name** field, and we should be able to see our new field in our report, like so:

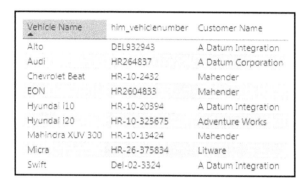

Vehicle Name	him_vehiclenumber	Customer Name
Alto	DEL932943	A Datum Integration
Audi	HR264837	A Datum Corporation
Chevrolet Beat	HR-10-2432	Mahender
EON	HR2604833	Mahender
Hyundai i10	HR-10-20394	A Datum Integration
Hyundai i20	HR-10-325675	Adventure Works
Mahindra XUV 300	HR-10-13424	Mahender
Micra	HR-26-375834	Litware
Swift	Del-02-3324	A Datum Integration

We can use other visualization controls based on our requirements.

You can find more information on creating Power BI reports at `https://docs.microsoft.com/en-us/power-bi/visuals/power-bi-report-add-visualizations-i`.

10. We can use the **Format** option to format different sections of the report:

Now, our sample report is ready, so let's upload it to Dynamics 365 CE.

Deploying a Power BI report to Dynamics 365 CE

We can place a Power BI dashboard or Power BI tiles in Dynamics 365 CE dashboards. We are going to create a Power BI dashboard and we will deploy this dashboard in Dynamics 365 CE. First, we need to publish our report to Power BI online; then we can create a dashboard to use it in Dynamics 365 CE. Let's take the following steps to use our sample report on Dynamics 365 CE:

1. Click on **Publish** to publish our report to Power BI online and follow the numbers given in the following screenshot:

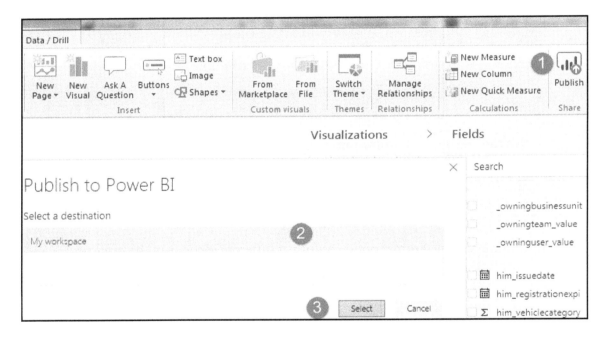

2. Open Power BI in the browser and verify our report:

3. Click on the report to open it and create a new dashboard using the **Pin Live Page** option:

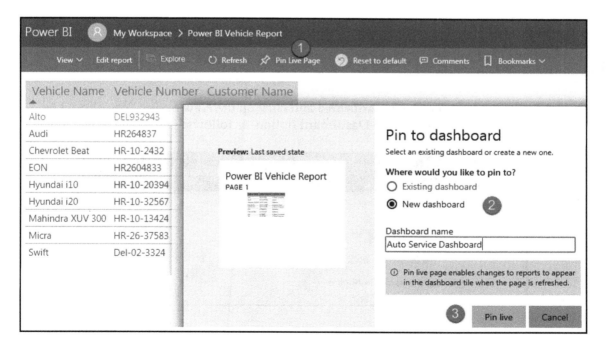

Select the **Go to Dashboard** option from the pop-up dialog; it will open a Power BI dashboard, which we can use in Dynamics 365 CE.

4. To deploy our Power BI dashboard to Dynamics 365 CE, first, we need to enable a setting for Power BI. So, navigate to **Settings** | **Administration**, click on **System Settings**, and enable the option as shown here:

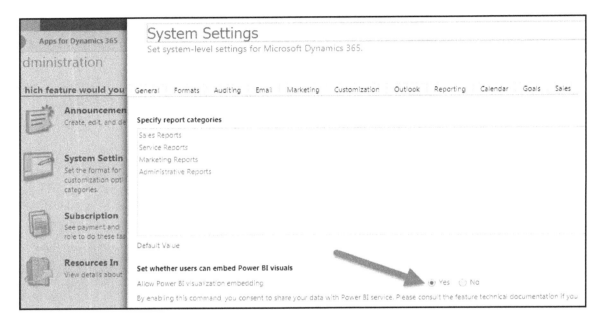

5. Navigate to the **Dashboards** area and click on the **New** option. You should be able to see the **Power BI Dashboard** option, as follows:

6. It will show a dialog with Power BI dashboards. Select our dashboard and click on **Save**, like so:

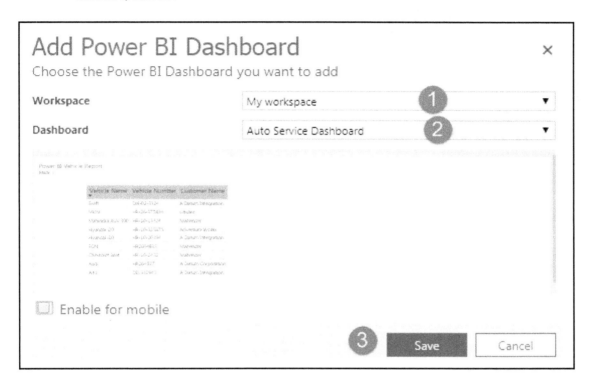

After that, we should be able to see our Power BI dashboard as follows:

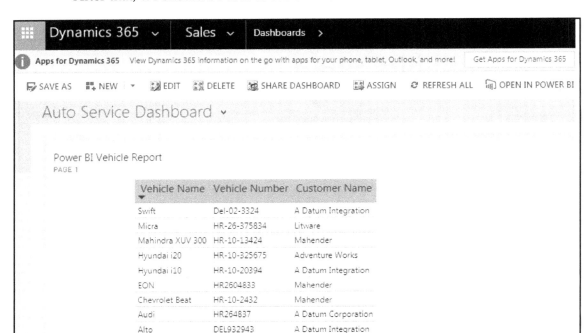

This is how we can develop Power BI reports and dashboards and deploy them to Dynamics 365 CE.

Summary

In this chapter, we learned about different reporting options for Dynamics 365 CE. We discussed how business users can use the Report Wizard to create a report for Dynamics 365 CE. We also discussed how to develop reports using SQL Server Data Tools for Visual Studio. We learned about adding grouping and filtering to reports with custom parameters by using the Option Set field. Finally, we discussed Power BI reports and how to develop Power BI dashboards for Dynamics 365 CE.

In the next chapter, we are going to discuss the testing phase—both manual and automated testing approaches—as well as how to conduct end user training.

10
Testing and User Training Planning

This chapter will help you understand how to prepare a test plan document and what common sections are included. We will discuss the different options for testing Dynamics 365 CE, such as manual or automated testing. You will also learn the difference between manual testing and automated testing. Later, we will discuss **User Acceptance Testing (UAT)** and how to perform it. Finally, we will discuss how to prepare an end user training plan and how to conduct end user training to make the implementation of Dynamics 365 CE successful.

The main topics that we are going to discuss in this chapter are as follows:

- Preparing a test plan
- Conducting manual testing
- Conducting automated testing
- Conducting UAT
- Preparing an end user training plan

Technical requirements

Although this chapter will help you conduct testing and planning with UAT, you should be familiar with testing concepts. In order to write automated test cases, you need to have programming knowledge. You should also be familiar with using GitHub.

Preparing a test plan

We know how to customize and extend Dynamics 365 CE, so let's talk about testing our customization and developments. Depending on the methodology you are using, you may need to perform testing when the development stage is over, such as in the waterfall model or when you need to perform testing when the first sprint is over, for example, in the agile model. Whatever approach is selected, testing for our project is performed based on the test plan, so it is critical to have a plan in place before the testing phase is started. Before preparing a test plan, we need to understand what a test plan is.

What is a test plan?

A test plan is basically a document that explains the scope of the testing phase and all the activities that we are going to perform in the testing phase. The main objective of the test plan document is to verify the product or project design and its compliance with the requirements provided by customers. A test plan document provides complete guidelines for the testing process, which include testing environment details, testing resources, testing approach, testing activities, and a schedule. The test plan document is mostly created by the testing team manager or lead. Here are the main features of the test plan:

- It defines the testing procedure.
- It provides clear information about what is in the scope of testing and what is not.
- It provides details about testing activities, which help us estimate the effort required for testing.
- It provides details about testing resource requirements.
- It provides details about test deliverables.

Now that we have an idea about the test plan, let's discuss how we can prepare a test plan document.

How to write a test plan

A test plan can be created manually or can be created using test plan software. To write a test plan, the basic criteria are to understand the product that we are going to test, the target users who are going to use the system, and why the customer is implementing this new system. If we are not clear about these details, it is difficult to write a good test plan document. It is recommended to read the requirement gathering document and learn basic details about Dynamics 365 CE.

Another key aspect of writing a test case is to know about the scope of testing: which module of Dynamics 365 CE is implemented for a customer and which specific functionality are they going to use? This helps us set the scope of our testing. We should also be clear about our testing approach. It should be mentioned in the test plan document whether we are going to perform testing manually or whether we will be using an automated testing approach. We should be aware of the end user expectations of those who are going to use this new system in their day-to-day activities. Our testing document should include the common sections listed in the following diagram:

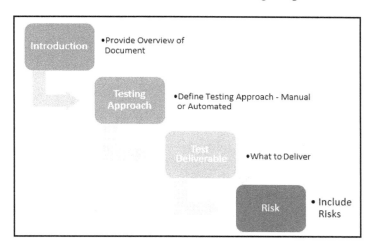

Let's discuss these sections in detail.

Introduction

As the name suggests, this section provides an overall summary of a testing plan document. We can include subsections under this section, which can provide details about test plan document objectives, scope, environment details, and required testing resources:

- **Objectives**: This section should provide the objective of the testing plan. We can include details about the proposed system and the tools that will be used to develop the proposed system. For example, in our case, we can include details here about what HIMBAP Auto Service Center is and what we are planning to achieve using Dynamics 365 CE. The following are some of the objectives of a good testing plan:
  - To test the proposed system against functional and non-functional requirements.
  - To make sure that we meet quality specifications provided by the customer.

- Issues should be identified and recorded for reporting purposes.
- All issues should be fixed before going live.
- It should also include details about UAT activities.
- **Testing Environment**: This section should provide details about the environment where we are going to perform testing, as well as access information.
- **Scope**: The scope of the test plan defines what needs to be tested. Here, we mention which of the functional or non-functional requirements are in scope, as well as which of the functional and non-functional requirements are out of scope.
- **Team members**: Here, we provide team member details about the testing team who are going to perform testing and what their role in the team is.

Testing approach

The testing approach depends on the project methodology that's used for project management, as well as the release cycle of your project. For example, if an agile implementation methodology is used, then the testing team will get an iteration after 1 or 2 weeks of testing. If a waterfall methodology is used, then testing will start once all the development is over, so this can depend on the project's methodology. But when talking about Dynamics 365 CE specifically, automated testing is a good option if we keep in mind that the two platform updates release per year and the subsequent small feature and security updates are released throughout the year by Microsoft.

Another thing that is mentioned here is whether we are going to use manual testing or automated testing. Let's go over these quickly:

- **Manual testing**: This is the oldest method of testing, where all the test cases are executed by the testing team manually. Testing is performed using test cases that are created based on the use cases. These use cases are associated with proposed solution features. Any bug/issue that's captured during testing is reported in the bug tracking system. The bug tracking system can be software or a simple Excel sheet. Based on these bugs, a test report is prepared and shared with the development team to fix these issues.
- **Automated testing**: This is another option for testing, where test scripts are written in the form of code to automate test case execution. In the case of automated testing, test scripts are also written using automated testing tools. There are many automation testing tools available on the market. Companies select tools based on their expertise and requirements. The main objective of using automated testing is to increase testing efficiency and improve the proposed system quality. A bug report is prepared once testing is completed for submission.

Now that we know about these two testing approaches, let's look at the differences between the two procedures:

Manual testing	Automated testing
The tester writes and executes test cases manually.	We can use an automation tool to write and execute test cases.
Writing and executing test cases is a time-consuming process.	Automation testing is faster than manually testing as not much human interaction is required.
Manual testing requires investment in experienced testing resources.	We need to invest in automation testing tools.
Manual testing can have errors.	This is automated fully so there is less chance of errors, considering all the test cases are designed correctly.
This testing can't help us to perform performance testing of an application.	We can perform performance testing and stress testing using automation testing tools.
It is not suitable if repetitive testing is required.	It is suitable for repetitive testing.

The preceding table helps us to understand the basic difference between manual and automated training approaches—we can use either based on our requirements. Now, let's see what the main deliverables are for the testing phase.

Test deliverables

This section provides details about the document that we are going to provide to the customer. There is no specific list of the test deliverables, but the following sections are commonly found in the document that's given to customers:

- The test plan document
- Test scripts
- Test scenario details
- Test data
- Bug reports
- Testing reports
- An overall test status report

Risk

In this section, we provide risk details, if any. For example, the following points could be common risks for any project:

- **Undefined product scope**: If the project scope is not clearly defined, it can delay the testing process.
- **Insufficient resources**: If testing resources are not sufficient, it can delay testing.
- **Frequently changed requirements**: If requirements are changing continuously, we may need to retest the functionality.

Now that we know the common sections that are included in the test plan document, in the next section, we are going to discuss how to conduct manual testing.

Conducting manual testing

Manual testing is conducted based on a test script or test cases, which are created by the testing team lead or senior testing resource. These test cases can be created manually or with automated testing tools. There are many steps involved in conducting manual training. The following diagram depicts the standard manual testing life cycle:

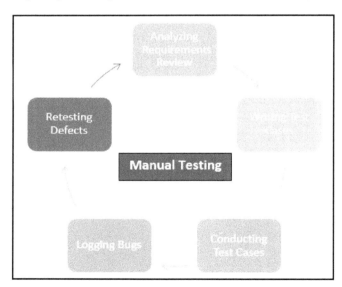

Let's discuss the test steps in detail, one by one.

Analyzing requirements review

This is the first step in the manual testing process. In order to conduct testing, it is critical to understand the requirements completely. The testing team can review the requirement document that's generated at the beginning of the project and can understand the requirements. It helps them understand what needs to be tested. Once the requirements are clear, the next step is to write test cases.

Writing test cases

Another critical step is to create a test case. A test case is basically a set of instructions that are executed by a tester to verify the functionality of an application or product. These instructions clearly define what specific input should be entered into the source application and what output should come as a result of these inputs. While writing test cases, it is recommended to include instructions in a simple manner so that they are easy to understand. We can use the following common fields while writing test cases for Dynamics 365 CE:

- **Case ID**: Every test case should be identified using its unique ID. We can create a case ID based on the modules or based on the features, depending on our requirements.
- **Module**: In the **Module** field, we can provide details about the topic or module that we are writing test cases for. For example, if we are writing test cases for customer functionality, we can make use of `Customer Management` in the module name.
- **Test Case Description**: This field provides information about the test case description. For example, if we want a test to create a customer record in Dynamics 365 CE, then our test case description could be `Create New Customer`.
- **Purpose**: We can also include this field, which provides the objective of a particular test case. For example, for the **Create New Customer** test case, our objective is to make sure the customer record is created and saved without any issues in Dynamics 365 CE.
- **Detail Steps**: This field provides detail steps for performing an action to test some functionality. These steps contain complete navigation details as well as test data that we need to feed into the application.
- **Expected Result**: This field provides details about the output that should be generated after performing detail steps. For example, in our **Create New Customer** test case, the customer record should be created without any errors.

- **Actual Result**: This field provides details on whether we received output based on the expected result or not. Normally, this field has two options, **Pass** or **Fail**, which the tester can select based on the output.
- **Comments**: This test can provide some additional details about the actual result. These comments can be helpful for developers to reproduce and fix a particular issue.
- **Author**: This field provides details about the author of the test case.
- **Tested By**: This field provides details about the tester who executed the test case.

Now, we know about the common fields that are added to the test case template. We can write test cases in Excel or any other editor based on availability. The following is the sample test case for customer creation:

Case ID	101
Module	Customer Management.
Description	Create a new customer.
Purpose	To make sure a user can create a new customer record without any issues.
Detailed steps	• Log in to the Dynamics 365 CE environment. • Navigate to **Auto Service	Customers** and click on the **New** button. • Create a customer with the following details: • **Name**: HIMBAP • **Phone**: 12324341 • **Website**: himbap.com • **Relationship Type**: Customer • Click on the **Save** button.
Expected result	A new Customer record is created with all the information that is filled out.
Actual result	
Comments	
Author	Diksha Rana.
Tested by	

Similarly, we can write another test case to update an existing customer record, create a contact, and update an existing contact record. We can also create a test case for other auto service-related entities. For example, the following is a sample test case for a vehicle entity:

Case ID	501
Module	Vehicle Management.
Description	Create a new vehicle record.
Purpose	To make sure a user can create a new vehicle record without any issues.

Detailed steps	• Log in to the Dynamics 365 CE environment. • Navigate to **Auto Service | Vehicle** and click on the **New** button. • Fill in the following details: • **Vehicle Name**: Alto Black • **Vehicle Number**: HR 26-1029 • **Customer**: Select Mahender from the lookup • **Issue Date**: 09-05-2016 • **Make**: Select Maruti Suzuki from the lookup • **Model**: Select Maruti Alto K10 from the lookup • **Manufacturing Year**: Select 2015 from the lookup • **Vehicle Type**: Hatchback • **Vehicle Category**: Automatic • Click on the **Save** button.
Expected result	A new vehicle record is created with all the information that is filled out.
Actual Result	
Comments	
Author	Diksha Rana.
Tested By	

We can create a test case based on the sample test cases we just covered. Once our test case is ready, the next step is to execute it.

Conducting test cases

In this step, a tester executes test cases that have been written based on the functionality or module of the application. All the test cases should be executed as is, without assuming anything. It is recommended that the tester should have basic knowledge of Dynamics 365 CE in order to execute test cases for Dynamics 365 CE.

Logging bugs

Once we have executed all the test cases, we log reported issues to the issue-tracking system. We can use bug-tracking applications from different vendors or can create our own in-house application using Dynamics 365 CE. Once all the issues have been logged, the tester can prepare a bug report and submit it to the project manager for review.

Retesting defects

This is the last step in testing, where all the defects are retested after the developer has fixed them. Once everything is fine, the product or application is ready for UAT.

This is how manual testing is conducted. Now that we have an idea of manual testing, we can discuss it in detail.

Conducting automated testing

Another option when it comes to conducting testing for the proposed system is automated testing. We have already discussed the differences between manual testing and automated testing. Automated testing is done mostly when we have fewer resources and we need to perform repetitive testing. Similar to manual testing, the automated testing process also has a life cycle, as shown in the following diagram:

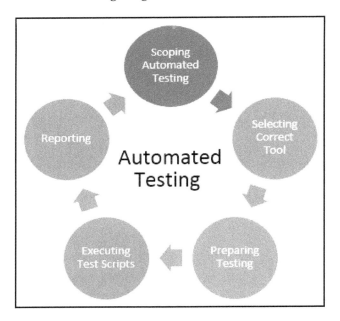

Let's discuss these stages one by one.

Scoping automated testing

In this stage, we set up the scope of automated testing. While setting up the scope, a feasibility check for automated testing is performed to make sure it is possible to perform automated testing for the target system. In most cases, automated testing is planned once we have manual test cases. We can review the existing test case and can find out the feasibility of automating testing for the existing test cases. We perform the following activities at this stage:

- Identify test cases that can and can't be automated
- Identify modules that can be fully tested using automated testing
- Identify resources to use for automated testing

Once we have defined the scope for automated testing, we can move on to the next stage.

Selecting the correct tool

In this stage, we identify the correct tools that can be used for automated testing. This activity is critical for automated testing as this testing is dependent on the automation testing tools, so we need to find the right tool based on our requirements. While finding a tool, we need to keep our technical skills and costs in mode if we are planning to use a paid tool. Since we are discussing testing options for Dynamics 365 CE, let's discuss some automated testing tools for Dynamics 365 CE.

EasyRepro

This is an open source framework provided by Microsoft for Dynamics 365 CE UI automated testing. This framework provides support for Dynamics 365 CE versions 8.2 to 9.1. This framework can be downloaded from `https://github.com/microsoft/EasyRepro` and contains the following sample for both the Dynamics 365 CE **Unified Interface** (**UI**) and the web client.

We can use this framework's APIs for quick UI testing. These APIs contain core Dynamics 365 CE commands that we use in our day-to-day work. For example, the following is a sample test from GitHub for creating account entity records by setting the `name`, `telephone1`, and `websiteurl` fields. In this sample test, we can see that it acquires the necessary credentials in order to connect with Dynamics 365 CE and then navigates to the `Accounts` subarea from the `Sales` area and creates an account record:

```
public class CreateAccount
{
    private readonly SecureString _username = System.Configuration.ConfigurationManager.AppSettings["OnlineUsername"].ToSecure
    private readonly SecureString _password = System.Configuration.ConfigurationManager.AppSettings["OnlinePassword"].ToSecure
    private readonly Uri _xrmUri = new Uri(System.Configuration.ConfigurationManager.AppSettings["OnlineCrmUrl"].ToString());
    [TestMethod]
    public void WEBTestCreateNewAccount()
    {
        using (var xrmBrowser = new Api.Browser(TestSettings.Options))
        {
            xrmBrowser.LoginPage.Login(_xrmUri, _username, _password);
            xrmBrowser.GuidedHelp.CloseGuidedHelp();
            xrmBrowser.ThinkTime(500);
            xrmBrowser.Navigation.OpenSubArea("Sales", "Accounts");
            xrmBrowser.ThinkTime(2000);
            xrmBrowser.Grid.SwitchView("Active Accounts");
            xrmBrowser.ThinkTime(1000);
            xrmBrowser.CommandBar.ClickCommand("New");

            xrmBrowser.ThinkTime(5000);
            xrmBrowser.Entity.SetValue("name", "Test API Account");
            xrmBrowser.Entity.SetValue("telephone1", "555-555-5555");
            xrmBrowser.Entity.SetValue("websiteurl", "https://easyrepro.crm.dynamics.com");
            xrmBrowser.CommandBar.ClickCommand("Save & Close");
            xrmBrowser.ThinkTime(2000);
        }
    }
```

You can find more details about this framework on GitHub.

Apart from this, there are some automated tested tools available that can be used by developers for unit testing. Let's discuss some of the available tools.

FakeXrmEasy.365

This is an open source framework that was developed for unit testing Dynamics 365 CE code. Starting from Dynamics CRM 2011 to Dynamics 365 CE, we can use FakeXrmEasy to unit test our code. The best part of this framework is that it provides mock objects so that we can connect with Dynamics 365 CE. For example, it provides mock objects for `IOrganizationService` and a plugin context from the memory. Running unit testing becomes easy and fast as it does not connect with actual Dynamics 365 CE service objects.

For example, we can simply use the following lines to get our service and the plugin context object:

```
var context = new XrmFakedContext();
var PlugCtx = context.GetDefaultPluginContext();
var service = context.GetFakedOrganizationService();
```

Developers can develop their unit tests within Visual Studio and run them if and when required. You can find out more, as well as instructions, at https://dynamicsvalue.com/ home.

You can download FakeXrmEasy from GitHub at https://github.com/ jordimontana82/fake-xrm-easy.

xrm-ci-framework

This is another tool that will help you automate Dynamics 365 CE solution testing and deployment. It uses the DevOps pipeline, which makes it easy for you to deploy your Dynamics 365 CE solutions more frequently with added consistency and quality.

You can download this tool from https://github.com/WaelHamze/xrm- ci-framework.

Moq

Another unit testing framework that can be used for Dynamics 365 CE is Moq. This framework also provides a mock object that we can use to connect to Dynamics 365 CE service objects and perform unit testing. For example, to set up a service object, we can use the following statement:

```
var Dynamics365serviceMock = new Mock<IOrganizationService>();
IOrganizationService OrgService = Dynamics365serviceMock.Object;
```

In the preceding code, we are creating an object of the Mock type that can act like Dynamics 365 CE's organization service, which we learned about in Chapter 7, *Extending Dynamics 365 CE*. We can use this object to perform organization service operations.

You can download and get more details about Moq from `https://github.com/moq/moq`.

Preparing for testing

Once the automated testing tools have been identified, we can prepare for testing. In this phase, different activities are performed, such as preparing and setting up a testing environment; guidelines are prepared for test script creation; guidelines are prepared for the test data based on the modules developed; and finally, guidelines are set up for defect logging and reporting. Responsible teams start preparing test cases based on the features or the module of the new system.

Executing test scripts

In this stage, test scripts are executed. Test scripts that have been prepared in earlier stages are executed and target the test environment's setup. Test scripts can be executed if they're targeting multiple environments and platforms to make sure our new system is compatible with all the environments or platforms that customers use. While executing test scripts, all the bugs are collected and reported to the development team.

Reporting

This is the final stage of the testing life cycle. In this phase, the team works on collecting a report for all the bugs that have been reported based on the modules. Bug reports are prepared based on the modules to identify which of the modules has a greater number of bugs that have been reported. Once the reports have been prepared, they are shared with all the relevant teams, such as development teams and stakeholders.

This is how we perform automated testing on our system. So far, we've learned about the high-level steps that are involved in manual and automated testing. Now, we are going to discuss how to perform user acceptance testing.

Conducting UAT

User Acceptance Testing (UAT) is conducted once the testing team confirms the system is bug-free. Testers are technical resources and they validate the new system based on the requirement's specification document. They interpret the requirements according to their knowledge about Dynamics 365 CE. But in UAT, the user conducts testing to make sure the system works based on their requirements. The outcome of the UAT is user acceptance sign-off for the Dynamics 365 CE solution developed. In UAT, end-to-end business processes are tested to make sure the system is based on customer expectations. UAT is performed basically using key users who know the system very well and use the system to perform their day-to-day activities. A separate environment is prepared that is similar to the production environment and has sample data similar to production data. The following diagram shows us when UAT is conducted in any project and highlights how, compared to other phases, UAT has much more weight:

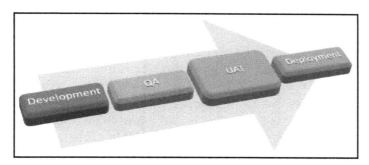

Once UAT has been conducted, the final results are analyzed by the customer to prepare the results of the UAT. The UAT process gives the customer a chance to know how the final system is going to run. They may realize they need to add some new functionality after conducting UAT, which is normally done in the enhancement phases.

Why UAT is important

UAT is an important phase of any project because it doesn't matter how many functional and unit tests are performed—the system may still behave differently when tested with real business data and by actual end users. The following are the critical reasons why we should perform UAT:

- It provides an opportunity to verify functional test cases before the system is used by end users.
- It provides optimal opportunities to identify issues and fix them at an early stage.

- It helps improve the quality of the system based on the client's feedback.
- As UAT is done by the end users and clients, it verifies whether a new system is developed based on client specifications or not.
- It helps us get final confirmation from the client before the system is ready for production.

To conduct UAT, the following steps should be taken:

1. **Planning and preparing a UAT checklist**: The first step is to plan UAT activities, and preparing the UAT checklist helps us stay focused. We can follow this checklist in order to make UAT successful. This checklist should include all the tasks that we are going to perform during the UAT phase. This helps us understand which of the tasks are completed and which of the tasks are not completed.

2. **Define the acceptance criteria**: Before conducting UAT, it is very important to prepare acceptance criteria. UAT acceptance criteria may include only critical business processes because it's not practical to test a complete application again during the UAT phase. The project manager should work with the customer to identify critical business requirements and prioritize them. All the acceptance criteria should be documented for the UAT sign-off.

3. **Identify key users**: UAT is performed by key users, which include different types of users such as admin users, also known as power users; executives; managers; and team members. It is important to get a user list from the customer to set up their users before UAT begins. After setting up the users, we need to also set up their security roles based on their job profiles to make sure they have access to areas that are relevant to their day-to-day duties.

4. **Set up the UAT environment**: Another important task is to set up the environment for UAT. It is important to conduct UAT in a separate environment, which should be similar to the production environment. It may contain a copy of historical data, if any, or should have sample business data where end users can perform their testing.

5. **Train key users**: This is another important step where we should train key users and stakeholders so that they are familiar with the new system. They may be using an old system with different navigation, so in the new system, they should be aware of the new navigation in order to access their work area.

6. **Assisting key users during UAT**: Even though we will have provided training to key users, it is important to assist them during the UAT phase. A team of functional consultants can be assigned to help key users. This helps us complete UAT in the agreed time.

7. **Listening to key users**: During the UAT phase, it is important to hear key users' feedback about the new system. It helps increase the usability of the system as key users may suggest some UI changes to make them more comfortable with the new system.

8. **Bug reporting procedure**: Before UAT begins, we should have our UAT bug report process defined so that all the UAT members are aware of the procedure to report any bugs that occur during UAT. Later, those bugs should be collected, which helps us determine whether the current product is ready for production release or not.

9. **UAT sign-off**: Once UAT is over, we should get UAT sign-off from the UAT team. UAT sign-off verifies whether the product is ready for production use or not.

This is how we can perform UAT for our application or product. Now, let's learn how to prepare a user training plan.

Preparing an end user training plan

The successful implementation of any Dynamics 365 CE project depends on how much the end user knows about the new system. End user training is one of the keys to the successful implementation of Dynamics 365 CE. End user training makes users more comfortable when using Dynamics 365 CE in production. The more they use Dynamics 365 CE for their day-to-day activities, the more the Dynamics 365 CE implementation will be considered successful. The most common reason for Dynamics 365 CE implementation failure is not using the Dynamics 365 CE application for day-to-day activities, and this could be for many reasons, such as lack of proper training, the slowness of the application, or performance issues. We'll talk about user training in more detail the next section.

Why we need end user training

A new implementation of Dynamics 365 CE in an organization could be a big change for most end users because they may have been using a different CRM system previously or using an earlier version of Dynamics CRM. It can be difficult to adapt to new Dynamics 365 CE changes. Depending on which version a customer was using previously, they may see a different UI, new command buttons, and new functionality in Dynamics 365 CE. Dynamics 365 CE end user training helps the user understand why and how to use new Dynamics 365 CE functionality to perform their day-to-day activities.

Sometimes, an organization skips end user training, which leads to Dynamics 365 CE user adoption failure. End user training can truly help with the implementation of Dynamics 365 CE and ensure maximum efficiency in the output. End user training can be conducted by a consulting company or a professional trainer that's been hired by the customer themselves. While planning end user training for a Dynamics 365 CE implementation, it is important to identify an end user's daily activities so that end user training can include topics accordingly. End user training should also include a practical example of the client's business process because it helps end users see how Dynamics 365 CE fits into their business flow.

Benefits of end user training

The following are the benefits of end user training:

- End users can be more productive as they know the system well before using it; there are fewer chances that they will not be aware of some functionality.
- During their training, they understand the purpose of the new Dynamics 365 CE implementation, so it helps them work efficiently by using new Dynamics 365 CE features.
- Increased productivity and efficiency of the end user leads to a return on the investment made in implementing Dynamics 365 CE.
- End user training increases user adoption.
- There are fewer chances of the wrong data being entered into the system.

Now that we know the advantages of end user training, let's discuss how we can conduct an end user training session and the main steps that we need to carry out.

Conducting end user training

To conduct end user training, we can follow the end user training steps in the following screenshot. This normally starts with understanding users and ends with capturing end user feedback:

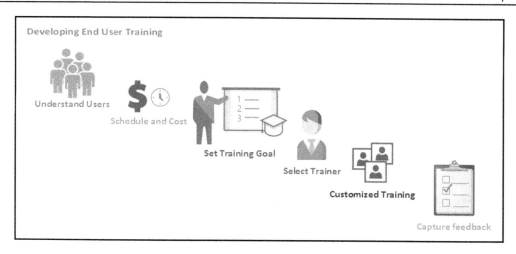

Let's discuss these steps in detail:

1. **Understand Users**: Before conducting end user training, it is important to understand end users. We should know who we are going to train and what their technical competences are. Do they already know about Dynamics 365 CE or early Dynamics CRM versions? Every organization has different types of users; for example, we may have users who will use new Dynamics 365 CE only for some tasks, such as generating reports and to review customer data, or users who will use Dynamics 365 CE extensively. But it is important to understand that every user needs training and support based on their job profile.

2. **Schedule and Cost**: We need to define the training schedule and budget before conducting end user training. While conducting training, we need to make sure all the training sessions are completed within the training schedule. It is also important to share the training schedule with the customer beforehand to make sure they can make all the required arrangements.

3. **Set Training Goal**: Before conducting end user training, it is important to set up a training goal first. The main objective of end user training is to increase the efficiency of the end users. While setting up a training goal, we need to keep the end user's needs in mind. For example, for the service department, we may have to set different goals than for the sales department – training goals are different.

4. **Select Trainer**: End user training should be conducted by a certified Dynamics 365 CE trainer who knows the Dynamics 365 CE application very well. They should be aware of the customer objective for implementing Dynamics 365 CE.

5. **Customized Training**: Apart from generic Dynamics 365 CE training, the trainer should prepare customized training for users with sample lab exercises. There may be different users from departments with different roles, so we need to make sure we prepare the training according to all the possible roles in the organization.

6. **Capture Feedback**: While conducting training, we should always capture users' feedback. This can be done during training sessions or can be captured once the training is over. It helps us understand user interest in the new Dynamics 365 CE, as well as their experience in the training sessions.

Here, we have discussed the main steps that are required to develop end user training plans. All of the preceding steps are very important, whether it is understanding the end user or capturing feedback after the training. Understanding the users gives us the opportunity to conduct training efficiently based on their requirements, while capturing feedback helps us track the effectiveness of the training. Now, let's discuss some sources for Dynamics 365 CE training.

Dynamics 365 CE training references

In this section, we're going to be talking about Dynamics 365 CE training, so let's talk about the references that we can use for it.

Dynamics 365 CE SDK

One of the popular, and free, places to learn about Dynamics 365 CE is the Dynamics 365 CE SDK, which is available online. We can access all the documentation for Dynamics 365 CE from `https://docs.microsoft.com/en-in/dynamics365/`, like so:

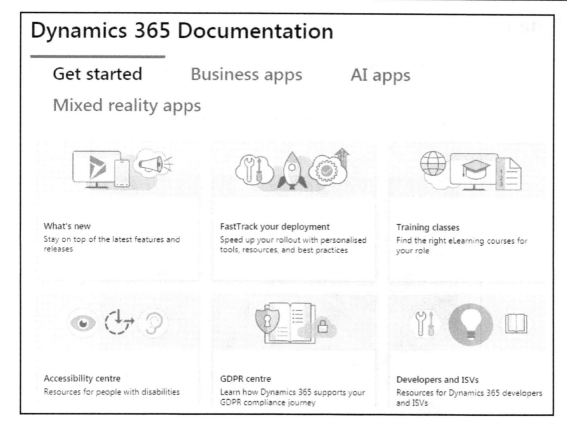

This documentation provides all the details about Dynamics 365 CE. As shown in the preceding screenshot, we can see different navigation options to get details about Dynamics 365 CE. We can see what has recently been released in the **What's new** section; we can see best practices for Dynamics 365 CE development under **FastTrack your deployment**; and we can find eLearning courses from Microsoft on this page.

Navigate to `https://docs.microsoft.com/en-us/learn/dynamics365/` for different learning paths for Dynamics 365.

Dynamics Learning Portal

If you are a Microsoft partner or part of the 365 Talent Portal, then you can access the Microsoft Dynamics Learning Portal. Here, you can get training materials for Dynamics 365 CE exams and lots of eLearning resources. You can access the Dynamics Learning Portal at `https://mbspartner.microsoft.com/Home`:

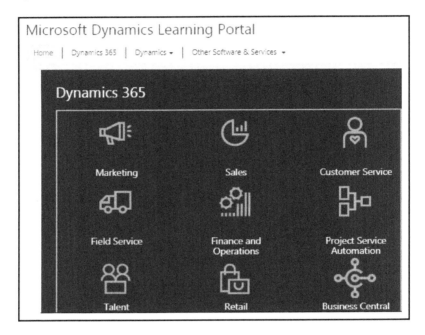

As shown in the preceding screenshot, we have training options available for all the apps for Dynamics 365.

Microsoft Training Partners

Microsoft Training Partners are training companies who are partnered with Microsoft to provide training for Dynamics 365 CE. We can look for the Microsoft Training Partners in our area by navigating to `https://www.microsoft.com/en-us/learning/partners.aspx`.

Apart from the preceding training sources, there are other sources available, such as YouTube's Dynamics 365 CE channels, the Dynamics 365 CE team, and Dynamics 365 CE community blogs.

Summary

In this chapter, we learned about testing the Dynamics 365 CE application. We discussed how to create a test plan and what sections we should include in our test plan document. Then, we discussed manual and automated testing approaches. We also learned why UAT is important for Dynamics 365 CE implementation and how it can be performed. Lastly, we discussed how to conduct end user training for Dynamics 365 CE implementation.

In the next chapter, we are going to discuss different paths we can follow in order to upgrade to Dynamics 365 CE from earlier versions of Dynamics CRM, as well as how we can migrate our existing data to Dynamics 365 CE.

Migration and Upgrade

11

This chapter will help you to get to know the options for upgrading to Dynamics 365 **Customer Engagement** (**CE**) from earlier versions. We will discuss different upgrade activities that you need to perform and what the different paths that you can take to upgrade are. We will discuss what we need to review in our current Dynamics **Customer Relationship Management** (**CRM**) version in order to upgrade it to Dynamics 365 CE. We will also discuss how to upgrade our Dynamics CRM solutions and code to make them compatible with Dynamics 365 CE. Finally, we will discuss data migration options for Dynamics 365 CE. You will learn about using the out-of-the-box data import wizard and using the **SQL Server Integration Services** (**SSIS**) Integration Toolkit from KingswaySoft to import data into Dynamics 365 CE.

The main topics that we are going to discuss in this chapter are as follows:

- Upgrading to Dynamics 365 CE
- Upgrading solutions
- Upgrading code
- Migrating data
- Importing data into Dynamics 365 CE

Technical requirements

This chapter has the following technical requirements:

- Knowledge of earlier versions of Microsoft Dynamics CRM
- Access to the latest Microsoft Dynamics 365 version
- **SQL Server Data Tools** (**SSDT**) for Visual Studio 2012
- KingswaySoft SSIS Integration Toolkit for Dynamics 365 CE
- Access to the Microsoft Dynamics 365 CE **Software Development Kit** (**SDK**)

Upgrading to Dynamics 365 CE

We have discussed details about Dynamics 365 CE in all the previous chapters, but here, we are going to discuss how to upgrade to Dynamics 365 CE if you are using earlier versions of Dynamics CRM—for example, if you are working with Dynamics CRM 2011, 2013, 2015, or 2016. How you can upgrade to Dynamics 365 CE depends on which Dynamics CRM version and deployment you are using currently. For example, for online customers, it is mandatory to upgrade to the latest version after a specific duration that is determined by Microsoft. Here, there is no control over the online deployment, and you have to move to the latest version. But if you are working with an on-premises deployment, then you can choose when you want to upgrade to the new version.

If you are working with an earlier Dynamics CRM version that is closer to Dynamics 365 CE, such as Dynamics CRM 2016, then it is going to take less time compared to versions earlier than Dynamics CRM 2016. This is because there is no direct way to upgrade to Dynamics 365 CE if you are using Dynamics CRM versions earlier than 2016. For example, the following screenshot shows you the process of upgrading to Dynamics 365 CE from Dynamics CRM 2011:

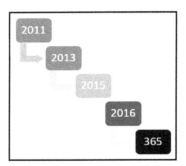

This means if we are using Dynamics CRM 2011, we need to upgrade our environments one by one, starting from Dynamics CRM 2011 to Dynamics 365 CE. Another thing we need to keep in mind if we are working with earlier versions is that we need to work on upgrading the code as well as the customization upgrade. This is because our Dynamics CRM may be using methods and service references that are deprecated already.

While planning for the upgrade or suggesting an upgrade for any customer, the first question that comes to mind is: *Why should we upgrade?* The most common reason to upgrade any software system is to gain benefits from the features released in the new version. In Chapter 1, *Introduction to Dynamics 365 CE*, we discussed the top 10 features of Dynamics 365 CE, which should give us at least one good reason to upgrade our existing Dynamics CRM to Dynamics 365 CE.

Another question that we face is: *How do we upgrade to Dynamics 365 CE?* If we are using online versions, then we don't need to bother about this question as online deployment is upgraded by Microsoft, but we need to take care of upgrading our customization and code. Also, keep in mind that Microsoft now releases a platform update twice a year (April and October), and normally, about 9 weeks prior to the update, they release update notes. After about 1 week, customers have the ability to apply early access to this update with a sandbox environment, to test all customization and coding. But, if we are working with an on-premises environment, then we need to plan our upgrade depending on different points. For example:

- Does the existing server support Dynamics 365 CE configuration?
- Do we have new servers in case we want to set up Dynamics 365 CE on new servers?
- Do we have the required IT team to take care of setting up the environment for Dynamics 365 CE?
- How much downtime is supported in case we want to use our existing infrastructure for Dynamics 365 CE?

All of the preceding points decide how we are going to upgrade and what our upgrade activities will be. We can list down the upgrade process using the following diagram, where we have common steps that we perform for any type of upgrade:

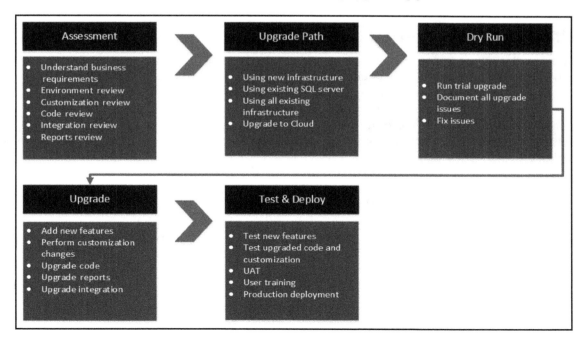

Before the upgrade, our first step is to prepare an assessment report that includes all the details of our current Dynamics CRM environment. After that, we work on the deployment plan that we are going to select based on our requirements, and it is recommended to do a trial upgrade to understand the complications involved in the upgrade. Finally, we perform testing on the upgraded environment, which involves functional testing as well as **user acceptance testing (UAT)**, before it is released to the end users.

Now that we have introduced the high-level details of a Dynamics CRM upgrade, let's discuss those high-level activities in more detail.

Dynamics 365 CE upgrade activities

A Dynamics 365 CE upgrade is a step-by-step process, and the activities you will perform during an upgrade depend on the deployment type. For example, if we are working with an on-premises upgrade, we may need to work on setting up the environment and setting up the application and SQL servers, along with reporting and email servers. Once the servers are set up, we have to install software and the required patches, which is a time-consuming process. Apart from setting up infrastructure, other activities are mostly the same for upgrading Dynamics 365 CE Online and in an on-premises deployment. Let's discuss the high-level activities, one by one.

Preparing an assessment report

The first thing before doing an update is to create an assessment report, where a comprehensive review of the current business and environment is done to understand the requirements of the upgrade and to create a plan to upgrade to Dynamics 365 CE. It is recommended to first understand how our customer is using Dynamics CRM currently, which Dynamics CRM modules they are using, and which of the new Dynamics 365 CE features could help them to increase their business efficiency. In our assessment report, we include the activities listed next.

Backing up your environment

Before starting any upgrade activity, you should first take a backup of your existing organization. This backup can help us if something goes wrong during the upgrade. We can always use our backup to restore our organization and make sure our environment is up and running quickly.

Cleaning your Dynamics CRM database

It is recommended to clean your Dynamics CRM database before upgrading. You may not want to take your old historical data that is not required—for example, completed system job records. You can refer to `https://support.microsoft.com/en-us/help/968520/performance-is-slow-if-the-asyncoperationbase-table-becomes-too-large` to clean async operation data.

Reviewing the customization

Before upgrading our environment to Dynamics 365 CE, we need to review the customization to check whether any unsupported customization is available in the customer environment. Unsupported customization can stop our upgrade process. Apart from that, we also need to review Microsoft or other vendor solutions that we have used for our customers to make sure they are still available for Dynamics 365 CE versions. Similarly, we may be using community solutions for an earlier version, so we need to check whether a similar solution is available that is compatible with Dynamics 365 CE. If not, we may need to develop an equal solution for Dynamics 365 CE.

The following is the list of customizations that are deprecated in Dynamics 365 CE v9:

- **Voice of the Customer (VoC)**: This was used for creating a survey in Dynamics CRM, but this solution is deprecated in Dynamics 365 CE. Now, we have a different solution, called Microsoft Forms Pro, which can be used to create a survey. You can find more details about Microsoft Forms Pro here: `https://formspro.microsoft.com/en-us/`. We need to replace the survey that we created with Microsoft Forms Pro.
- **The Blackberry app**: Microsoft has deprecated the Blackberry app for Dynamics 365 CE. Although Microsoft will continue to provide security and other updates for the Blackberry app, it will soon be removed from the app stores. So, if our customer is using a Blackberry app, we need to plan to migrate them to the Dynamics 365 CE for phones app.
- **The Outlook add-in**: Microsoft has deprecated the Outlook add-in for Dynamics 365 CE, which also includes features such as offline mode and synchronization in Dynamics 365 for Outlook. So, we need to plan to migrate our Outlook app customers to the Dynamics 365 CE app for Outlook. This app provides more features; for example, it's a user-responsive design. We can drill down to view record details within the app; it provides contextual information from Dynamics 365 CE. Now, it's easy to associate an Outlook email or appointment with a Dynamics 365 CE record, with a single click. This app works with server-side sync.

- **Service scheduling**: If you are a service-providing company using service scheduling under a custom service module, you need to start planning on using the new **Universal Resource Scheduling** (**URS**), which is available in Unified Interface.

- **Dialog changes**: Dialogs provide us with the option to design multi-screen processes where we can provide user output based on their inputs. Dialogs are also used widely by many service-based customers to process requirements based on user queries. But dialogs are deprecated in Dynamics 365 CE, so we need to plan on using a business process flow, or we need to design canvas apps to implement our requirements. However, keep in mind canvas app embedding to an entity form is only available for Dynamics 365 CE Online.

- **Contract entities**: All contract entities, such as Contracts, Contract Line Items, and Contract Templates are deprecated in Dynamics 365 CE. If your customer is using these entities, we need to implement their requirements using Entitlement entities in Dynamics 365 CE.

- **Standard SLAs**: In the earlier version of Dynamics CRM, we had the option to use two **service-level agreements** (**SLAs**): Standard and Enhanced. But in Dynamics 365 CE, Standard SLAs are deprecated; we can only use Enhanced SLAs, which provide more flexibility, such as case-on-hold support, auto-pause and resume, and support for success actions.

- **Relationship roles**: Relationship roles have been around since Dynamics CRM 4.0, but now, these are deprecated from Dynamics 365 CE, and we need to start using connection roles instead.

- **Mail Merge changes**: The Mail Merge feature is also deprecated. Now, in Dynamics 365 CE, we need to use a server-side document generation feature, where we can generate Word and Excel documents using Word and Excel templates.

- **Announcement changes**: Announcements were used to share information with other Dynamics CRM users, but they are also deprecated.

- **Legacy attribute for business process flow**: In earlier versions of Dynamics CRM, when business process flow was enabled for the entities, it automatically added some fields to the entities, such as `processed`, `stageid`, and `traversedpath`, which are deprecated. Now, in Dynamics 365 CE, we have a separate entity for business process flow.

We need to check customers' customizations for the deprecated customizations mentioned in the preceding list, and we need to plan accordingly using the new features of Dynamics 365 CE.

Code review

Another important thing we need to do is a code review. We need to perform a code review of our customer's environment, where we check client-side as well as server-side code. Keeping in mind the different clients for Dynamics 365 CE, there are many Dynamics 365 CE JavaScript methods that are deprecated.

 You can get a full list of the deprecated methods here: `https://docs.microsoft.com/en-us/dynamics365/get-started/whats-new/customer-engagement/important-changes-coming#some-client-apis-are-deprecated`.

We can use the following code validation from the tools available:

- **Microsoft Dynamics CRM 2015 Custom Code Validation Tool**: We can use this tool to validate our code and check for any deprecated methods from Dynamics CRM 2015. It will help us to validate whether any unsupported code is written where code is manipulating the **Document Object Model** (**DOM**) object or any APIs that are deprecated used in code. This tool provides a solution that can be installed in your Dynamics CRM 2015 or 2016 organization to validate code. If you have started upgrading from Dynamics CRM 2011, it will show all the Dynamics CRM 4.0 code to update it. You can download this tool from `https://www.microsoft.com/en-us/download/details.aspx?id=45535`.
- **Dynamics 365 V9 JavaScript Validator**: This tool is developed to validate any code that is not compatible with Dynamics 365 CE. We can connect to our organization and can use this tool to scan all of our web resources to see which of the web resources have a method that is deprecated in Dynamics 365 CE V9. It also detects **Simple Object Access Protocol** (**SOAP**) endpoints used in service code to query data from entities.

You can download XrmToolBox here: `https://www.xrmtoolbox.com/`.

- **Legacy Feature Check Tool**: Apart from the client-side code, we also need to review our server-side code if we are upgrading from Dynamics 2011 to Dynamics 365 CE. In the case of Dynamics CRM 2011, your code may contain a reference to 2007 endpoints, so you need to find and remove all those references. To check this, we can use the Legacy Feature Check Tool provided by Microsoft. It can be downloaded from `http://go.microsoft.com/fwlink/p/?LinkID=309565`. If we try to upgrade our organization without removing these references, our upgrade will fail. It is better to check this before any upgrade process is started.
- **Remove any unsupported database objects**: Dynamics 365 CE and earlier versions of Dynamics CRM do not support any changes in the database, although it is technically feasible. In order to make our upgrade smooth, we should remove any unsupported changes to the CRM database that a customer has made—for example, any custom triggers, stored procedures, and so on.
- **Try a test upgrade**: Apart from the preceding activities, it is also recommended to first try your upgrade using the virtual machine, if possible. It helps us to identify potential issues that could occur during the upgrade. It also helps us to plan our upgrade activities and checklist accordingly.

Apart from these tools, we can also use PowerApps Checker from XrmToolBox as well as SnapShot!. SnapShot! is a powerful tool to get detailed documentation of your environment for solution components. You can get more details from `https://www.xrmcoaches.com/snapshot/`.

Now, we understand all the upgrade activities that we need to perform and we have discussed the important sections that we need to include in our assessment report. Once that is done, it's time to look into all the activities in detail. In the next section, we are going to discuss our solution upgrade.

Upgrading solutions

When we upgrade our Dynamics CRM organization to Dynamics 365 CE, all of the customizations are also upgraded automatically. However, we still need to work on our customizations to adjust them based on the new Dynamics 365 CE interface. If anything unsupported is done, we need to remove it to make sure everything is working with Dynamics 365 CE correctly. We may need to change our navigation based on Dynamics 365 CE. Depending on which version we are upgrading from, we need to work on the customization. Before Dynamics 365 CE, we used to develop custom solutions for features that were not present in Dynamics CRM—for example, multi-selection dropdowns. This feature was not available in earlier versions, but now, we have this feature out of the box. We should always try to use out-of-the-box features of Dynamics 365 CE instead of writing any custom solutions. In earlier versions of CRM—for example, Dynamics CRM 2011—we used to write lots of code for screen validation, but this code can now be replaced with business rules that are easy to configure, and you don't need to write any code. Any business user can develop business rules without any programming knowledge.

Depending on which client your customer is going to use, you may need to work on the entity forms, views, and other entity components. For example, if your customer will be using the Unified Interface, then you need to change your form design. You need to design your navigations, especially custom navigation, which was added to web clients for earlier versions. You need to set up a view configuration for the Unified Interface as, by default, all views are not available in the Unified Interface, so you need to change them using the app designer. Keep in mind the legacy web client is deprecated for 2020 release 2, so now, it is mandatory to upgrade to the Unified Interface.

You can refer to a post on how to show all the web client views in the Unified Interface here: `http://himbap.com/blog/?p=3646`.

So, we've learned about how our solution is upgraded to the new version and what the main areas are in which we need to make changes after upgrading. Apart from the customizations upgrade, the next important part is upgrading our custom code. In the next section, we are going to discuss that.

Upgrading code

Upgrading code is a critical activity for an upgrade, especially if you are upgrading from an earlier version such as Dynamics CRM 2011. There are some client-side methods that are deprecated to make it easy to move from one client to another. So, even if you are upgrading from Dynamics CRM 2016, you need to upgrade your client-side code to make it compatible with Dynamics 365 CE. Although old methods can work due to compatibility support, they will stop working in some major Dynamics 365 CE releases. Let's discuss high-level changes that we need to make in our Dynamics CRM 2016 code, as follows:

- `Xrm.Page`: In Dynamics CRM 2016, the `Xrm.Page` object was used to refer to entity forms and fields from JavaScript written on entity forms as well as HTML web resources. But now, using `Xrm.Page` to access entity forms and fields in the script written for entity forms is deprecated. Instead of using `Xrm.Page`, we need to use `formContext` to refer to an entity and its field. We can get `formContext` from `executionContext`, which we can pass from `form` and `field` events. We can use the following code to get `formContext` from the `method` parameter:

  ```
  AccountName_OnChange:function(executionContext)
  {
  //get formContext from execution contextvar formContext =
  executionContext.getFormContext();
  }
  ```

  In the preceding code, we are getting the `executionContext` parameter, which is configured to pass from an event definition.

  The use of `Xrm.Page` in HTML web resources is still supported if we have an HTML web resource that is using `Xrm.Page`. We don't need to change anything there.

- `Xrm.Page.context`: `Xrm.Page.context` was used in Dynamics CRM 2016 to get contextual information about where our code is executing—for example, to get the client URL, organization name, and organization language code. But now, we need to change our code to use `getGlobalContext` from `Xrm.Utility`. This object can be used to get details about the following three settings:
  - `client`: This returns information about the client where our code is executing—for example, web for web client and the Unified Interface client, Outlook, and mobile.

- `organizationSettings`: We can use this to get details about our organizations—for example, organization ID, language code, and default currency code. All the methods that we use to get organization-related information will be replaced with `globalContext.organizationSettings` using `Xrm.Page.context`.

- `userSettings`: We can use this to get details about the current user—for example, current user security roles, user ID, username, and time zone information. So, any method that we used earlier to get user setting details such as `Xrm.Page.context.getUserLcid` needs to change to `globalContext.userSettings.languageId`.

Apart from the preceding objects, `getContext` also has some methods available that help us to get the current client URL to make Web API service code, the client version, the current app name, and the app URL.

- `Xrm.Page.context.getQueryStringParameters`: In CRM 2016, if we wanted to pass any query string parameter, we used the `Xrm.Page.context.getQueryStringParameters` method. Now, in Dynamics 365 CE, we have to change it to `formContext.data.attributes`.

- `Xrm.Utility.alertDialog` and `Xrm.Utility.confirmDialog`: `Xrm.Utility` contain many methods that were used earlier to display a prompt to users, such as an alert or confirm dialog, but now, we have to use `Xrm.Navigation` for these prompts. For example, let's change the following code of CRM 2016:

```
Xrm.Utility.alertDialog("Please provide account phone number!");
```

We'll change it to the following:

```
Xrm.Navigation.openAlertDialog(AlertMsg).then(
function success(result) {
//code which we want to execute after alert
},
function (error) {
//capture error and write in console
console.log(error.message); //in case any error write it under
cosole.
} );
```

Similarly, we need to change the `confirmDialog` code as well.

- `Xrm.Utility.isActivityType`: This method was used to know about the entity type. It returns and informs us whether the entity is an activity-type entity or not. This method has been replaced with `Xrm.Utility.getEntityMetadata`. We can use this method to get entity metadata.

- `Xrm.Utility.openEntityForm`: This method was used to open an entity form to create a new record, or to open any existing record. But now, it has been replaced with `Xrm.Navigation.openForm`. We can use this method as follows:

```
var entityFormOptions = {};
entityFormOptions["entityName"] = "account";
entityFormOptions["openInNewWindow"] = true;
var parameters = {};
//set account number
parameters["accountnumber"] = 1101;
Xrm.Navigation.openForm(entityFormOptions, parameters).then(
function (success) {
//do nothing
},
function (error) {
console.log(error.message);
  });
```

You can find more details about `openForm` at `https://docs.microsoft.com/en-us/powerapps/developer/model-driven-apps/clientapi/reference/Xrm-Navigation/openForm`.

- `Xrm.Utility.openQuickCreate`: This method was used to open quick create forms in Dynamics CRM 2016, but now, we can use the `XrmNavigation.openForm` method to open quick create forms. To open a quick create form, we need to set the `useQuickCreateForm` parameter as follows in `Xrm.Navigation.openForm`, under `entityFormOptions`:

```
entityFormOptions["useQuickCreateForm"] = true;
```

- `Xrm.Utility.openWebResource`: `openWebResource` from `Xrm.Utility` was used to open any HTML web resource in CRM 2016, but in Dynamics 365 CE it is replaced with `Xrm.Navigation.openWebResource`. We can use this method with the following syntax:

  `Xrm.Navigation.openWebResource(webResourceName,windowOptions,data)`

  Where `webResourceName` is the name of the web resource that we want to open, `windowsOptions` are the windows-related options such as height, width, and `openInNewWindow`. The `data` parameter is used to send a data collection to the web resource that we want to populate.

 We need to change all of the preceding methods from CRM 2016 code to Dynamics 365 CE-compatible code. You can find more details about deprecated methods at `https://docs.microsoft.com/en-us/dynamics365/get-started/whats-new/customer-engagement/important-changes-coming#some-client-apis-are-deprecated`.

If we are upgrading from CRM 2016, we don't need to upgrade any server-side code as there are no changes to the server-side methods. But if you are upgrading from CRM 2011, you definitely need to remove any references to the 2007 endpoint from your code. You can utilize the tools that we discussed in the *Code review* section. Now, we know all the activities that we need to perform while upgrading to Dynamics 365 CE. Another thing we need to perform is data migration, when we are moving from one server to another, or we are coming to Dynamics 365 CE from any other legacy system. In the next section, we are going to discuss different data migration options that we can use to import data in Dynamics 365 CE.

Migrating data

Customer data is very important for any business, so it is critical to migrate customer data correctly. We need to perform data migration activities when we are upgrading from earlier versions to Dynamics 365 CE or implementing a fresh Dynamics 365 CE version for a customer. We also need to perform data migration if we are using an on-premises system and our customer wants to upgrade to Dynamics 365 CE Online. So, depending on the scenario, the data migration activity is performed accordingly.

To perform data migration, we can use the following options:

- **Database restore**: We can use this option for an on-premises upgrade. We can take a backup of our Dynamics CRM database and can restore it for the new SQL server. Once the database is set up, we can use the deployment manager to import our organization using the restored database.

- **Using Dynamics 365 Data Import**: One option is to use the Dynamics 365 Data Import utility if the number of entity records is few. We can download the data import template for the entities from **Settings | Data Management | Templates for Data Import**. Dynamics 365 CE allows us to import data using different formats, such as `.xml`, `.csv`, `.txt`, `.xlsx`, and `.zip` files. We can get data files from the old system and prepare import files. We can import a maximum of 32 MB of files at a time. While importing reference data, it important to keep in mind that all reference data should exist in the system first. For example, if we are importing contact entity data, all the parent accounts should already exist in the system; otherwise, we will get a **Reference Source Not Found** error.

- **Using a third-party migration tool**: We can also utilize third-party migration tools. The most commonly used tools are SSIS Integration Toolkit and Scribe. These tools use the Dynamics 365 service to transfer data to Dynamics 365 CE. Some third-party tools, such as Scribe, provide easy configuration options from the user interface whereas, in some tools, we need to write some scripts, such as the SSIS Integration Toolkit. We can set up the mapping of the entity and field for data transfer. We can directly connect the old system to Dynamics 365 CE, or if we have flat files, we can use them for importing data.

- **FastTrack**: Microsoft runs this program to support their customers. Microsoft helps customers who have more than 250 full user licenses to move to the Dynamics 365 CE cloud. The FastTrack program basically helps the customer to move to the cloud for services such as Office 365, Azure, and Dynamics 365. When a customer is selected for FastTrack, Microsoft assigns a solution architect from the Dynamics 365 group who becomes the main point of contact for the whole transition. Solution architects from Microsoft make sure to complete this process successfully based on experiences with other customers.

- **A utility developed in-house**: Another option is to develop our own utility to migrate our data to Dynamics 365 CE. We can use the Dynamics 365 CE web service or Web APIs to connect to Dynamics 365 CE entities and upload data into them. This process requires experienced Dynamics 365 CE developers.

Now we know about all the options, we have to move data into Dynamics 365 CE, so let's discuss that in the next section.

Importing data into Dynamics 365 CE

In `Chapter 8`, *Integrating Dynamics 365 CE with Other Applications*, we discussed how to use the Dynamics 365 CE SDK to import data into Dynamics 365 CE. Now, let's discuss some more options for feeding data into Dynamics 365 CE. First, we are going to discuss Dynamics 365 CE's out-of-the-box data import wizard.

The Dynamics 365 CE import wizard

The Dynamics 365 CE import wizard is a good option for importing a small amount of data. We can use this wizard to create or update Dynamics 365 CE data. To create new data, we can download data import templates from the **Data Management** area by taking the following steps:

1. Navigate to **Settings** from the top navigation bar and select **Data Management**, or log in to `admin.powerplatform.microsoft.com`. Select your environment, then click **Settings** | **Templates for Data Import** templates.

2. When you click on **Templates for Data Import**, a dialog window will open, as in the following screenshot, where we can select our entity name from the drop-down list:

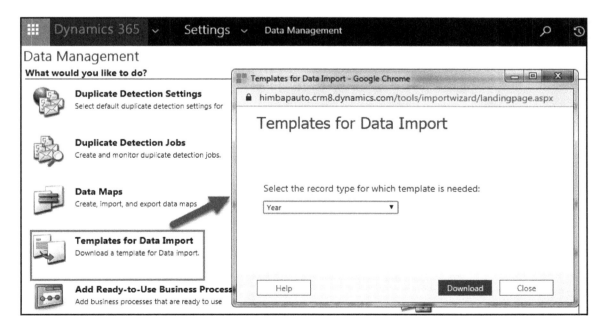

3. When we click on the **Download** button, it will download an Excel template that includes all the fields that are available on the main entity form. While trying to download the data import template, keep in mind that your entity should not have two fields with the same display name; otherwise, you will get an error.

Let's say we want to import data into our **Year** entity. We can take the following steps to import data:

1. Download the data template from the **Data Management** section by selecting the **Year** entity from the dropdown.
2. Open the `Year.xlsx` file, fill in the year details under the **Name** column, and click on **Save**.
3. Navigate to **Settings** | **Data Management** | **Import.**
4. Click on the **Import Data** button on the command bar.
5. Click on **Choose File** and browse our `Year` file, as shown in the following screenshot:

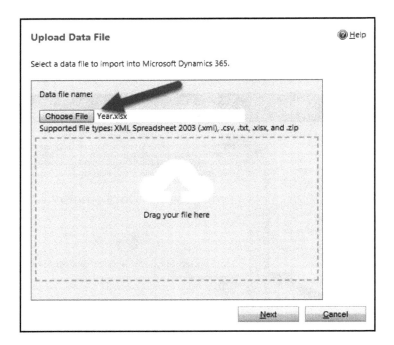

6. Click on the **Next** button to go to the next screen, which is shown in the following screenshot:

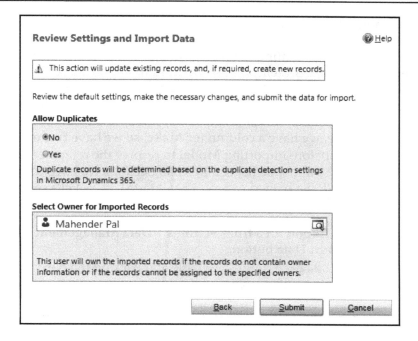

On the preceding screen, we can select an option for the **Allow Duplicates** question. If we select **No**, it will validate data based on the duplicate detection rule created for the current entity. It will mark all the records that are duplicates based on the duplicate rule conditions. But if we select **Yes**, it will bypass any duplicate detection rules and will import data as it is in our import file. We can also configure the owner of the records here.

7. Click on the **Submit** button and it will start the import process. We can track our import process from the **My Imports** view, as follows:

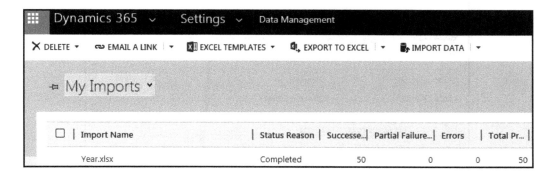

This is how we can use the data import template to import data into Dynamics 365 CE. Now, let's see how we can import our **comma-separated values** (**CSV**) files into Dynamics 365 CE. This is useful if we are getting flat files from customers and we don't have time to put that data into the data import template, so we need to import those files directly. Let's say we want to import data into the **Make** and **Model** entity using CSV files. As discussed earlier, in order to import data with a reference, we need to make sure the reference data is available in Dynamics 365 CE, or we can import both pieces of data at the same time. For example, in our **Model** file, we have a column for **Make**, so we have two options—either we can import **Make** data before importing **Model** to resolve the reference correctly, or we can import both files at the same time using a ZIP file. Let's say we have combined both **Make** and **Model** into a ZIP file named `AutoMakeAndModel.zip`. Let's see how we can do that here:

1. Navigate to the **Import** area from **Settings** | **Data Management** | **Import** and click on the **Import Data** button.
2. Browse our `AutoMakeAndModel.zip` file and click on the **Next** button.
3. The next screen will show us all the files under the `ZIP` folder, as follows:

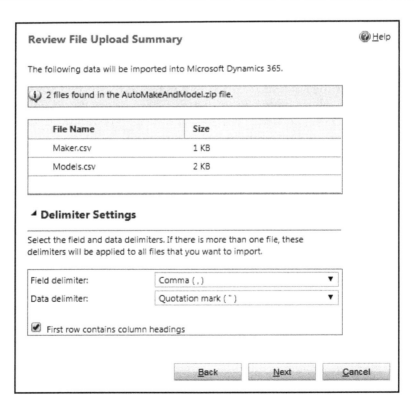

Under **Delimiter Settings**, by default, a comma will be selected, but if we have used any other delimiter, we can select that from the dropdown.

4. Click on the **Next** button and select **OK** in the confirmation dialog for the delimiter.
5. The next screen will show us all the **Data Maps** available under Dynamics 365 CE. If we created a data map earlier, we can select it to map the field for the entity; otherwise, we can select the **Default** option, as in the following screenshot:

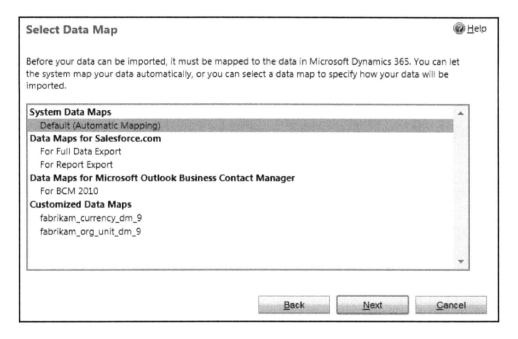

The **Default** option selects the field mapping between our CSV file and entity based on the field display name.

6. Click on the **Next** button and select the mapping for the entity, as in the following screenshot:

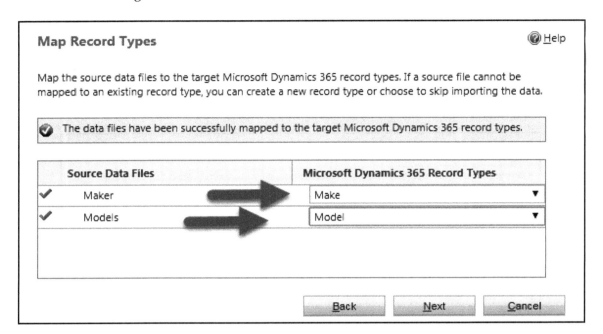

We can also use `make.powerapps.com` to load data into our entity. For more details, you can refer to `https://docs.microsoft.com/en-us/powerapps/maker/common-data-service/data-platform-cds-newentity-pq`.

7. Click on the **Next** button and set the field mapping for all entities. We can select the source field from our CSV file and the target field from the right-hand side of the Dynamics 365 CE entity, as shown in the following screenshot:

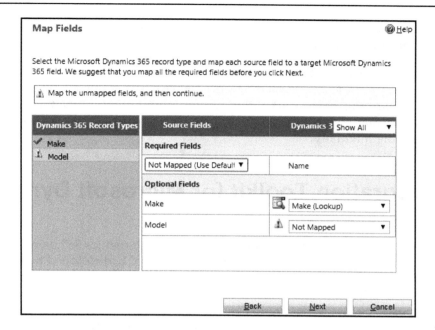

8. Click on **Next** twice and click on **Submit** on the last screen. We can also store our field mapping, as follows:

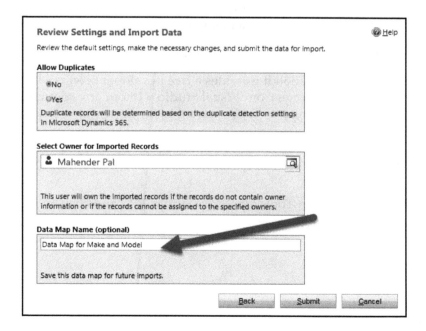

Now, next time we need to reimport this ZIP field, we can select this mapping on the **Select Data Map** screen.

Now, it will import both files. So, this is how we can use the data import wizard to import data into Dynamics 365 CE. The main difference between using the data import template and CSV files is mapping. In the case of the data import template, Dynamics 365 CE automatically does mapping for the entity and its field, whereas in the case of CSV files, we need to do mapping manually.

SSIS Integration Toolkit for Microsoft Dynamics 365

Another option we want to discuss is to import data into Dynamics 365 using SSIS. We are going to use the SSIS Integration Toolkit for Dynamics 365 CE, developed by KingswaySoft. As the name suggests, it uses Microsoft SQL SSIS packages to import data into Dynamics 365 CE. It provides different connectors to connect with different databases for data migration purposes, but we are going to discuss uploading CSV files using the SSIS Integration Toolkit for Dynamics 365 CE. You can download the SSIS Integration Toolkit from the https://www.kingswaysoft.com/products/ssis-integration-toolkit-for-microsoft-dynamics-365/download page and set it up in your development environment. Make sure to review the software prerequisites on their website in order to use this toolkit. We are using this toolkit in the development environment for demo purposes.

We are using SQL Server Data Tools for Visual Studio 2012 for our demo.

 SSIS Integration Toolkit provides a free developer license where we can run our SSIS package from Visual Studio without any commercial license. You can refer to FAQs related to the license at https://www.kingswaysoft.com/purchase/licensing-faq.

Let's take the following steps to create our SSIS package to import data into Dynamics 365 CE:

1. Start SQL Server Data Tools for Visual Studio 2012 and click on **New**.
2. Select an option and fill in the details based on the following numbering:

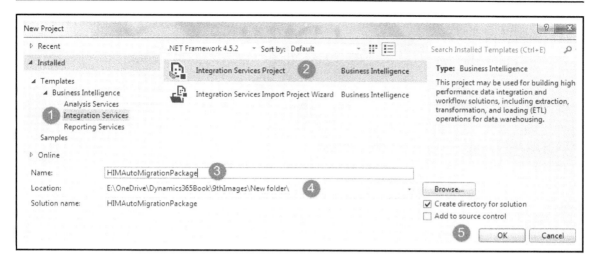

3. Right-click on **Connection Managers** and select **New Connection...**, as shown in the following screenshot:

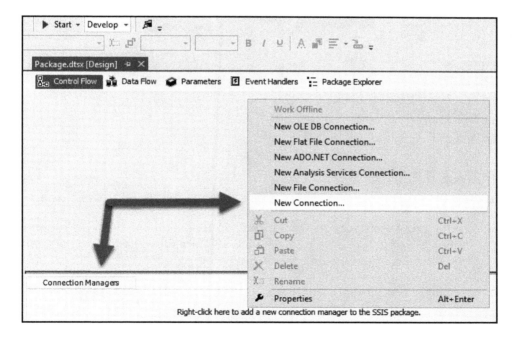

4. Select **Dynamics CRM** under **Connection Manager Type** and click on the **Add** button.

5. Fill in the information in the **CDS/CRM Connection Manager** dialog based on the following numbering, and click on **OK**:

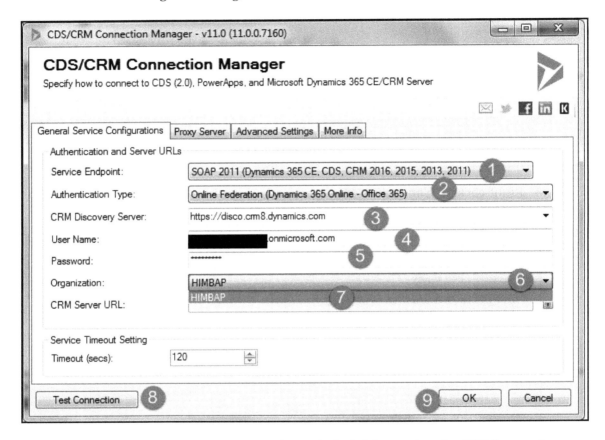

6. We are going to import our **Make** and **Model** data using the SSIS Integration Toolkit. So, first, let's drag two instances of **Data Flow Task** onto the **Control Flow** tab, as in the following screenshot:

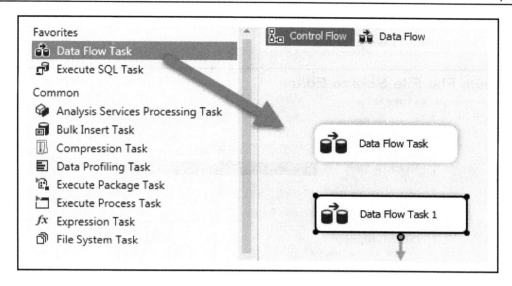

7. Right-click on the first **Data Flow Task** and let's rename it `Import Makers`, and similarly, rename **Data Flow Task 1** as `Import Models`. Once that's done, double-click on the **Import Makers** under **Data Flow Task** and drag **Premium Flat File Source** to the **Data Flow Task**, as follows:

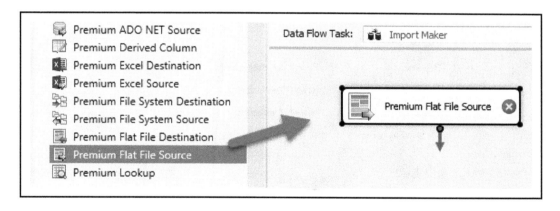

8. We need to double-click on **Premium Flat File Source** and configure the editor, using the following numbering:

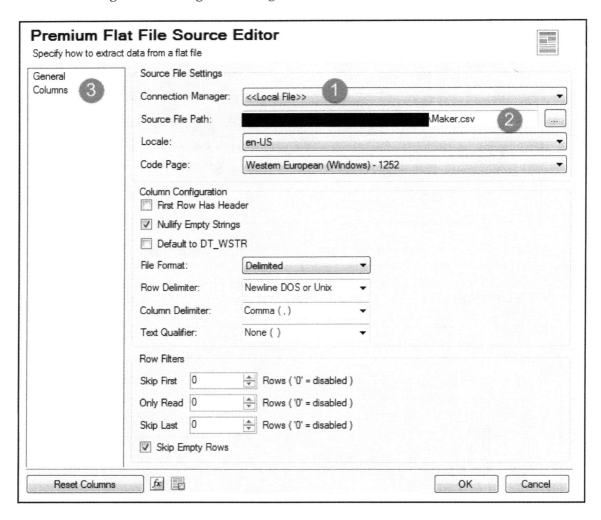

9. Click on **Columns** to review the columns. If required, we can also rename the columns using the **Column Properties** window, as follows:

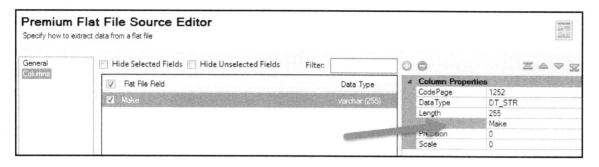

10. Click on the **OK** button to close **Premium Flat File Source Editor**. Now, we need to load data from our CSV file to Dynamics 365 CE using the **Dynamics CRM Destination** component.

11. Drag the **Dynamics CRM Destination** component and connect the **Premium Flat File Source** component with the **Dynamics CRM Destination** component. Now, we need to double-click to configure the properties of the **Dynamics CRM Destination** component. We need to set the following properties under the **General** tab:

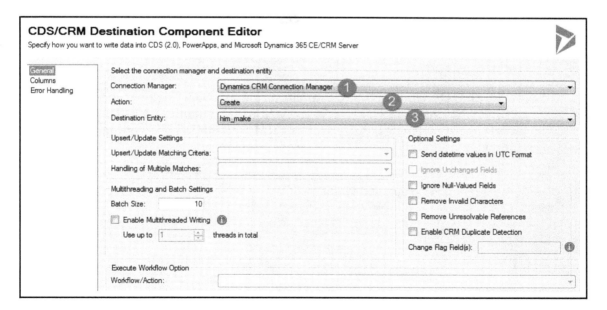

12. We need to set up the mapping. We have just one field for the **Make** entity so we can set it as follows, under the **Columns** tab:

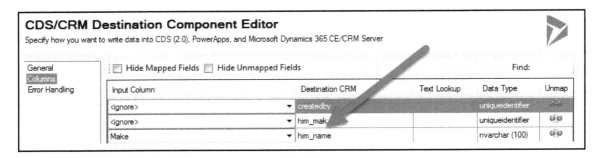

13. Take the same steps and add **Premium Flat File** for the **Model** entity, and set its properties as follows:

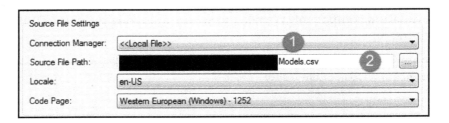

14. Now, drag **Dynamics CRM Destination** from the SSIS Toolbox, and you need to connect the **Premium Flat File Source** arrow to **Dynamics CRM Destination**. After that, double-click on **Dynamics CRM Destination** and configure it as in the following numbering:

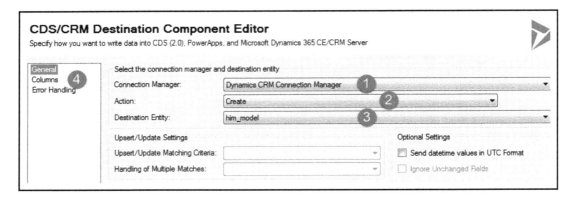

15. Under the **Columns** tab, we need to map columns. We need to add the name of the model and its maker, as follows:

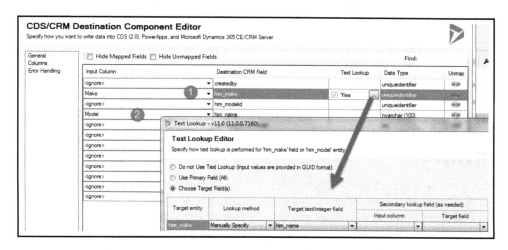

16. Finally, we can click on the **Start** button or press *F5* to test our package. It will first import the **Maker** records into Dynamics 365 CE, and then, it will upload the **Model** data. Once that is complete, we should be able to see the **Control Flow**, as follows:

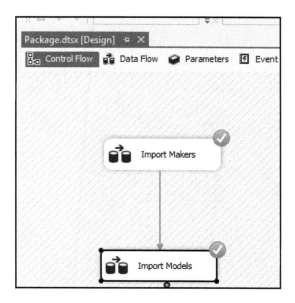

This is how we can use the SSIS Integration Toolkit to import one or more files into Dynamics 365 CE. We have done a simple import for **Makers** and **Models** for our auto service solution. But we can use the SSIS Integration Toolkit for Dynamics 365 CE for more complex scenarios.

 You can find more details about how to use the SSIS Integration Toolkit for Dynamics 365 CE from their help manuals at `https://www.kingswaysoft.com/products/ssis-integration-toolkit-for-microsoft-dynamics-365/help-manual`.

Summary

In this chapter, we learned about Dynamics 365 upgrade and data migration options. We discussed different paths that can be used to upgrade to Dynamics 365 CE and we also discussed different activities that we need to perform during an upgrade. We discussed which tools can help us to upgrade our solution and code to Dynamics 365 CE. Later, we also discussed options available to migrate our historical data to Dynamics 365 CE. We discussed how we can use the Dynamics 365 CE import wizard and the SSIS Integration Toolkit to import data into Dynamics 365 CE.

In the next chapter, we are going to discuss deployment and go-live support. We will discuss how to prepare a go-live checklist and the configuration that is required before we go live.

12
Deployment and Go-Live Support

This chapter will help you to understand how to deploy Dynamics 365 **Customer Engagement** (**CE**) solutions to another environment. You will learn how the deployment process can be done using manual steps, as well as which tools are available to automate the deployment process. You will also learn about common checklist items for Dynamics 365 CE go-live.

We will then discuss the configuration required before go-live. We will further discuss why we need to have post-go-live support, and what options are available to get post-go-live support.

Finally, you will learn about the maintenance activities required for on-premises Dynamics 365 CE.

The main topics that we are going to discuss in this chapter are as follows:

- Deploying Dynamics 365 CE solutions
- Preparing a go-live checklist
- Configurations required before go-live
- Post-go-live support
- Maintaining Dynamics 365 CE

Technical requirements

You should have a basic understanding of Dynamics 365 CE and access to a Dynamics 365 CE environment. The following is a list of the technical requirements for this chapter:

- Access to the internet to download the tools mentioned in the *Automated deployment* section
- Microsoft Excel
- Office 365 admin rights in a Dynamics 365 CE environment

Deploying Dynamics 365 CE solutions

After completing Dynamics 365 CE development and testing, it's time to deploy our changes to the production environment. In Chapter 6, *Customizing Dynamics 365 CE*, we discussed Dynamics 365 CE solutions that we can use to deploy our changes to other environments. We also discussed the points that can help us to select a managed or unmanaged solution. Depending on the type of deployment, we do what we need to in order to plan it accordingly. For example, if we are moving some updates to production, we can do it after working hours, but if we are going to roll out a complete application, it will require a good amount of downtime. Most of the time, these types of rollouts are done on weekends. If we are doing an upgrade, solution deployment may or may not impact the business—for example, if we are doing a side-by-side upgrade where the old application is still functional, we can deploy our application without any issues. In Chapter 11, *Migration and Upgrade*, we discussed different options that we can use to deploy a Dynamics 365 CE solution from one environment to another environment. For solution deployment, we have two main options available:

- Manual deployment
- Automated deployment

Let's look at them in detail.

Manual deployment

As the name suggests, in manual deployment, we export and import solutions manually. We can export our solution as managed or unmanaged, and install it in another environment. Depending on the release, we may deploy our full solution if we are doing it for the first time, or we can deploy a partial solution if we are not doing it for the first time. A partial solution only includes new changes that we want to deploy to the targeted environment. If required, we also need to do other related deployments manually. For example, we may need to import our master data in order for our customization to work properly. We can take the example of a field service app for Dynamics 365 CE. We discussed field service apps in `Chapter 1`, *Introduction to Dynamics 365 CE*. If we are using a field service app, we need to set up a number of data entities such as Resources, Territories, Field Service Products, and Incident Types, and we need to perform these imports manually, but once done, we can move them to another environment using a data migration tool. This process is suitable if we have a simple solution that does not include dependencies on other solutions or integration, and especially if we don't require frequent deployment.

Exporting solutions

In `Chapter 6`, *Customizing Dynamics 365 CE*, we discussed how to create solutions and add the components that we want to customize. To export this solution, we can use the **Export** button from the **Solutions** toolbar if your **Solutions** editor is already open. At the time of writing this chapter, Microsoft has changed the process of working with solutions. Now, when you navigate to **Settings | Solutions,** even from a classical web client, it will open a new **Solutions** editor, as shown in the following screenshot:

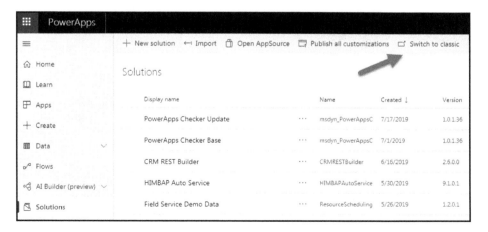

But we can click on **Switch to classic** to open the classic editor to work with a solution. In PowerApps, when we try to export our solution (following the numbering in the next screenshot), we will get the following dialog:

This dialog allows us to publish any customization that is not published yet. Another new thing we will find here is the **Solution checker**, which helps us to find potential issues in the solution. We can click on the **Run** button to run the **Solution checker** and see a list of issues in our solution. Once the checking process is completed, we can see potential issues, as shown in the following screenshot:

In the preceding screenshot, you can see that it is showing one of the scripts has the **debugger** keyword for the debugging script.

Once all the issues are resolved, we can start the export process again by selecting our solution and clicking on the **Export** button. We can click on the **Next** button, and we will get the dialog shown in the following screenshot:

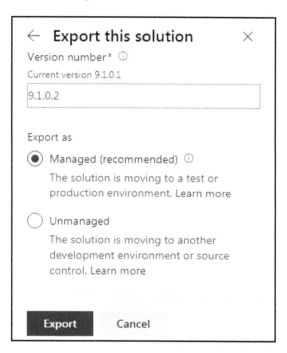

Here, we can select a version of our solution and select whether we want to opt for a **Managed** or an **Unmanaged** solution.

Finally, we can click on the **Export** button to export our solution. Keep in mind that Microsoft has included solution numbering automation, which automatically updates the solution version number. If we are manually exporting a solution twice without making any changes—for example, if we are exporting both a managed and unmanaged solution—we need to manually set the version number to the same number, as the solution numbering automation by Microsoft will automatically increase the version number.

To import our solution into the target environment, we can use the **Import** button by navigating to **Settings | Solutions**. We can browse our ZIP file and follow the screen to import the solution. Make sure to keep **Enable any SDK message processing steps included in the solution** enabled to activate the workflow and plugin steps that are part of the solution, as shown in the following screenshot:

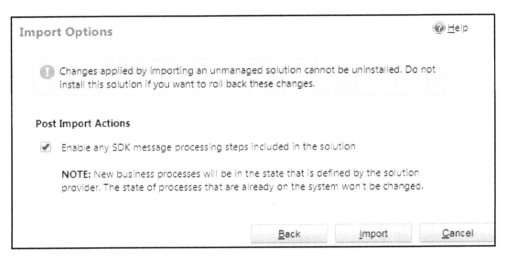

If we are importing an unmanaged solution, we need to publish our solution after import, whereas if we are importing a managed solution, it will be published automatically by the Dynamics 365 CE platform.

Automated deployment

In automated deployment, the tasks that we want to perform for our solution deployment are all handled by the software tool. This process requires no, or minimal, manual efforts. Automated deployment is well suited when we need to release our solution frequently. We can use software that can perform all the necessary steps for solution release, or we can use tools that can just deploy our solution after it is built or exported from the source environment manually. Depending on the development environment—whether we are using a single server or multiple dev servers—we can use tools to build our solutions after extracting solutions from different development environments. Let's discuss some of the tools that we can use with Dynamics 365 CE to automate our solution release process. Some of the tools can perform this process completely, and some of them help us to automate this process partially.

SolutionPackager

This tool comes with the Dynamics 365 CE **Software Development Kit (SDK)**, and it is very useful if multiple developers are working in parallel and sharing the same customization. This tool extracts the solution into multiple XML files that we can use to store in the source control, and we can use this tool to recreate solutions to deploy into a **quality assurance (QA)** environment. By extracting individual components, we can easily identify changes that happened in our environment. This helps to complete components if required. It generates a specific file structure, which we can refer to here: `https://docs.microsoft.com/en-us/dynamics365/customerengagement/on-premises/developer/solution-component-file-reference-solutionpackager`.

We can import the solution generated from the SolutionPackager tool manually, or we can use further automation to deploy the solution to an environment from the SolutionPackager output.

 You can find more details about SolutionPackager and its commands at `https://docs.microsoft.com/en-us/dynamics365/customerengagement/on-premises/developer/compress-extract-solution-file-solutionpackager`.

Package Deployer

This is another tool released by Microsoft that we can use to deploy our package. A package can contain different components, such as solutions, custom screens, configuration data, and custom code. We can use both the SolutionPackager tool and this tool to automate our Dynamics 365 CE build process.

 You can find more details about this tool at `https://docs.microsoft.com/en-us/power-platform/admin/deploy-packages-using-package-deployer-windows-powershell`.

You can download the Dynamics 365 SDK tool at `https://docs.microsoft.com/en-us/dynamics365/customerengagement/on-premises/developer/download-tools-nuget`.

Microsoft Dynamics 365 Developer Toolkit

Another toolkit we can use to automate deployment and make our development easy is the Developer Toolkit for Dynamics 365 CE, released by Microsoft. This is a Visual Studio add-on that we can install on Visual Studio. After that, we can develop and deploy extensions for Dynamics 365 CE, such as plugins, custom workflows, and web resources from Visual Studio itself.

 You can download Microsoft Dynamics 365 Developer Toolkit at `https:/ /marketplace.visualstudio.com/items?itemName=DynamicsCRMPG. MicrosoftDynamicsCRMDeveloperToolkit`.

Dynamics 365 Build Tools

This is another build tool, developed by Wael Hamze, Microsoft Dynamics **Most Valuable Professional** (**MVP**), that can be downloaded from the marketplace. This tool is a combination of different tools that make the build process easy. We can use this tool to automate solutions built in Dynamics 365 CE as well as PowerApps. Using this tool, we can deploy solutions more frequently, if and when required.

PowerApps Build Tools for Azure DevOps

PowerApps Build Tools is a collection of PowerApps-specific Azure DevOps build tasks that we can use to automate solution deployment. We can perform different tasks using these tools, such as the synchronization of solutions between development environments, updating source control, and setting up new environments. You can get more details about this tool from `https://marketplace.visualstudio.com/items?itemName=microsoft-IsvExpTools.PowerApps-BuildTools`.

So, now we know that we can make our deployment automated using the aforementioned build tools, or can perform the deployment process manually by exporting solutions from one environment to another environment. In the next section, we are going to discuss a checklist that is important for any go-live.

Preparing a go-live checklist

A Dynamics 365 CE go-live checklist is a list of the items that should be completed before the end user starts using the system for their day-to-day work. This checklist can help us to ensure that we have not missed anything important. It is recommended to prepare a checklist in the initial project phase and verify each item listed in the checklist before releasing the new system to users. Depending on the project type, this checklist may be different. For example, if we are working on an upgrade, it may have different items than if you are working on a fresh Dynamics 365 CE implementation. The following table includes common checklist items:

Production Deployment Checklist		
SrNo	**Description**	**Completed**
1	Are all user stories complete?	No
2	Is UAT complete?	No
3	Is user training complete?	No
4	Get a list of production users	No
5	Is the production environment setup complete?	No
6	Is all historical data uploaded?	No
7	Is the change request procedure setup complete?	No
8	Is the documentation complete?	No
9	Sample testing	No

Let's discuss these checklist items for a Dynamics 365 CE implementation one by one, as follows:

- **Are all user stories complete?**: We need to make sure that all the agreed user stories are completed for this release. These user stories are agreed upon during project planning. We need to make sure that all the user stories are tested and verified by the testing team as well as the **User Acceptance Testing (UAT)** team.

- **Is UAT complete?**: We discussed the UAT process in detail in `Chapter 10`, *Testing and User Training Planning*. Before releasing the system to end users, we need to make sure UAT is completed and signed off. UAT ensures that the new system is based on the customer's expectations and that there are no gaps in the functionality developed.

- **Is user training complete?**: User training is critical in making a Dynamics 365 CE implementation successful. It helps us to improve user adoption. If the user only knows about the new Dynamics 365 CE functionality that we used to build the new system, then they won't be able to use the new system properly.
- **Get a list of production users**: We should verify whether we have got a list of production users and their respective security roles from the customer to make sure that all users can be set up in the production environment before go-live.
- **Is the production environment setup complete?**: Another checklist point is to make sure the production environment is set up correctly. If we are going to use any integration in our project, it should also be set up correctly.
- **Is all historical data uploaded?**: Data is a critical part of any business application, so we need to make sure that if there is a master, it is present in the system—for example, setting up products, price lists, and currencies. If a customer has historical data, it should be imported and verified in the new system by the customer so that users can refer to it, if and when required.
- **Is the change request procedure setup complete?**: When the user starts using the new system, they may want to modify some of the existing processes, or perhaps they'll want to add some new functionality. It is important to make sure the change request procedure is set up so that users can request new changes and we can plan for adding those functionalities in the next release.
- **Is the documentation complete?**: Documentation is another critical checklist item, where we need to make sure that we have documented all the functionality that our customer is going to use. This is very helpful if any changes are required and for providing knowledge transfer to new project resources or customer team members.

All the preceding points should be documented and verified one by one against the production environment. The preceding checklist is common in a Dynamics 365 CE implementation, but we can add more checklist items based on our projects.

Although the new system is tested completely and UAT is also completed successfully, we should create a quick sample test in the production environment to make sure all the functionalities are working perfectly.

Now, we have a list of the common checklist items that we need to complete before go-live. In the next section, we are going to discuss the main configurations required before go-live.

Configurations required before go-live

Before going live, there are some critical configurations that need to be completed, and we need to verify that they are working correctly because these configurations can impact end users' operations from day one, which can lead to a bad impression. These configurations can also vary from project to project, but let's discuss some common configurations required for Dynamics 365 CE projects, as follows:

- **User setup**: This is a critical requirement for go-live. We need to make sure to set up all users correctly in the production environment. Their security roles should be set up based on the customer's requests. If a customer will be using teams, we need to make sure users are created and all users are added to their respective teams. If a customer is using field-level security, then respective users should be added to the field-level security profiles; otherwise, they may get an error when creating, updating, or viewing entity records.

- **Mailbox setup**: Before go-live, we need to make sure the mailboxes for all users are set up correctly. We can use the **TEST & ENABLE MAILBOXES** button to enable mailboxes for users. After that, we can review the test run status, **Incoming Email Status,** and **Outgoing Email Status** to verify that the email is configured correctly and is working fine. As you can see in the following screenshot, the **TEST & ENABLE MAILBOXES** button will be enabled only after selecting the mailbox record:

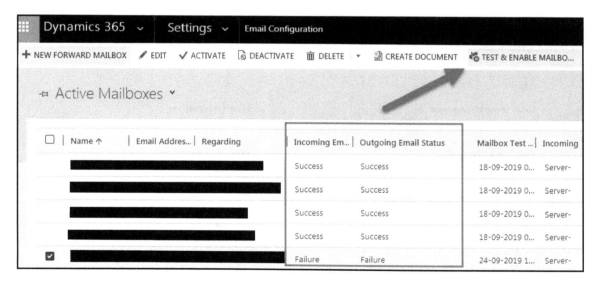

If the customer uses email templates for sending emails, also verify that they are configured correctly.

- **Workflow activation**: If we have created a workflow to automate any tasks, we need to make sure these workflows are configured correctly and activated. We need to also make sure the scope of the workflow is configured correctly. We discussed workflow scope in `Chapter 8`, *Integrating Dynamics 365 CE with Other Applications*.
- **Administration and business management setup**: We discussed Dynamics 365 CE configuration in `Chapter 5`, *Configuring Your Dynamics 365 CE Organization*. Before go-live, we need to make sure all the administrative setup (such as **Languages**, **Auto-Numbering**, **Skype**, and **Yammer**) and business management setup (such as **Fiscal Year Settings**, **Business Closures**, **Queues**, **Sales Territories**, and **Currencies**) is done. We can configure Dynamics 365 CE settings by navigating to **Settings | Administration**, as shown in the following screenshot:

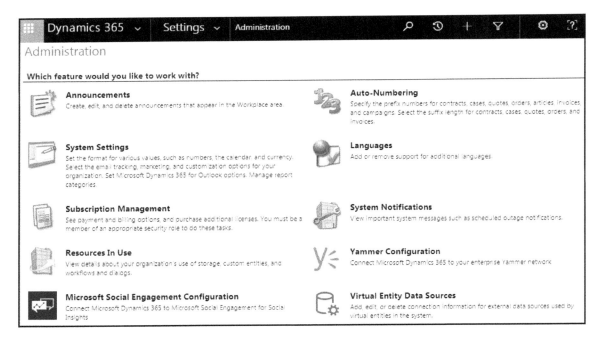

Apart from this, all the other important configurations—such as **Duplicate Detection**, **Document Management** if using **Document Management Features**, and **Field-Level Security** profiles—need to be configured.

- **Report and dashboard configuration**: Reporting is an important part of any business application, so we need to make sure all the reports and dashboards are configured properly for customers. All users should be able to access their reports and dashboards based on their security roles.
- **App access**: If a customer is going to use an app to access our new application, we need to make sure that the application is accessible to the user from that app. For example, if a user will be using the Outlook app, we need to make sure that the user is added to Dynamics 365 App for Outlook.

 You can find more details regarding Dynamics 365 App for Outlook at `https://docs.microsoft.com/en-us/dynamics365/outlook-app/deploy-dynamics-365-app-for-outlook`.

If the customer will be using other apps, such as the Resco Field Service app, we need to make sure users have the correct security role assigned to them to access the app.

- **Whitelisting the Dynamics 365 CE URL**: This is another critical configuration that must be done; otherwise, it can impact the performance of Dynamics 365 CE. We need to make sure that, if we are using any anti-virus software, the Dynamics 365 CE URL is whitelisted.

All the preceding configurations are common to Dynamics 365 CE, but you can refer to `https://docs.microsoft.com/en-us/dynamics365/customerengagement/on-premises/deploy/post-installation-configuration-guidelines-dynamics-365` for Dynamics 365 CE on-premises-specific configuration.

Post-go-live support

Once a Dynamics 365 CE implementation or upgrade is done, the post-go-live support phase starts. Every Dynamics 365 CE implementation partner company provides post-go-live support for a period of between 2 to 6 months. Sometimes, post-go-live support plays a critical role in selecting a Dynamics 365 CE implementation partner. Normally, while discussing the project plan, the project's go-live support duration is also included in the project timelines. As part of the post-go-live support, the project implementation team addresses any implementation issues instead of making new changes.

A post-go-live support contract can be implemented using different models. Sometimes, post-go-live support is handled by new vendors. These support vendors can be partnered with the implementation team or the customer directly. Customers can receive support from their partners for all the technologies they are using, based on their contract.

Before looking into post-go-live support options, let's first consider why we need post-go-live support. The following diagram details the common reasons for post-go-live support being required:

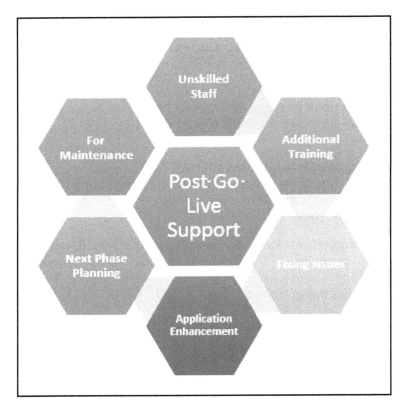

Let's discuss these topics one by one in detail, as follows:

- **Unskilled Staff**: The first, and most common, reason for post-go-live support being required is unskilled staff. Not all customers have an in-house team to handle their day-to-day change requests or quick queries about how to perform a specific task in Dynamics 365 CE. Even though the implementation team provides training for both end users and admin users, not all employees will remember what they have learned during Dynamics 365 CE training. As such, the customer requires someone who can support them after go-live.

- **Additional Training**: Sometimes, the training classes provided during the implementation of Dynamics 365 CE are not sufficient for all users or specific users. This can decrease user productivity, and if they don't have time to go through the user manuals provided to them, the customer may require some additional training for their teams. During these training sessions, users can learn about some more detailed content that is not covered in standard user training sessions, as well as getting answers to any questions they may have after using the new system.

- **Fixing Issues**: At times, we may face issues in the application sometime after the go-live date. These issues may or may not be showstoppers, but if they are, it is critical to fix them as soon as possible. These issues can be specific to the code development done for the application or can be related to new updates released by Microsoft. In cases where the issue is introduced by code development, we need the help of technical resources to fix the issue. Sometimes, the issue is related to bugs in Dynamics 365 CE, in which case we need to report the issue to Microsoft to fix it.

- **Application Enhancement**: Sometime after application go-live, the user becomes familiar with the new system, and they start suggesting enhancements to the application. These enhancements can be related to the application design, navigation changes, screen changes, or—perhaps—enhancing reports. Customers may need post-go-live support to enhance the application. These suggestions could be small or could require a good deal of development effort. Customers can decide whether they want to make these changes as an enhancement, or whether they want to include these changes in the next phase of the implementation project. They can include these new enhancements in their implementation roadmap plan.

- **Next Phase Planning**: Sometimes, customers also need support for planning their next phase. They need help to set up the roadmap for their Dynamics 365 CE journey. They may want to integrate Dynamics 365 CE with more applications. Sometimes, they want to make a small **proof of concept** (**PoC**) before including a solution in their roadmap. They may need the help of technical resources to understand the feasibility of the solution.
- **For Maintenance**: We also need IT resources for maintenance purposes. If we don't have IT resources in-house who can work on maintenance activities, we may need to get support from outside of the organization.

Now we have an understanding of the common reasons why we need post-go-live support, let's discuss the possible options for getting that support, as follows:

- **Support from the implementation team**: We can get post-go-live support from the implementation team who implemented Dynamics 365 CE for us. While discussing the project initially, we can discuss post-go-live support with the implementation team. We can check details such as what the duration of the post-go-live support will be; whether there is any limit for the post-go-live support, such as a case per day or per month; in what timeframe we can expect the resolution of the issue reported; and what the terms and conditions of the post-go-live support are. Getting post-go-live support directly from the implementation team is always helpful as they know the system very well and can take less time to resolve any issues, compared to new vendors.
- **Using a new vendor**: If the implementation team doesn't provide post-go-live support, we can look for another vendor to provide that support for us. We can find this vendor from the **Microsoft Partner Network** (**MPN**), but initially, this process can take time as they will need to first understand the system before providing any support. When selecting a different vendor, we should consider whether they have Dynamics 365 CE capabilities.
- **Microsoft support**: Microsoft support especially comes into the picture when we are facing an issue specific to Microsoft. We can raise a support ticket with Microsoft from the Office 365 portal and provide details of the issue we are facing. You can get more details on Microsoft support at `https://dynamics.microsoft.com/en-in/support/`.
- **Hiring contract resources**: Another option we have is to hire Dynamics 365 CE contract resources for the duration of the support. We can hire skilled resources who have good experience in Dynamics 365 CE as well as experience in providing Dynamics 365 CE support.

- **Using Dynamics 365 community forums**: Getting support from Dynamics 365 community forums is also very common, but this support option can only work when we have skilled technical resources if any new extensions are required. But if we want to extend the capability of Dynamics 365 CE and we don't have any technical resources, then community forum support is not very helpful. Functional consultants can also get support from the community regarding any issues related to functionality or customization.

 You can refer to the different Dynamics 365 community forums at `https:/ /community.dynamics.com/f`.

- **Dynamics 365 CE community blogs**: If we have in-house technical and functional resources, Dynamics 365 CE community blogs can be very helpful for resolving day-to-day issues. Dynamics 365 CE has a huge list of blogs where we can find very useful information. If required, you can contact the blog writers to get more details.

 You can find different Dynamics 365 CE blogs at `https://community. dynamics.com/365/b`.

- **Dynamics 365 documentation**: Dynamics 365 documentation has very useful information. I did not see this much documentation available for earlier Dynamics **Customer Relationship Management** (**CRM**) versions, before Dynamics 365 CE. Now, we have documentation available for all the apps available in Dynamics 365.

 You can access the Dynamics 365 documentation at `https://docs. microsoft.com/en-in/dynamics365/`.

All of this documentation is tailor-made based on levels, roles, and so on. In the following screenshot, you can see the learning options available for the Dynamics 365 CE **Field Service** app:

Now, we know how to provide post-go-live support to our customers after Dynamics 365 CE implementation. Another activity that is very important in Dynamics 365 CE is maintenance. In the next section, we are going to discuss maintenance activities. We will learn about maintenance activities we may need to do for Dynamics 365 CE.

Maintaining Dynamics 365 CE

Depending on the deployment type (online or on-premises) we are using for Dynamics 365 CE, we'll need to work on Dynamics 365 CE maintenance activities. These maintenance activities involve organization data backup, rollup or patch updates, and performance improvements. If we are using Dynamics 365 CE Online, we don't need to work on many of the maintenance activities, as most of them—from backing up organization data to installing the latest updates—are done by Microsoft. But if we are using the Dynamics 365 CE on-premises system, we'll need to perform these activities ourselves. So, let's discuss the main maintenance activities that Dynamics 365 CE requires.

Dynamics 365 CE backups

This is a critical maintenance activity for Dynamics 365 CE. Dynamics 365 CE data backup can help us to recover our data when required. In the case of Dynamics 365 CE, an online daily backup of our organization is done by Microsoft, but if required, we can also make a backup by using the **New backup** button, as shown in the following screenshot:

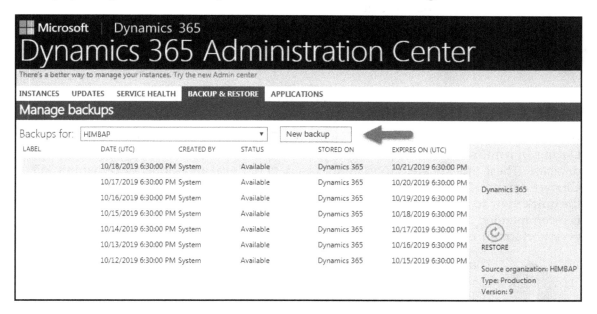

In the previous screenshot, you can also see details of the backups that have been done in the past, and we can select any backup and restore our organization to that backup when required. Microsoft retains backups based on the Dynamics 365 application. For example, if we are taking a backup of a production environment where we have Dynamics 365 applications, Microsoft will keep it for up to 28 days. On the other hand, if a production environment does not have any Dynamics 365 applications, its backup is retained for up to 7 days.

 You can get more details about backup and restore from `https://docs.microsoft.com/en-us/power-platform/admin/backup-restore-environments`.

In the case of Dynamics 365 CE on-premises, we need to take a full backup of Dynamics 365 CE databases, such as the `OrganizationName_MSCRM`, `MSCRM_CONFIG` and `ReportServer` databases. This helps us to recover the databases in the event of a failure. We can also set up scheduled backups through the **Maintenance Plan** wizard from SQL Server.

 You can find more details about database backup and recovery for Dynamics 365 CE on-premises at `https://docs.microsoft.com/en-us/dynamics365/customerengagement/on-premises/deploy/back-up-the-microsoft-dynamics-365-system`.

Index maintenance

Another activity that is required for Dynamics 365 CE maintenance is index maintenance. During Dynamics 365 CE setup, many indexes are created in the Dynamics 365 CE database. These indexes are important for fast data retrieval and for better Dynamics 365 CE performance. New indexes are created when we create a new custom entity or modify the quick view to add more search columns. After using Dynamics 365 CE for some time, it is recommended to review these indexes and rebuild them if you are facing poor performance in Dynamics 365 CE.

 You can find more details about rebuilding indexes in SQL Server at `https://docs.microsoft.com/en-us/sql/relational-databases/indexes/reorganize-and-rebuild-indexes?redirectedfrom=MSDNview=sql-server-ver15`.

In the case of Dynamics 365 CE Online, we don't need to worry about this as Microsoft takes care of the maintenance activities for us.

Installing SQL Server updates

Another activity involved in the case of Dynamics 365 CE on-premises is installing updates. These updates can be specific to SQL Server security or reporting service updates. We can get these updates from Microsoft Windows Updates as well. These can be downloaded automatically, and we can also delete them manually.

 You can find more details about updating Dynamics 365 CE on-premises at `https://docs.microsoft.com/en-us/dynamics365/ customerengagement/on-premises/deploy/update-microsoft-dynamics-crm`.

Installing updates for Dynamics 365 CE

From time to time, Microsoft releases updates for Dynamics 365 CE to fix issues or release new features. In the case of Dynamics 365 CE Online, Microsoft takes care of installing any updates for their customers, whereas in the case of the on-premises version, we need to install these updates based on our Dynamics 365 CE version. The following screenshot provides a list of the updates available for Dynamics 365 CE on-premises at present:

Cumulative updates available for Microsoft Dynamics CRM 9.0

The following table lists the available cumulative updates for Microsoft Dynamics CRM 9.0. These cumulative update rollups include all the hotfixes that were released for limited distribution. These cumulative update rollups also include all earlier update rollups listed in the associated table.

Download links for these cumulative updates are available within each article in the links below.

Article number	Article title	Release date	Version
4533102	Microsoft Dynamics 365 (on premises) Update 0.12	January 2020	9.0.12.4
4526080	Microsoft Dynamics 365 (on premises) Update 0.11	December 2019	9.0.11.9
4521749	Microsoft Dynamics 365 (on premises) Update 0.10	November 2019	9.0.10.10
4515519	Microsoft Dynamics 365 (on premises) Update 0.9	October 2019	9.0.9.4
4513177	Microsoft Dynamics 365 (on premises) Update 0.8	September 2019	9.0.8.0005
4508724	Microsoft Dynamics 365 (on premises) Update 0.7	August 2019	9.0.7.7
4504521	Microsoft Dynamics 365 (on premises) Update 0.6	July 2019	9.0.6.9
4500497	Microsoft Dynamics 365 (on premises) Update 0.5	June 2019	9.0.5.5

You can see a full list of Dynamics 365 CE updates at `https://support.` `microsoft.com/en-gb/help/3142345/microsoft-dynamics-365-` `onpremise-cumulative-updates.`

Summary

In this chapter, you learned about Dynamics 365 CE solution deployment options and go-live support. We discussed the different options available for deploying solutions from one environment to another. We also discussed both manual and automated options for deployment. Later, we discussed Dynamics 365 CE go-live checklists and configuration. We also discussed why we need post-go-live support and how we can get it. Finally, we discussed Dynamics 365 CE maintenance activities.

We started our journey of Dynamics 365 CE implementation with the introduction of different implementation methodologies. We discussed different approaches that we can use to gather requirements and perform requirement analysis. We also discussed different customization steps and learned how to customize different components of Dynamics 365 CE.

We learned how we can integrate Dynamics 365 CE with other modern applications. We gained an understanding of the different options for writing reports for Dynamics 365 CE using the out-of-the-box reporting wizard, as well as using Visual Studio. We also saw how we can write test cases and perform testing for our changes. Sometimes, our customer will be using an old version of Dynamics CRM; for such cases, we discussed different options for migrating existing data and upgrading the earlier version of Dynamics CRM to Dynamics 365 CE. We finished off by looking at the different deployment options and how to provide post-go-live support.

Other Books You May Enjoy

If you enjoyed this book, you may be interested in these other books by Packt:

Mastering Microsoft Dynamics 365 Business Central

Stefano Demiliani, Duilio Tacconi

ISBN: 978-1-78995-125-7

- Create a sandbox environment with Dynamics 365 Business Central
- Handle source control management when developing solutions
- Explore extension testing, debugging, and deployment
- Create real-world business processes using Business Central and different Azure services
- Integrate Business Central with external applications
- Apply DevOps and CI/CD to development projects
- Move existing solutions to the new extension-based architecture

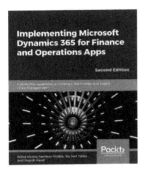

Implementing Microsoft Dynamics 365 for Finance and Operations Apps - Second Edition

Rahul Mohta, Sandeep Shukla, Et al

ISBN: 978-1-78995-084-7

- Understand the technical architecture of Dynamics 365 for Finance and Operations
- Become well-versed with implementing Dynamics to manage finances in your business
- Get up to speed with different methodologies and support cycles of the Microsoft Dynamics architecture
- Explore different best practices to analyze the requirements or scope of your business
- Understand the technique of data migration from legacy systems
- Use the capabilities of Power BI to make informed business decisions
- Manage all your upgrades with the help of One Version service updates

Leave a review - let other readers know what you think

Please share your thoughts on this book with others by leaving a review on the site that you bought it from. If you purchased the book from Amazon, please leave us an honest review on this book's Amazon page. This is vital so that other potential readers can see and use your unbiased opinion to make purchasing decisions, we can understand what our customers think about our products, and our authors can see your feedback on the title that they have worked with Packt to create. It will only take a few minutes of your time, but is valuable to other potential customers, our authors, and Packt. Thank you!

Index

goal metric 140
grid events
  about 232
  reference link 232
grid methods
  reference link 228

H

hierarchy security, types
  manager 201
hierarchy security
  about 200
  position 201
HIMBAP Auto Service Center
  application layer 109
  integration layer 109
  user interface 109
  users 109

I

IFrame events 232
Independent Software Vendor (ISV) solution 78,
  80, 159
indexes, SQL Server
  reference link 388
Internet Facing Deployment (IFD) 25
internet-facing deployment (IFD) 107
IOrganizationService Interface
  reference link 244

K

Kanban 54
Kanban board
  Finished queue 54
  In Progress item 54
  To Do list 54
KingswaySoft
  reference link 360
Knowledge Base (KB) 111, 141
knowledge base search control events 232

L

Legacy Feature Check Tool
  about 346

download link 346

M

mailboxes 155
main form
  body 186
  footer 187
  header 186
major.minor.build.revision format 161
manual deployment, Dynamics 365 CE solutions
  exporting 371, 372, 373, 374
manual testing
  about 318
  bugs, logging 323
  conducting 320
  defects, retesting 324
  requirements review, analyzing 321
  test cases, conducting 323
  test cases, writing 321, 322
  versus automated testing 319
Marketing app 10
Microsoft Dynamics 365 Developer Toolkit
  about 376
  reference link 376
Microsoft Dynamics 365
  SSIS Integration Toolkit, using 360, 362, 364,
    366, 367
Microsoft Dynamics CRM 2015 Custom Code
    Validation Tool
  about 345
  reference link 345
Microsoft Dynamics Marketing (MDM) 10
Microsoft Forms Pro
  reference link 343
Microsoft Partner Network (MPN) 384
Microsoft Sure Step methodology 50
Microsoft Training Partners
  about 336
  reference link 336
migrate email router data 155
Moq
  about 327
  reference link 328
Most Valuable Professional (MVP) 376

N

non-functional requirements
  about 67
  application availability 67
  performance 67
  reliability 67
  scalability 67
  security 67
  usability 67

O

on-demand data integration 259
OneDrive for Business 152
OneNote integration 151
openForm
  reference link 350
Organization service, method
  create method 243
  delete method 244
  execute method 244
  retrieve method 241
  RetrieveMultiple method 241
  update method 243
Organization service
  using 241
organization-level entity
  creating 170
outlook and mobile, option
  mobile app, enabling 172
  offline capability, for Dynamics 365 for Outlook 172
  phone express, enabling 172
  reading pane, in Dynamics 365 for Outlook 172

P

Package Deployer
  about 375
  reference link 375
personal charts 209, 210
personal settings options
  activities 118
  configuring 117
  email 119
  email signatures 119

  email templates 118
  formats 118
  general 117
  languages 120
  privacy 120
  synchronization 118
phases, Microsoft Sure Step methodology
  about 52
  analysis 53
  deployment 53
  design 53
  development 53
  diagnostic 52
  operation 53
phases, project management methodologies
  executing phase 39
  finishing phase 39
  initiating phase 39
  planning phase 39
  testing phase 39
platform layer
  about 217
  business entities 218
  custom workflow assemblies 218
  Dynamics 365 CE web services 217
  plugin assemblies 218
plugin code
  debugging 254, 256
  deploying 251, 252, 253
plugin registration 251
plugin registration, options
  DataBase 252
  disk 252
  GAC 252
plugins, stages
  MainOperation 245
  PostOperation 245
  PreOperation 245
  PreValidation 245
plugins
  used, for implementing custom logic 244, 245, 246
  writing 246, 247, 248, 249, 250
post-go-live support
  about 381, 382, 386

rapid 52
standard 51
upgrade 52
proof of concept (PoC) 384
public queue 136

Q

quality assurance (QA) 111
QueryByAttribute class
about 242
reference link 242
QueryExpression class
about 242
reference link 243
queues 136, 137
queues, types
private queue 136
public queue 136
quickForms methods
reference link 227

R

RAD, phases
prototype, developing 49, 50
release 50
requirement planning 49
testing 50
Rapid Application Development (RAD) 49
relationship roles 139
Report Wizard
using 288, 289, 290, 291, 292
report
deploying 300
filter, adding 302
grouping, adding 300, 301
parameter, adding 303, 304, 305
pre-filtering support, adding 302, 303
requirement analysis 68
requirement documents 39
requirement gathering 68, 69
requirement gathering, techniques
brainstorming 75
closed-ended questionnaire 73, 74
closed-ended questions 71
interview 70

open-ended questionnaire 72
open-ended questions 70
prototype 75
questionnaire 71
workshops 74
resource groups 140
respective teams 82
Retail app
about 13
reference link 13
RetrieveMultiple method, QueryByAttribute class
QueryByAttribute class 242
QueryExpression class 242
Ribbon Workbench
reference link 215
rollup field
reference link 183
Rollup Query 139

S

Sales app
about 8, 9
reference link 9
sales territories 137
sample application, for Dynamics 365 CE
download link 244
Scrum calls 45
Scrum methodology 46
Scrum methodology, phases
backlog refinement 48
daily standup 48
product backlog 47
sprint planning 47
sprint review 48
server-side logic
implementing 240
Organization service, using 241
server-side synchronization monitoring 156
service management settings
configuring 142
entitlement 144, 145
Routing Rules Sets 143
SLAs 143
service-level agreement (SLA) 132, 171, 344
SharePoint document location 151